DATE DUE

DATE DUE			

DEMCO 38-296

men OF color
FASHION, HISTORY, FUNDAMENTALS

LLOYD BOSTON

FOREWORD BY
QUINCY JONES

INTRODUCTION BY
ANDRÉ LEON TALLEY

All black-and-white-toned prints were custom-made exclusively by
ARISTA PHOTO SERVICES in New York City.

Text copyright © 1998 by Lloyd Boston
Foreword copyright © 1998 by Quincy Jones
Introduction copyright © 1998 by André Leon Talley
Original photographs copyright © 1998 by Matthew Jordan Smith
Archival photographs: credits listed on page 256

Excerpt on page 183 reprinted with permission from
The Autobiography of Malcolm X, published by Ballantine
Books, a division of Random House, Inc.

Published in 1998 by Artisan
A Division of Workman Publishing Company, Inc.
708 Broadway, New York, New York 10003–9555
www.workman.com

Editor: SIOBHÁN MCGOWAN
Designer: SUSI OBERHELMAN
Production Director: NANCY MURRAY

Library of Congress Cataloging-in-Publication Data
Boston, Lloyd
Men of Color: Fashion, History, Fundamentals/by Lloyd Boston;
foreword by Quincy Jones; introduction by André Leon Talley.
p. cm.
ISBN 1–57965–167–4
1. Afro-American men—Costume. 2. Costume—United States.
3. Fashion—United States. I. Title.
E185.86.B637   1998
391'.1'08996073—dc21   98–22189
                    CIP

Printed at Arnoldo Mondadori Editore, Verona, Italy

10   9   8   7   6   5   4   3   2   1

First paperback edition, 2000

page 1: At the turn of the century, a group of well-suited Black men
gathered on Mount Olive in North Carolina.

page 6: In 1942, during the Second World War, Harlem residents
lined up for food rations: In spite of tough economic times, men
of color maintained their appearance, dressing in suit, tie, and hat,
even attending to the essential shoe shine.

Tommy Hilfiger U.S.A., Inc., is a proud sponsor of
Men of Color: Fashion, History, Fundamentals

Johnnie Walker® Black Label® is a proud sponsor
of *Men of Color: Fashion, History, Fundamentals*

Kodak Professional

Rush Communications

To my "wildflower," Mrs. Lynell Boston Kollar,
for being a mother and a father extraordinaire,
and for letting me choose my own "garanimals."
I love you, Mom.

And for the countless men of color who have
come before me and paved the sometimes
bloody way with a survival skill called style,
this one is for you.

Contents

Miles Ahead 18

THE SUIT
Interview with Wynton Marsalis

JAZZ
Guest essay by Thomas Terrell
Interview with George Benson
Expert advice from Martin Cooper

Measuring Up 40

THE PANT
Interview with Bill T. Jones

R&B
Guest essay by David Thigpen
Interview with Isaac Hayes
Expert advice from Jeffrey Banks

Front and Center 64

THE SHIRT
Interview with Ed Bradley

TELEVISION
Guest essay by Nick Charles
Interview with Bryant Gumbel
Expert advice from Tommy Hilfiger

Fade to Black 84

ATTITUDE
Interview with Samuel L. Jackson

STAGE & SCREEN
Guest essay by Deborah Gregory
Interview with Billy Dee Williams
Interview with André De Shields
Expert advice from Shaka King

Cool Points 110

RELAXED ELEGANCE
Interview with Ahmad Rashad

SPORTS
Guest essay by Craig Rose
Interview with Reggie Miller
Expert advice from Anthony McIntosh

On the Good Foot 132

THE SHOE
Interview with Gregory Hines

DANCE
Guest essay by George Faison
Interview with Savion Glover
Expert advice from Star

Just Above My Head 154

THE HAT
Interview with LL Cool J and Russell Simmons

HIP-HOP
Guest essay by Julia Chance
Interview with Sean "Puffy" Combs
Expert advice from Rod Springer

Say It Loud 178

HAIR
Interview with Maxwell

ROCK N' ROLL
Guest essay by Michael Gonzales
Interview with Lenny Kravitz
Expert advice from Ademola Mandella
    and Orin Saunders

Facing the Rising Sun 202

ETHNICITY
Interview with Cornel West

LUMINARIES
Guest essay by Constance C. R. White
Interview with Jesse Jackson
Expert advice from Moshood

If It Ain't Got That Swing 224

THE DETAILS
Interview with Renauld White
Interview with Tyson Beckford
Expert advice from Leonard Bridges

FOREWORD

African-American men have always maintained a sense of pride in the way we present ourselves. The root of this can probably be traced back to the motherland, where festive adornment was part of our culture. In Africa, the way men and women dressed bespoke tribal allegiance, social standing, and religious affiliation. But it was our colorful style execution that distinguished us. Dressing was elevated from basic necessity to visual celebration, and that spirit is still with us today. Despite the centuries of suppression we suffered during slavery, when we weren't allowed to practice our religions, speak our languages, or create our art, we somehow managed to maintain our sense of self-expression. As newly freed men, we optimistically adopted the dress of our White counterparts, hopeful of being accepted into mainstream society. Whenever possible, we put our own spin on style.

There has always been a unique correlation between style and music. From performers such as The Mills Brothers and Louis Armstrong in the thirties and forties, to Count Basie, Cab Calloway, Nat "King" Cole, Billy Eckstein, Duke Ellington, Dizzy Gillespie, and Miles Davis in the fifties, to the individualistic, rebellious, and Afrocentric styles of Jimi Hendrix, James Brown, Marvin Gaye, Sly Stone, and George Clinton during the sixties and seventies, to the flamboyant ebullience of Michael Jackson and the hip-hop culture of the eighties and nineties, musicians have always displayed a cutting-edge style. Perhaps because music is an art form that cannot be contained by cultural boundaries, images of musicians are accepted and adopted more readily by society at large.

I was born in Chicago, and grew up in the forties in Bremerton, Washington, where I would try to emulate the styles of the various jazz bands that came through town. Whether it was the Ellington, Jimmy Lunceford, or Basie Band, all of the members exuded a hip, almost regal, dignity. That dignity, that carriage, that style, created an aura alien to the majority of African Americans at the time. The philosophy of Black pride was instead an unwritten, unspoken anomaly, one that could only be perceived. Musicians were not the only ones to adapt traditional dress, but they became the prime purveyors of the message, and subsequently inspired African-American men across the country with their unfettered creativity. It is a quality in musicians that I have admired from the time I was a boy. I became a musician myself not only because I love music on so many different levels, but also because I was inspired by the pride musicians exuded through their style. To this day, the influence of musicians can be seen in the proliferation of hip-hop style all over the world.

In *Men of Color: Fashion, History, Fundamentals*, we finally have the opportunity to reflect on, revel in, and learn about the living legacy that is Black male style. I applaud Lloyd Boston for bringing to life this fascinating, informative, long-overdue volume, one that I hope will live on for generations of us to reflect upon.

QUINCY JONES

INTRODUCTION

Lloyd Boston's *Men of Color: Fashion, History, Fundamentals* is a glorious accomplishment, a treasure chest of cross-cultural cadences. As I think about what the book means above and beyond the boundaries of its bindings, I float back to a text by the Harlem Renaissance writer Zora Neale Hurston on spirituals and neo-spirituals. In her essay, Hurston defines true spirituals as more than mere songs. Rather, she declares, "They are unceasing variations around a theme." Boston has achieved the literary equivalent of such soulful spirituals, simultaneously celebrating the subtle nuances and setting forth a sweeping overview of a single, central theme—the undeniable stylishness of the Black man.

And what nuances! The subject of hair alone merits its own chapter: From the brilliantine 'dos of the fifties, when men of color thought kinky hair was something to be controlled and when a pot of pomade was as vital to personal hygiene as a toothbrush, to the far-out Afros of the sixties and seventies, to the elaborately carved fades of the eighties and the smooth domes of the nineties, the Black man's coif is as unique as its owner.

The Black man is a sartorial force to be reckoned with: His influence is international. For example, Michael Roberts, an American photographer and fashion critic based in Paris, wears polo shirts and khaki trousers when working in his atelier. On the road, traveling for professional purposes, he favors sleek, single-breasted Hugo Boss and Giorgio Armani suits, Manolo Blahnik brogues, and an efficient Woolrich parka in winter. "Suits are time-savers," Roberts states. "They eliminate the question of what to wear, give me time to do other things. And as with any other uniform, a suit eliminates indecision. Plus, it prevents people from judging you based on what you wear, prevents them from jumping to conclusions."

Witness Maxwell, age twenty-four, one heartbeat away from Marvin Gaye's ethos. The native New Yorker doesn't have to resort to stomping on stage in satin pajamas to evoke sexual heat, or sexual healing. His aura? Subtle, sensual, mysterious. "At present, my style is minimalist, the externalization of the evolution of my own inner confidence. I don't feel the need to be flashy today, but tomorrow, who knows how I might want to express myself?" In December 1997, that self-expression unfurled into a light fantastic when the singer took the stage at a gala black-tie event in Manhattan: Strategically positioned at the inner and outer corners of each eye were mirrored chips. No makeup. "I had wanted to play with light centered around the eye for a long time," the singer explained. "The idea was inspired by my own personal problems with eye-to-eye-contact, with people staring right into my soul."

With just one look, the Black man had launched another trend. Karl Lagerfeld was so impressed with Maxwell's ocular adornment that the image fueled his Chanel Spring/Summer 1998 collection. "I admire Maxwell," the über-designer proclaimed. "He made a very modern statement, but one that was also reminiscent of the brilliant Man Ray photograph of the hyper-real glycerine teardrops."

Dr. Janis A. Mayes, associate professor of African-American Studies at Syracuse University in New York, confirms the impact of the Black man on fashion: "Bold colors, rich patterns—what men of color wear, other people want to wear. Black male style is endlessly imitated and re-appropriated by other races." American culture is both frightened by and fascinated with Black beauty. "The politics of eroticization are nowhere more evident than in the media representations of the Black male body," Dr. Mayes continues. "Mass culture is constantly in conflict, simultaneously desiring and fearing the Black man."

What motivates a well-dressed man of color? Is he not engaging in a performance of sorts, a play for respectability? The man of color uses his style to individuate himself, to identify himself. His appearance expresses his social status, professional power, personal achievement, sex appeal. The fabulous, flamboyant fashions proudly worn by the African-American brother ultimately celebrate his evolution, from the castrated slave to the empowered, procreative, unstoppable superman.

ANDRÉ LEON TALLEY

Author's NOTE

DON'T FLIP THE BRIM ON A BLACK

man's hat, caress his well-coifed hair, or extend an embrace that may wrinkle his crisply starched shirt. And never, under any circumstances, step on a brother's shoes—a simple "excuse me" will *not* suffice. Sound harsh? Maybe. But for many African-American men living in the twentieth century, garments are considered as valuable as financial portfolios, luxury vehicles, and real estate. Trespassing on the "grounds" that we've called duds, threads, vines, rags, and even gear is more than an invasion of personal space, it's an assault on the only element of our image that we have fully controlled: our style.

Be it social, political, or economic, our struggle for self-expression has left an indelible mark on what

Duke Ellington held tight to his personally molded hat on the set of *Belle of the Nineties* in 1934 *(top)*. The Jimmy Lunceford Orchestra took to the skies in smart three-piece suits and ties *(above)*. Dressed in fluidly draped double-breasted suits, The Mills Brothers posed with Bill "Bojangles" Robinson in 1933 *(right, Robinson center)*. Red-hot music made for some mad jitterbugging at the Savoy Ballroom in 1947, although no amount of heat could deflate the smooth style of these two Harlemites *(opposite)*.

the world views as American. In business, politics, sports, and the arts, our influence is undeniable. Our impact on style is no exception.

Clothes have always been a necessity, but culture, religion, environment, and ego are all factors that affect what we wear. For Black American men in particular, who have emerged from a history of slavery and segregation, and who continue to be stereotyped and stigmatized, clothing has always served a symbolic purpose. What we wear signals where we are and, more important, where we want to be. Whether the look is tough, affluent, Afrocentric, or preppie, our sartorial skill is also a survival skill.

Black male style has always been more about the "how" than the "what," emphasizing the way an item is worn as opposed to the item itself, and focusing on detail. For a Black zootie in the forties, a high shine on a two-toned wing tip wasn't complete until the excess polish was removed with a toothpick from the shoe's decorative perforations. A seventies soul brother could be just as meticulous about the symmetrically aligned, home-braided cornrows he wore to bed at night as he was about the precision-cut blowout he wore by day. And when break-dancing broke in the eighties, creased pants were as important then as they were in forties—in fact, when a hard-pressed crease wouldn't last through the acrobatic feats of this dance craze, b-boys took it upon themselves to stitch in a vertical thrust that made their Lees stand permanently at attention.

Black male style is no coincidence: A lineage of strength and pride filters into fabrics we've sewn, standards we've twisted, traditions we've abandoned, and trends we've ignited. African-American men have developed a science to dressing that has expanded the parameters for all men. Ironically, styles born of a struggle for self-definition have often been whimsically appropriated by mass-market fashion. From Dizzy Gillespie's bebop beret to White beatnik chic; from the street hustle of the uptown player to John Travolta's

The seventies saw the rise of both urban-hustler and Afrocentric styles. Wide-brimmed fedoras and tight double knits were essential to any true player's wardrobe *(opposite),* **while loose-fitting, graphically printed caftans became the unofficial uniform on college campuses** *(above).* **Afros crowned the heads of neo-Nubian princes, creative facial hair kept it funky.**

finger-pointing, disco-dance-floor version in *Saturday Night Fever;* and, of course, from Michael Jordan's personal preference for longer basketball shorts to their eventual acceptance on and off the court—Black male style always makes its way into the mainstream.

As we are many, we are one. Each of us embraces a style unique to our state, city, town, and even 'hood. We share a common ingredient of original expression that can't easily be defined because it manifests itself in so many different ways. For me, to step out the door each day without first having planned my outfit down to the last detail has never been an option. I'm sure this is a typical ritual for most Black men.

Before sitting down to write *Men of Color: Fashion, History, Fundamentals*, I had to first stand in front of the mirror and ask myself what made my clothing different. In those honest moments, I began to understand the meaning behind such Black collo-quialisms as "smooth as silk." For newly freed men raising their families, building communities, creating businesses, and developing a vision for a solid future, a focus on "clean" dressing informed America that we, too, wanted our share, while our emphasis on color and texture reaffirmed our ties to Africa. As a product of this dual legacy, I celebrate the self-defined image that leads, inspires, and makes no apologies. When I secure my belt and glance over my entire ensemble, I smile at the sight of Adam Clayton's creases, Martin's light starch on my collar, Ossie's felt-tipped brim, and Malcolm's high shine. They will undoubtedly carry me through my own daily battles.

It is not enough to give accolades to the brand names we've loved, or to cite the perpendicular angles on which we've propped our hats, or to classify the pos-tures and near-choreographed gaits that the world has deemed "cool." My wish at the outset of writing this book was to document a true celebration of Black male style in America. Since so few texts exist to confirm our style contributions, it was important to me that the book

be as accurate and elegant as possible. I asked myself what I would want to see in such a volume, and the answers spilled forth: an array of beautiful archival photographs from the turn of the century to the pre-sent day; original images of my favorite celebrities, accompanied by their stories and secrets for great personal style—in their own words, as told to me in brother-to-brother conversations; fundamental "how-to" information on building a functional, high-quality wardrobe; and an insightful dialogue between Black men, one that would explain and validate what I always knew to be true about our style. It is my hope that I have achieved exactly this, an unprecedented gathering of Black men who respect the impact Black male style has had on the world. (And no such celebration would be complete without a word or two from a few of our sisters, for who better to appreciate the beauty of a Black man than a Black woman?)

This volume is intended to pay homage to a spirit of strength that has channeled itself through style—a style spawned from bloody struggle, from a genuine need to be heard firsthand, seen eye-to-eye, counted on our feet. Black male style, this mystifying twist on necessity, is the outward expression of an on-going fight to keep from being rendered invisible.

Menswear designer John Bartlett makes it a point to feature Black male models in his collections (*opposite*), and he explains his choice with conviction: "African-American men are unafraid of expressing themselves through their clothes. Elegant peacocks, they perfectly balance street gear and status labels. They wear the clothes with a swagger that conveys the masculinity and sexiness of my designs. Men of color seem to have a unique ability to mix classic clothing with pieces that are more ethnic or exotic. Such ensembles marry the various multicultural elements that influence style. In the world of men's fashion, many designers either shy away from using Black models on their runways or use them in a way that connotes hip-hop style. But for me, men of color have a confidence that translates across the board, from the most traditional to the most experimental clothing looks."

Miles AHEAD

the suit

jazz

"... there was a world in which you wore your everyday clothes on Sunday, and there was a world in which you wore your Sunday clothes every day."

RALPH ELLISON

THE suit

of clothing, the suit has served as a sort of leveling device for Black men. Be it the hard-earned indulgence of a day laborer or the hand-me-down received from an older relative, be it custom-tailored or home-sewn, there's no denying the air of respectability gained by a man wearing a suit. Sartorially, it was the ultimate assimilator.

Imagine the pride a colored man must have felt when donning a full suit—jacket, trousers, and, in some instances, waistcoat—for the first time. By assuming what for a man is probably the highest order of dress outside of full military regalia, he hoped to be looked upon with respect. Consciously affected speech and mannerisms went hand-in-hand with a studied approach to style. By combining tailored clothing and social graces, he confronted the challenge to appear correct. For Black men, the traditional suit has always been an external manifestation of an inner determination to be seen as equal, from head to toe. In the endeavor, brothers embraced the suit as a core wardrobe item. It provided a palatable foreground, strongly stating its owner's self-assurance.

In the twenties, with the help of the electric sewing machine, Black men became self-taught valets, relying on their own resourceful styling instead of buying prefabricated garments. Necessity taught us how washing, pressing, and proper fittings helped lesser-quality suits come to life. When injected with inventive flair, such suits—and their owners—were a force to be reckoned with.

For many style-conscious men regardless of race, the classic, tailored suit has been viewed as a wardrobe stifler, limiting self-expression. But for Black men with integration on their minds, displaying individuality was

Single- or double-breasted suits, accented with waistcoat, watch chain, or bow tie, outfitted the VanDerZee men in 1909 (previous spread, left). Count Basie embodied jazz style in his sharp double-breasted suit (previous spread, right). In 1910, a southern businessman's staunch belted suit with peaked lapel and cargo pockets mirrored military regalia (top). Fitted waists, featured in both the radical zoot (above) and the more conservative work suit (opposite), held brothers together in the forties.

not the goal. For former slaves and sons thereof, discarding most cultural expression posed little problem, since our acceptance up to that point had depended on a careful balance between Euro- and Afrocentric sensibilities. But by the thirties, when stars such as trumpeter Louis Armstrong hit the scene, many blue-collar Black men began to aspire to a look that would dazzle the neighborhood as much as the jazzman dazzled his audiences. Armstrong, whether wearing a double-breasted, cream wool suit with three-inch cuffs or his rarely seen "plus fours" (the affectionate name for knickers), argyle socks, and newsboy cap, set forth an eclectic example of all that our style could be.

As we approached the middle of the century, guided by the jazzy sensibilities of the swing and bebop eras, we created regional suit styles and accompanying swaggers that would cross-pollinate state-to-state, region-to-region, like the latest dance steps: Harlem's zoot suit, with its elongated jacket, wide lapels, and super-wide-brimmed felt hat; Atlanta's refreshingly southern seersucker day suit, topped with a madras-banded straw hat; Chicago's own black velvet zip-front suit, best complemented by a coordinating, maxi-length opera coat complete with removable cape. Be it the forties, fifties, or seventies, signature styles like these were destined for a town near you.

"Suiting up" for an occasion has always meant knowing the intended venue and its roster of guests. At the Savoy Ballroom in the forties, the suit was worn high, with rubber-soled "gym shoes" for swinging. Grafton Trew, a seventy-seven-year resident of Harlem, recalls, "Italian silk and shantung were the fabrics of choice for evening suits in the forties. . . . In the winter, you would wear your wools and stripes, your dark suits for weddings or funerals or informal dances." Comfort

At Morehouse College in the sixties, stylish students favored streamlined versions of standard suitings *(above)*. In 1954, New York congressman Adam Clayton Powell, Jr.'s already-epic stature next to Liberian president William Tubman was further enhanced by an elegant pinstriped suit *(right)*. Fueled by Blaxploitation films of the seventies, brothers dressed to excess in flamboyant attire, including loud plaid jackets and "elephant-leg" flares *(opposite)*.

was obviously important in the oversized-yet-fitted, frankly rebellious, zooty take on the traditional suit. In spite of wartime fabric restrictions set by the government in 1942, style pariahs were always a step ahead. Blacks celebrated the extremes, igniting the going palette of staid grays and greens with sunset yellows and celestial blues. Hiking up the waistline by doubling the rise. Darting the jackets mid-section to emphasize the waist. Eliminating inches of fabric at the cuff to "peg" the leg to the point of impeding circulation. Angling the shoulders to create a shelf effect with disproportionate amounts of padding. The combined effect? The male take on an hourglass figure. Go figure.

Although zoot suit inventor Hal Fox felt the ensemble was the "end to end all ends" ("zoot" appropriately beginning with the coolest, alphabet-closing letter), many established entertainers, including the natty Nat "King" Cole and the suave Bobby Short, disagreed. "I had to take a firm stand about my own personal sense of style," Short remembers. "A zoot suit was clown stuff . . . I wore my tight white tails instead." The timeless sophistication of such artists evolved into a separate sect of forties Black style, and paved the way for trendsetters like vocalist Joe Williams and balladeer Johnny Mathis.

In the fifties, most Black men wore conventional square suits with narrow lapels and full pants. Thin ties were standard fashion accessories, as were felt fedoras. But as barriers were broken, so were most of the very trends we'd set. Sixties suits had a softer shoulder, one that was able to be turned away in the face of "separate but equal." They had a leaner leg, one that could endure countless miles marched in hope. And they were notched with a thin tie, stretched to the breaking point by traditions that were choking our dreams. With the advent of synthetic, silklike fabrics such as sharkskin or shantung, which weighed much less than wool, Black men once again created a new aesthetic: the "continental suit." Its razor-sharp pant creases could cut an innocent passerby. Slimmer in shape overall, with a longer line from the shoulder down to the tapered, cuffless leg, it became the signature look of brothers who sang in harmony, such as the pendulum-swinging Four Tops, who broke in 1963 with their first Motown hit, "Baby, I Need Your Lovin'."

As our celebrities' style evolved, we followed suit. In 1973, when The Four Tops asked, "Are You Man Enough?," we responded with suits cut so tightly in certain areas as to give the world a resounding "Yes!" Double-knit polyester bell-bottomed trousers hugged our hips. Belted suit jackets with brocade-flap pockets topped high-rolled collar, tropical-fruit-colored, nylon fitted shirts. Some of us completed the suit with a simple silk scarf knotted at the neck and an elevated slip-on "croc" in at least two tones. Of course, there were leaders of this new school who pushed the envelope, layering gold chains in place of a simple sash, tipping in six-inch platform shoes, and carrying a brass-capped walking stick. For the Black man in the decade of "The Mack" and "Sweet Sweetback," excess was the benchmark of true player suit style. But did we play ourselves?

Many brothers who spent the seventies sequestered in the halls of Morehouse or Harvard may have thought so. Our charge into the last two decades of the twentieth century has been led by a suited regiment of business mavericks. As the CEO of Beatrice Holdings, Wall Street power broker Reginald Lewis struck an authoritative chord with his pinstriped power suits. On television, Blair Underwood's staunch yet softly elegant, double-breasted, earth-toned Hugo Boss suits sat solidly on the back of the fictional *L.A. Law* firm's Black attorney. In contrast, on the hot, sandy shores of Miami, Phillip Michael Thomas, as "Detective Rico Tubbs," kept his cool in pastel-colored, single-buttoned, silk/rayon suits that transcended their individual labels to become the *Miami Vice* look.

Without question, Black men have embraced the suit like a long-lost sweetheart. Polished with our careful attention to detail, this tailored coat of arms has helped place us among the greatest warriors of business and entertainment. The suit has protected us like a well-crafted security system of style.

The future "King of Pop," Michael Jackson, kept
the seventies "soul brother" look intact with
his custom-made, white polyester, bell-bottomed
suit, trimmed with braided silver for added star
quality *(above, left)*. In the eighties, the corporate
maverick made his mark in designer duds *(left)*.
The zoot suit, updated with exposed shirt cuffs
and ever-longer proportions, reaffirmed its influence in the nineties *(above, right)*.

Wynton MARSALIS

"THE SUIT"

Suits are my work clothes, they're what I wear onstage. A tailored suit projects a clean, streamlined image, and when people see that you're clean, they know that you're serious. It makes them pay attention. Moreover, suits lend a sense of ceremony to what I do, and my performances are ceremonious occasions. My favorite suits are made by Joseph Abboud—I love his classic proportions, earthy palette, and the newness of his designs. I also like suits by Dimitri, Hugo Boss, Canali, Armani, and Versace.

Braces are my accessory of choice. They don't rumple the waist of my pants the way a belt can, and they rarely need adjusting, which is important when I'm performing. I wear them in different colors and patterns. It makes for a nice effect when my jacket flies open. Color is another key element of my style. I'm inspired by the works of Matisse. Oftentimes I try to emulate his bright color combinations in the way I put my ensembles together.

I grew up in the seventies, which, in my opinion, was a decade without much style—from those awful polyester leisure suits to the big platform shoes. Instead, I referred to the legends of jazz for style inspiration. Some of the cleanest cats were Duke Ellington, Miles Davis, and, of course, Louis "Pops" Armstrong. The Duke in particular had a knack for unexpected color. Many people don't know it, but Duke Ellington was also a talented painter who gave up a Fine Arts scholarship to Pratt Institute in order to pursue jazz. His artful approach to color was evident in his clothing, both onstage and off. Miles, on the other hand, was simply cool, and so very clean in the early years of his career. He had a real sense of what style meant, as was evident in his slim, fitted suits. But it was Louis Armstrong's image, probably more than any other, that influenced the clean look I aspire to. Many of today's young lions seem to be asserting more of a rock and roll persona, wearing T-shirts and jeans to gigs. It's too bad they're not helping to carry on the style started by legends like Miles and The Duke.

Brothers should own at least one beautifully crafted, bad-ass Italian hat—a Borsalino being my personal favorite. Black men can wear hats better than anyone on the face of this Earth! They should also have three basic suits: a classic navy that's either solid or pinstriped, a herringbone, and a charcoal-gray flannel. I recommend single-breasted jackets, because I find them to be more versatile, but it's a matter of choice. I also prefer a three-button model, because varying the number of buttons you close can change the whole look of a suit. Besides, I like the number three. The trumpet has three valves, there's the Father, Son, and Holy Ghost, the three-act play. The blues has three sections, as does the human body. It's an important number for me.

JAZZ

BY THOMAS TERRELL

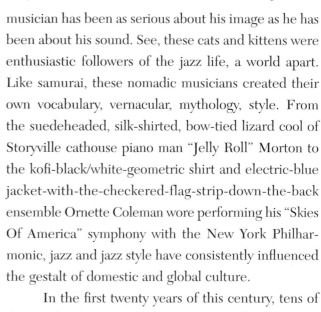

FROM JUMP, THE CONSUMMATE JAZZ

musician has been as serious about his image as he has been about his sound. See, these cats and kittens were enthusiastic followers of the jazz life, a world apart. Like samurai, these nomadic musicians created their own vocabulary, vernacular, mythology, style. From the suedeheaded, silk-shirted, bow-tied lizard cool of Storyville cathouse piano man "Jelly Roll" Morton to the kofi-black/white-geometric shirt and electric-blue jacket-with-the-checkered-flag-strip-down-the-back ensemble Ornette Coleman wore performing his "Skies Of America" symphony with the New York Philharmonic, jazz and jazz style have consistently influenced the gestalt of domestic and global culture.

In the first twenty years of this century, tens of thousands of African Americans migrated primarily to the industrial centers of Kansas City, Chicago, and New York City. Inevitably, the flow pulled jazz musicians right along with it. Each of the cities began to develop an individual band scene with its own bona fide superstar (Benny Moten's Kansas City Orchestra, Chicago's King Oliver's Creole Jazz Band, New York's Fletcher Henderson Orchestra). The jazz life in these cities had strict style codes. In KC, the music had to be low-down and jumpin', the look: big-brimmed fedoras, three-piece suits, double-breasted overcoats, wool sox, wing tips. In Chi-town, jazz was syncopated rhythm and dance solos, the look: top hats, homburgs, pomaded hair, black tuxes, Brooks Brothers two-button suits, white sox, Florsheim two-tones. In NY, big bands played jungle swing, the look: derbies, fedoras, fur or cashmere overcoats, cutaway tuxes, baggy double-breasted suits, silk sox, English brogues. Dapper both on and off the stage, these musicians were the

Singer Joe Williams swathed his velvet throat in a silk ascot *(top)*. Trumpeter Louis "Pops" Armstrong sported a tailored three-piece suit, four-point pocket square, and chain-link bracelet in the thirties *(above)*. Legends Thelonious Monk, Howard McGhee, Roy Eldridge, and Teddy Hill, outside Minton's Playhouse in 1948, epitomized smooth jazz style *(opposite top, left to right)*. Who's the coolest cat? Nat "King" Cole, a class-act in a chalk-striped suit *(opposite, bottom)*. Trumpeter Dizzy Gillespie, the architect of bebop, structured his look around dapper French berets, dark-framed glasses, and a spunky goatee *(opposite, far right)*.

style councilors, the few beacons of Black creativity, empowerment, and pride in those trying times. Rank-and-file Black folk emulated the dress and style of these musicians. Many went so far as to make the jazz life their own.

During jazz's first golden era (1930–1944), big-band swing became both Black and White America's lingua franca. As always, Black folk not only invented the dances but also were the first to jump on the fashion trends set by the artists. Jazz musicians became the supermodels of the day. Taking their cues from

Pianist Earl "Fatha" Hines played it slim and trim in a fifties slender suit and skinny tie *(above, Hines in middle)*. **Avant-garde sax-man John Coltrane's music may have been "giant steps" ahead, but he favored an understated style of dress: single-breasted sack suits, button-down oxford shirts, and plain ties** *(right)*. **Thelonious Monk kept it cosmopolitan with his multicultural collection of hats** *(opposite, top)*, **while drummer Max Roach chose the casual, counting time in short-sleeved polo shirts** *(opposite, bottom)*.

the icons' styles—Coleman Hawkins's roomy double-breasteds, Cab Calloway's yellow zoot suit, Lester Young's porkpie hat, thin necktie, and private language, Earl "Fatha" Hines's shades, Duke Ellington's cigarette attitude and classically natty wardrobe—the young, hip masses of Black America added their own flavas: loud, coordinated colors, eccentric hat blocking embellished with freaky feathers, wide-ass lapels, gold jewelry, gold teeth, and wild-gravity conks.

As the forties waned, a new sound and style emerged to usher in jazz's next magic age. Bebop, a furious Black scream of manhood, was poised to rock the world. Its avatars played, and looked, like gods. Each had his own vision mojos: Dizzy Gillespie workin' that beret-goatee-rectangular-eyeglasses thing, Thelonious Monk topped with his kooky collection of caps, brims, and crowns (a white bamboo number comes to mind), Howard McGhee stylin' shades 24-7, Lucky Thompson parading his Monte-Carlo-chic profile. In the still-segregated, Korean War/Eisenhower fifties, beboppers were the only visual evidence of Black individuality. Defiantly non-status quo, boppers flipped the script by adopting the button-down Brooks Brothers Wall Street special as their own uniform. Cool music, cool clothes, cool life. (Footnote: The classic Blue Note Brooks Brothers LP cover look has perenially inspired youth from the UK to Japan.)

When Miles Davis upped the ante with cutting-edge drapes from London's Saville Row, his impeccable taste garnered him two "best-dressed" citations from *Esquire* magazine. As formidable as Davis's musical legacy is, his four decades of style innovations should not be forgotten. When he switched to continental cuts in the sixties, he sparked a change that was reflected in the trench-coated, sharkskin darkness of The Temptations and their young "playa" followers. By the Summer of Love, Miles began to feel constricted by both self-image and music. He found his next style in the funk of James Brown, the rockin' gospel of Sly Stone, the psychedelic spaces of Jimi Hendrix. Surrounding himself with younger, electri-

fied players, Miles's entire zeitgeist simultaneously expanded and devolved.

Ditching the suits, Miles relaxed, flowing effortlessly into the seventies Black freak groove. He began with a razor-cut Afro, hippie beads, ribbed wool henley shirts, velvet bell-bottoms, ankle boots, and progressed to wraparound specs, gold links, Comme des Garçons threads, suede boots. A true samurai mack-daddy, the trumpeter owned several Lamborghinis and Ferraris and lived in a chill crib decorated like a Casbah grotto.

Miles came back in the eighties with an upbeat, funky sound and a decidedly pan-global fashion view. In the spirit of the times, he was b-boy fresh: bicycle caps, shag hair weaves, Gaultier frames, Versace tops, Miyake sets, Bruno Magli kicks. Until his death in 1991, Miles Davis was the international paradigm of iconic jazz élan. His influence reverberates still.

Miles's sartorial gifts were truly rare, but other jazz lifers have left their marks in the sands of contemporary fashion. Count Basie had his yachtsman's caps. Wes Montgomery and Jimmy Smith popularized stingy-brim fedoras. Ray Charles hyped tortoise-shell Ray Bans. Sun Ra pioneered African robes. Sonny Rollins wore a Mohawk. Yusef Lateef made baldness a fashion statement. Elvin Jones swung Nehrus and medallions, Roy Haynes strutted Borsalinos, Lester Bowie jammed in a white lab coat (complete with pocket protector), Pharaoh Sanders invented the hip high-priest vibe, Don Cherry originated rooster-comb dreads. Wynton Marsalis viciously rocked Armani and Hugo Boss.

Whither tomorrow's new jazz style? The clues can be found in the electric pastels of Graham Haynes's Hush Puppies, in the insouciant classicism of Roy Hargrove's kit, in Joshua Redman's DKNY, Rodney Kendrick's greatcoats, Branford Marsalis's team-sports casuals. One thing is for sure—when/wherever jazz musicians style grandly, we will be compelled to follow.

Over the course of a career that spanned more than four decades, trumpeter Miles Davis earned a reputation as a style chameleon, constantly changing his look: In the seventies, he posed in front of his vast and varied wardrobe (opposite). Trumpeter Wynton Marsalis, in homage to his style idol Louis Armstrong, promoted a return to clean, classic suits, such as this off-white, single-breasted, three-piece outfit, accented with two-toned shoes and gold necktie (above).

George BENSON

"JAZZ"

My music heroes—Nat "King" Cole, Billy Eckstein, Duke Ellington, "King" Curtis—were the best-dressed men in music. And Miles Davis, of course. He never ceased to amaze me. He was really in the vanguard. His style was so thoroughly thought-out and he was always well-groomed. He'd hit the stage chipper, dressed to kill and ready to blow the roof off the place. Even when he'd reached his seventies, he still looked good. Of the cats today, actors Billy Dee Williams and Denzel Washington come to mind. Denzel's a little looser with what he wears, but there's a neatness to him. He can put on a T-shirt and a pair of pants and still look good. It's the *way* he wears his clothes. Wynton Marsalis's style has helped his image and the image of jazz in general. He comes across as talented and knowledgeable—a clean horn player with a clean image to match.

Back in the forties and fifties, it was not uncommon to see artists dressed to the max, 100 percent. They wore pinstriped zoot suits with those great big baggy pants, pocket-watches on chains, and big fedoras to top it off. Very sharp. It's not the style of dress, but the way you use your clothing to enhance your appearance that makes the difference.

Today's youth would say that the way I dress is a bit much—they like to dress down—but it's normal for me. I have a lot of nice pieces, and because I'm flexible, I can make almost anything work. I'm not a fussy dresser, but if I put on clothes that don't feel right I'll stand in front of my closet for twenty minutes trying to find something that makes the statement I want to make for that day.

I like wearing sports jackets, they're versatile. On the other hand, when I wear a suit I feel compelled to wear a shirt and tie. Wearing a suit with just an open-collar shirt can look a little sloppy. Trousers that complement my build are very important to me, and they must have a sharp crease.

Wearing a lot of jewelry is not my thing. To me, too much gold can spoil a look. Aside from my wedding ring, I wear a simple gold band. Also, I like wearing a nice watch, something sharp that gets noticed when your sleeve rises up.

In the early days of my career, I was not in a position to dress up, I didn't have the money. But my wife always suggested I do it anyway. She helped me to understand that paying attention to how I dressed would take me a long way. One time I went to a steakhouse for dinner wearing a T-shirt, and the maitre d' politely kicked me out. I was so insulted I called the mayor of the town and argued racial discrimination. But the mayor checked into it and got back to me: "The maitre d' said you were wearing a T-shirt." I admitted it was true. He then told me to go back to the restaurant the next day dressed appropriately, and to call him if I still had a problem. That next day I was sharp! I wanted to let the restaurant know I hadn't realized the importance of the dress code. I strolled on in wearing a suit and was treated much better.

Martin COOPER

DESIGN DIRECTOR, BURBERRY'S

Martin Cooper understands first-hand the power of the well-dressed man. As the director of design for Burberry's of London, Cooper oversees the creation of rainwear and tailored clothing collections for individual markets worldwide, including France, Italy, Germany, and the United States.

Cooper's success can be credited to his keen eye for detail and his accuracy in fit. He first developed his design talents and professional ethics working alongside top fashion designers such as Jeffrey Banks, Gloria Sachs, and Calvin Klein. He has been with Burberry's since 1994. A graduate of Parsons School of Design, Cooper resides in New York City.

The SUIT

Although Black men have a long tradition of fine suitings, today many of us think we're making informed decisions when in fact we're purchasing suits of secondary quality. When evaluating a suit, the following top-ten points should be kept in mind:

TAILORED FIT

Brutal honesty is the first step in approaching this important and often costly purchase. A man must evaluate his physical assets and attributes in order to accentuate the positive. Cooper regards buying a suit as striking a compromise, "finding a marriage between your own body type and a style appropriate for it." Whether tall and slim, short, stocky, or athletic in build, when buying a suit, size matters. Cooper insists, "Tailoring is everything." Find a good tailor to assist in adjusting an off-the-rack (store-bought, as opposed to custom-made) suit to your shape. For example, "I'm tall and skinny," Cooper continues, "and for that reason I always have my tailor do a 'waist compression,' completely scooping out the waist" in order to create the illusion of a broader shoulder. Developing a relationship with an experienced tailor will help you discover similar techniques to enhance your body type. With his expertise, a $200 suit can look like a million bucks.

VENTS

Vents are slits or cuts on the back of a suit jacket at the points where it covers the hips and buttocks. Not all jackets have them. Vents are stylized treatments, and ultimately a question of personal choice, but they offer definite advantages to certain body types. There are three basic variations of vents.

The first, the "center back" of the traditional American suit, covers a range of body types, particularly those of African-American men who often have muscu-

more of a "lip"—and Italian suits (left) are usually on the padded side. Cooper's experience has taught him that one style is not necessarily better than another for African-American men in general, but that each individual, adhering to the primary rule of honesty, should choose a shoulder that best complements his stature. For example, sloped shoulders may benefit from the boost provided by a British jacket, but a broad-backed man doesn't need to overstate the obvious with Italian padding.

SIZING

When selecting a suit, it's crucial to know the specifics of size—neck and shoulder width, sleeve length, waistline, and inseam (the measurement of the inside of the leg, from the center crotch to the top of the foot). Update measurements with the help of an experienced salesperson each season. A tailor can keep the numbers on file and notify you of any changes.

Even when selecting an off-the-rack suit, men have options to accommodate their build. "Athletic cuts," a relatively new development in standard-size suits, are made for larger proportions, specifically in the thigh, chest, and neck. Cooper notes that "most men may not even be aware of this choice, and may be squeezing into a 40 Regular when they could be easing into a 40 Regular Athletic Cut."

PANT LENGTH

True pant length is measured from the waist. Suit pants should fit comfortably, but without hanging off the waist, as might jeans or more casual trousers. A secure fit at the waist should allow for flat pleats and a fluid, vertical drape, or fall, off the leg. Pants should "break" slightly at the hem, the crease bending softly as it nears the shoe.

PANT CUFFS

Because of the added weight of the fabric, cuffs can help a suit's pant-leg fall in a clean line. Depending on fabric and pattern, cuffs can look less or more casual. Regard-

lar, athletic builds. The center back treatment gives a bit more ease in the behind without pulling the fabric.

The traditional English "double-vent," also referred to as a "twin" or "side" vent, has a vent on either side of the jacket, falling near the hipline. Originating in formal equestrian gear, where such vents proved functional for the rider on his mount, the double-vent, according to Cooper, "allows access to your pockets" without destroying the line of the suit.

The contemporary favorite of many Black men in America, the Italian "ventless" jacket (opposite), prohibits pocket access without rumpling the fabric. Cooper states that this choice "looks great from the front, but horrible from the back," because it often does not provide adequate coverage for more muscular or prominent hips, buttocks, and thighs.

SHOULDER

American-made suits have a narrow shoulder, English suits have a raised or "roped" shoulder—rope is actually inserted into the sleeve head to give the shoulder less of a suit's main purpose, be it business or leisure, Cooper recommends a standard inch-and-a-half cuff.

SLEEVE LENGTH

Sleeve length clearly delineates a tailored suit from a hand-me-down. In Cooper's opinion, "Sleeve length is based on shirt length. As a rule of thumb, the jacket's sleeves should always hit at roughly mid-palm." In general, five-eighths of an inch of cuff should be exposed, but this measurement can increase when wearing cuff links or French cuffs.

BUTTON CLOSURE

The age-old question of which buttons to close when wearing a suit jacket has no right answer. Cooper prefers the middle button, although a strong argument can be made in favor of the top button, which allows for better draping. Personal preference dictates the choice, but note that buttoning all buttons is always a no-no—it prevents ease of movement and even looks restrictive. Regardless of single- or double-breasted styles, the bottom button should always be left undone.

FABRIC

Wool gabardine—or "wool gab," as Cooper colloquially refers to it—is the most basic fabric for a versatile suit. "It may not be the most sophisticated choice in

the world, compared, for example, to wool crepe," he adds, "but you'll always fit in and you'll always feel comfortable." Taking into account today's advanced technology in fabrics, Cooper challenges Black men to once again embrace the latest in suits. Synthetic blends offer extra stability, while stretch fabrics provide a little give, allowing for options ranging from close-fitting silhouettes to fuller-cut suits.

POCKETS

Cooper cites four pocket options for jackets, all timeless. The first is the sometimes formal "besom," a slitlike opening made with two quarter-inch pipings. To preserve a jacket's line, it should remain closed. The second, the "flap" pocket, is inserted into the besom and is meant to cover the opening when the pocket is in use. The British "ticket" pocket is most often found on three-button suits: It holds a smaller pocket inside, similar to the coin pocket found on jeans, and, appropriately, is somewhat sportier in appearance. Lastly, Cooper himself dons an "over-the-patch" or "three" pocket, which includes a breast pocket in its equation.

Measuring UP

r&b

"Do a common thing in an uncommon way."

BOOKER T. WASHINGTON

THE pant

Paris, a vogue for illustrated pants gripped the city. These "painted" trousers were constructed of inexpensive materials printed with whimsical patterns, not unlike fabric wallpaper, and were sold at a low cost. One of the original styles, as described in *La Fashion*, a periodical of the day, was called the "Uncle Tom" and was "all covered with picaninnies." Popular American depictions of the "shiftless Negro" had made their way to foreign shores, and wandering minstrel shows—billed under such names as "The Burnt Cork Encyclopedia" and "The Crow Quadrilles"—helped to perpetuate the image internationally. Back in the States, our fascination with trousers, slacks, knickers, and drapes began when our coveralls were shed and our traveling pants were granted.

Of the many styles of pants Black men have embraced—including the woolen stovepipe trousers of the thirties, the pegged-legged blouson zoot pant of the war years, the coffee-can-cuffed dark blue Levis of the fifties, and the skinny, flat-front sharkskins in the decade to follow—all have had one thing in common: an interestingly awkward fit. Although many Black men adhere to careful measurements when having their trousers tailor-made, pants that are ready-to-wear present a perpetual challenge to the average physique. By the end of the sixties, the "pinched pant" had become a trademark look: Advertisements in magazines geared toward Black men and women proclaimed a new pant fit for "us," the "New Breed Slant" (from a clothing company of the same name), which accentuated the "capital assets of the black male" with a garment shaped to accommodate his special needs. But, oddly enough, by the time in African-American history when such options became available, the erotically obvious

Seven-inch coffee-can cuffs decorated the dungarees of Morehouse College men in the fifties (*previous spread, left*). R&B legend Jackie Wilson sang, split, and shimmied without a hint of sweat in pleated sharkskin pants (*previous spread, right*). Pinstriped wool trousers with three-inch cuffs properly outfitted a gentleman at the turn of the century (*top*). A forties jitterbug contestant combined comfort and style in his cuffed, stovepipe, saxony plaid pants (*above*). Ragging in tweed plus fours and roller skates, a little Harlem dandy put haberdashery in motion (*opposite*).

tension that resulted from our compressed "presence" in omnipresent off-the-rack trousers was exactly what we hoped to display. What better, more physical, proof of Black power? A style oxymoron, "confined freedom" from the bottom up!

Bell-bottoms were born from the hippie movement of the late sixties. Like most everything else of the era, bells represented the backlash against "the establishment"—in this instance, traditional "longline" or "continental" trousers. Cut tight at the waist and full at the leg, bell-bottoms made a sweeping statement, and were soon wardrobe staples of style-setting artists and entertainers.

Jazz legend Miles Davis, a St. Louis native who early in his career swore by the cuts and codes of his preferred preppie suit-maker, Brooks Brothers, found himself looking for a new bottom silhouette in the Afrocentric seventies. To accommodate his evolving, more active, stage persona, he turned to Black designer Stephen Burrows for a 180° switch. Patched suede bells did the trick. Burrows recalls his muse: "Miles's strong sense of individual style brought my clothing to life in a way that was totally unique and without apologies. In addition to my suede bells, he also wore my 'Mickey Mouse' pants, which were multicolored leather pants stitched together with leather cord, and he topped them with my signature bright-colored matte jersey T-shirts. He also had a few pairs of my fringed leather pants. His pride reminded me of a preening peacock, so confident, yet extremely sexy. As with the daring direction of his music, if he liked the threads he had on, he could care less what anyone else thought." Never

Rat-packer Sammy Davis, Jr. worked his sixties hip swagger in flat-front pegged-legs; hard creases marked his every dance step *(opposite)*. **From awning stripes to madras plaids, seventies flares set a funky pants precedent** *(above)*. **In linen, cotton, and seersucker trousers, Morehouse College students at a commencement day ceremony showcased forties southern style** *(right)*.

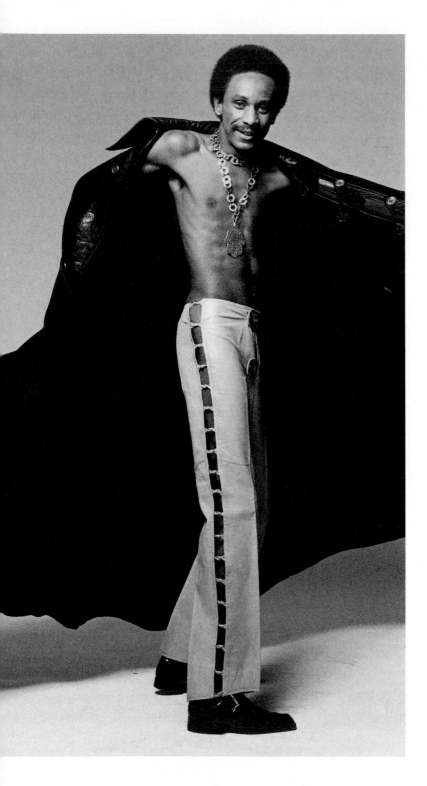

known for feeble commentary on anything, especially not his own style, Davis himself stated that "Niggers from St. Louis had a reputation for being sharp as a tack when it came to clothes. So couldn't nobody tell me nothing." His transformation was complete.

We watched our style heroes: on television, impeccably dressed on *The Jack Benny Show*; on newsreels, marching arm-in-arm for freedom in the Deep South; on the silver screen, as the "guess who" that came to dinner. These Black male icons sent a nonverbal message: Getting dressed starts with elegant, well-made pants, and when your style is smooth, you can be judged on what's inside. To this day, many Black men insist on a knife-sharp pant crease, often stitching it themselves, since no one else can do the detail quite as right. When the seventies brought the industrial dungaree back for a generation of hippies and White urban bohemians, many Black men held firm to dressier "player" looks inspired by both local hustlers and big-screen idols such as the muscle-clad Jim Kelly. As the title character in *Black Belt Jones* (1974), he wielded kicks and spins in his polyester fightin' pants—"spray can fit" in the seat, as described by author Ted Polhemus in *Street Style* (Thames & Hudson, 1994). In double-knit elephant-leg bell-bottoms with satin side stripes, or second-skin polyester leisure slacks, Black men of the seventies left a lasting impression.

Events of the late eighties dramatically changed the image of the Black man in America. Reverend Jesse Jackson placed second in the Democratic presidential primary, and made history with his electrifying speech at the 1988 party convention. Progressive politician Kurt Schmoke was elected the first Black mayor of Baltimore, and Kwesi Mfume earned a seat in the United States Congress. These pioneers preferred classic, conservative clothing: double-breasted navy suits, crisp white pinpoint cotton shirtings, jewel-toned ties, cap-toe oxfords. In sharp contrast to the buttoned-down politico chic of Capitol Hill, brothers on the street began to seriously loosen up. Customized

A seventies player was fit to be tied in his ladder-sided suede bell-bottoms; cutouts and a snug fit provided a sensual peek at the Black male myth *(above)*. Nineties supermodel Tyson Beckford catwalked the runway in classic, chalk-striped flannel trousers from Ralph Lauren's Fall 1997 collection *(opposite)*.

denim, authentic athletic uniforms, and ethnic accessories were mixed and matched with abandon.

A key element of this new silhouette was the oversized pant. Its dropped-to-the-hip "non-fit" was interpreted by many to be a style homage to a subculture of supposed drug dealers, gangsters, and slackers. Aggressively anti-fashion, the pants exposed underwear waistbands and sometimes more. Initially rejected by the mainstream for its controversial connection to criminal activity, the baggy pant has since become emblematic of hip-hop style, and has for the most part been claimed as another proud example of our fashion legacy.

The Reverend Jesse Jackson traced the "lazy waist" phenomenon to the influence of incarcerated Black men, who wore standard-issue prison pants low on their hips because belts—viewed as potential weapons—were forbidden in jail. Did the rage for baggy pants trickle out from the prison system onto city streets, or did it originate in the post-break-dance New York City club scene? Peter Paul Scott, a marketing executive and veteran of the eighties nightlife, believes dancers started the trend: "We wore our pants two, three sizes too large, for comfort when dancing at The Funhouse and MK's. We were slowly getting out of the fitted Lees that, as break-dancers, we worked the floor in. The new dance styles had us on our feet and in the air, and the 'baggies' kept us in flight. The bigger, the better."

Does source matter? Just as Black male style itself is diverse, so are its origins. The baggy pant is as important a cultural icon as the zoot suit, the Afro pick, or the "broke-down" Borsalino. It stands as an unmistakable example of our self-expression.

As an integral foundation element for most of our wardrobes, the pant has to be as agile as we are. Whether we're stompin' at the Savoy, leading a church revival, or staking our claim on the coveted trading floors of Wall Street, our trousers have helped us to take a stand with style.

More than any other article of clothing, well-fitting pants are essential to a Black man's wardrobe. Those bubble-butts of ours won't tolerate just anything. It's been an ongoing battle for me to figure out what cut of trouser gives me the best line, one that's elongating and slimming. Styles with a western pocket and straight leg usually do the trick. Prada makes a clean version, and I have some Comme des Garçons pants from the eighties that I still wear all the time.

Comfort is a key consideration for me when I get dressed. I've always feared what I call the "Rosie Grier effect." Grier is this huge, beautiful specimen of a man who always seemed stuffed into a suit. I've never liked the idea of my broad shoulders and long arms being crammed by a constricting jacket. Fortunately, styles have changed, and I've learned how to dress for my physique.

Bill T. JONES

"THE PANT"

My own style is very flamboyant. I like to break the rules about how to wear a sports jacket or how to pair pants with a particular top. The Black men in my adult life who have taught me the most about the joy of dressing and the confidence it conveys have been jazz musicians. Certainly Miles Davis was an example. He, Max Roach, and Julius Hemphill inspired me to indulge my innate sense of adornment, which I believe comes naturally to Black men.

I am a child of the sixties who very much identified with the counterculture of that time. As a teen, I was influenced by the styles of Jimi Hendrix. He had a certain finesse when it came to putting texture and color together, and I tried to imitate that. On the other hand, being the son of migrant workers and a working-class person myself made me gravitate toward simple clothes. They

had to be cotton, and they had to be wash-and-wear. I remember a time when owning more than one pair of shoes seemed sinful. But within the last fifteen years, as my career has expanded, I've begun to appreciate clothes that demand special care.

Sometimes if you are a "serious" artist, style can work against you. Stylishness can be mistaken for frivolousness. It's a very New York, avant-garde notion, a throwback to the sixties. It was liberating when I realized that, as an artist, I didn't have to look poverty-stricken all the time. The cuts and colors of what I wore could even serve as a sort of poetry, a commentary on who I was.

R&B

BY DAVID THIGPEN

FROM THE DELIRIOUSLY FLAMBOYANT

Marvin Gaye embraced a blue-blood aesthetic early in his career: preppie polo sweaters, flat-front pants, slim suits, even a yachtsman's cap *(above)*. **The Mills Brothers defined forties crooner style in clean jacket-and-tie combos; busboy jackets, slim satin ties, and pilgrim loafers were staples of the quadraphonic Four Tops in the sixties; James Brown pleaded for mercy in satin and sharkskin; the "dragonfly" bow ties, double-breasted ivory suits, and slicked-back hair of The Ink Spots set the style standard for many R&B artists** *(opposite, clockwise from top left)*.

getups sported in the fifties by Little Richard to the luxuriously retro-chic duds styled in the nineties by star crooner Maxwell, rhythm-and-blues performers have forever changed what's cool. Through their own ingenious riffs on the styles of the times, R&B musicians have established themselves as a force reaching beyond music into the world of fashion. In R&B's golden age of the late sixties and early seventies, stars such as James Brown, Sly Stone, and George Clinton became arbiters of young urban chic, with a style-setting power rivaling the Seventh Avenue houses. Their moves were closely watched, triggering trends and spawning imitators everywhere. The famous houses of Gucci and Yves St. Laurent found inspiration in the distilled refinement of Milan and Paris; R&B stars drew inspiration from less-polished precincts—from movies, from ghetto street corners, from colorful scenes happening right in the heart of American cities. The music and the clothes became inseparable, together symbolizing wealth, sophistication, sex, and an irrepressible individualism. By unhinging the rigid conservatism of mid-century America and allowing a new language of style to break through, R&B helped set off an explosion that resounds to this day. The music itself—rooted in the gospel and blues sounds of the early twentieth century—combined the sacred and the profane in a way that was irresistible to young listeners, promising transcendent pleasures and earthly gratifications. The clothes—a vital part of the package—offered the assurance of style. The fast, new, and vibrant culture of R&B became an ideal breeding ground for a fashion revolution. The style pioneered by Black men made a splash that rippled outward and circled the globe.

The staid world of the fifties was ripe for such a revolution. Bursting onto the national scene in 1955, Little Richard (born Richard Penniman) caused shock waves that, forty years later, reverberate in the styles of Elton John, Michael Jackson, and The Artist (formerly known as Prince). In an era that included the likes of Jackie Wilson (his love of rhinestone suits must have given Elvis ideas), Sam Cooke, and Ray Charles—whose uptown, sophisticated styles descended from the dapper twenties—Little Richard stood out from the pack. Silver lamé trousers, gold shirts, fuchsia jackets glittering with rhinestones—his outrageous style gleefully mowed down racial and sexual barriers. He made his appearances bedecked in a creamy white zoot suit, or a satin robe, or a mirrored overcoat. But the "common thread" in all his extravagant outfits was that each subverted the mold of Eisenhower-era conservatism. "I had to be different for people to know me," Richard explained. "Other guys looked more macho, so I made my hair higher and wore makeup so people didn't know where I was coming from." Richard's styles helped establish the R&B star as a larger-than-life figure.

By the sixties a bubbling brew of social and emotional turbulence was washing over America. Black Panthers were marching, cities were ablaze with protests and riots, a generation gap was widening, draft cards and brassieres were burning. Style fragmented, too. Miniskirts were in. Nehru collars were hot. So were Afros, neck medallions, and bell-bottoms. *Sweet Sweetback* was a hit in the cinemas, Richard Roundtree was a sex symbol, and Black Power was aborning. No one captured the rising updrafts of the times as did James Brown. Rakish, self-confident,

Piano man Ray Charles has maintained his classic cool for decades *(opposite)*. Stevie Wonder was one of the first artists to incorporate ethnicity into his image; his long, beaded cornrows celebrated the legacy of African adornment *(left)*. In the seventies, Marvin Gaye's style took a radical turn towards the Afrocentric—gone were the preppie captain's hats, replaced by knit kufis *(above)*.

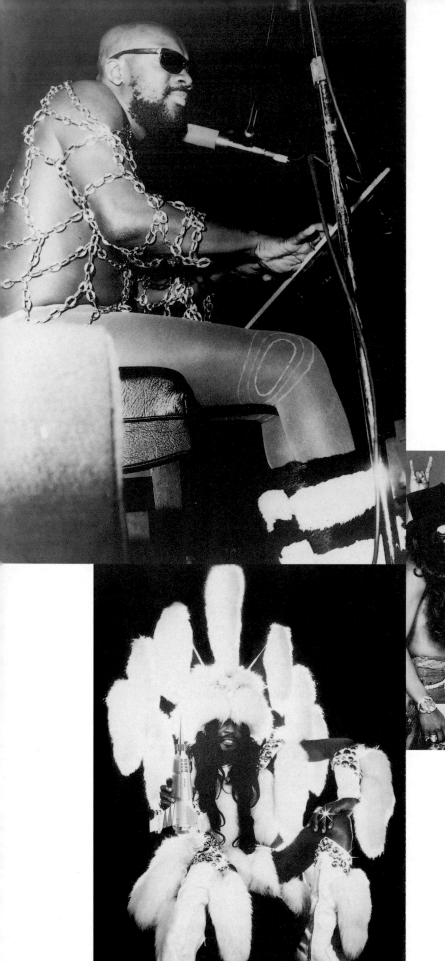

regal in his carriage, Brown developed a style that paralleled the rising Black Power movement. Almost never appearing without a suit, Brown reveled in being turned out, right down to the last ostentatious detail. In blindingly polished boots, skintight bell-bottoms, ruffled shirt, and silk cravat wrapped perfectly around his throat, Brown accomplished the impossible: He made a red, a yellow, an orange suit look sharp. Although he dripped with gold and diamonds the size of bottle caps, Brown brought a decidedly masculine flair to the style of the times, symbolizing the suave urban dandy whose self-pride was his bold statement to the world.

With perfectly matched suits and smoothly choreographed dances, the harmony groups of the late sixties presented an image of rooted calm, of sober

Soul maestro Isaac Hayes, aka "Black Moses," caused a sensation in a chain-metal creation custom-made by Hollywood designer Charles Rubin *(top, left)*. Captain of the Mothership George Clinton landed on Earth wearing riveted white leather platform boots with matching wristbands and a foxtail headdress *(bottom, left)*. Parliament Funkadelic set R&B style on fire with pounds of rhinestones, Day-Glo feathers and furs, skintight studded leather boleros, and stage takes on tribal makeup *(above)*. Funkateer Bootsy Collins's star-studded shades were symbolic of seventies fashion excess *(opposite)*.

middle-class prosperity. During their long careers, The Four Tops, The Spinners, and The Temptations ran the style gamut, from thin-lapelled business suits to sequined Vegas stage uniforms. In the sixties, suave was in. Detroit emerged as a hub of style and music, spawning the legendary Motown label and the natty, youthful figures of Stevie Wonder and Smokey Robinson, who belted out love songs whilst roaming the stage in classy three-piece suits. No less forgettable was The Jackson 5, who scored more points for music than for personal style. Later came the cool, reflective calm of Marvin Gaye. On the cover of *What's Going On?*, his best-selling album, he appeared in a trench coat. Understated style was in effect.

As the sixties wore on into the seventies, a new type of style symbol appeared, best exemplified by Sly Stone and Jimi Hendrix. Both represented an exuberant, powerful new youth culture that welcomed eccentricity, hungered for individualism, looked to a variety of styles, and gorged itself not just on R&B, but on rock and soul, too. The language of rebellion had become louder. Drawing on the outlandish legacy of Little Richard, Stone and Hendrix fashioned themselves as wildly flamboyant, princely figures. But they also embraced Black bohemia, taking their personal styles in equal measure from the more earthy hippie culture. Stone clearly had a foot in both camps, favoring fringe jackets, jeans, high-heel boots, and a huge Afro. Hendrix evolved one step further, donning headbands, western shirts, brocade vests, paramilitary jackets, and jewelry that bore spiritual significance. Hendrix and Stone were imitated by legions of fans, and their style lives on today, most visibly in the grunge finery of Lenny Kravitz.

It would be difficult to find a more memorably dressed duo than George Clinton and Bootsy Collins of Parliament Funkadelic, the greatest funk band of the seventies. Clinton's music was born of an untrammelled imagination, of fantasy and space travel, and he dressed for the part, uniformly outrageous. At times, sporting huge white cowboy hat, vest, and elephant bell-bottoms, he seemed to be a genetic mutation of Little Richard and Jimi Hendrix. In lavishly colored robes and glasses, he played the modern-day shaman. Bootsy Collins, in trademark supersized star spectacles, zebra-skin jackets, and gloves, had the aura of a mystical figure, a space-age futuristic brother. While Clinton and Collins were too extravagant to spawn many direct imitators, they had millions of followers. The infinite possibilities of the outrageous moved the fashion of the times forward. Isaac Hayes, another notable figure of the seventies, brought a hard-edged masculinity to his image. His penchant for revealing leatherwear made the display of skin hip.

With the emergence of Prince in the early eighties, fashion came full circle. Appropriating elements of the militaristic, quasi-regal wardrobe styled by Michael Jackson in the late seventies, Prince picked up where Little Richard left off, appearing in gender-blending outfits that suggested an updated version of unrestrained sexuality. Too much even for his most ardent fans, Prince nevertheless brought sexuality back to the fore of fashion vocabulary, and may have even influenced some of the exhibitionistic ensembles promoted by Jean Paul Gaultier and Karl Lagerfeld and popularized by Madonna. By the nineties, R&B's major fashion figures embraced a new style ethic, rebelling against the excesses of the past. Boyz II Men were the embodiment of virtuous luxury. Retro-soul-singer Maxwell and British R&B star Seal both found strong personal styles in refined simplicity—in dark, crushed-velvet jackets, Armani suits, and a generally conservative aura reminiscent of Marvin Gaye.

Through the styles of R&B stars, the fashion pendulum has swung back and forth, between youthful rebellion and mature reflection, casual sexuality and constrained sexual energy. R&B fashion often anticipated the mood of an era, and sometimes triggered a new trend. The future of soul style is a question, but the past tells us that tomorrow's stars will undoubtedly have a profound impact on image.

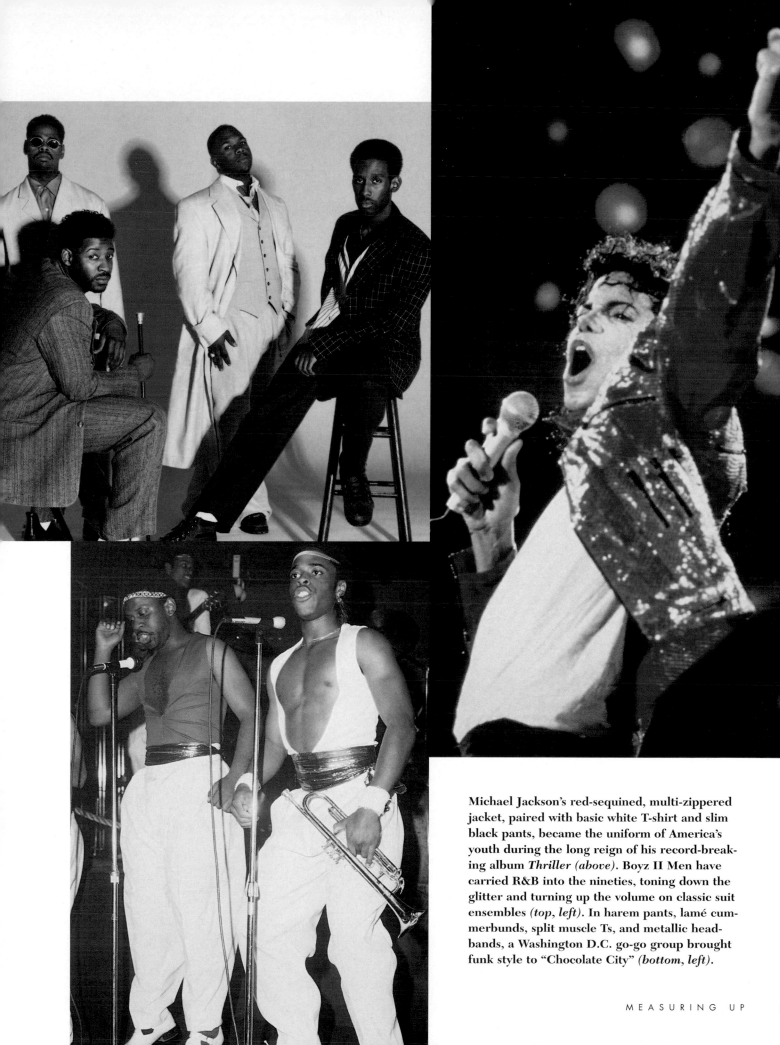

Michael Jackson's red-sequined, multi-zippered jacket, paired with basic white T-shirt and slim black pants, became the uniform of America's youth during the long reign of his record-breaking album *Thriller (above)*. Boyz II Men have carried R&B into the nineties, toning down the glitter and turning up the volume on classic suit ensembles *(top, left)*. In harem pants, lamé cummerbunds, split muscle Ts, and metallic headbands, a Washington D.C. go-go group brought funk style to "Chocolate City" *(bottom, left)*.

Isaac HAYES

"R&B STYLE"

Back in the seventies, I would watch a lot of acts go out onstage, where the first thing they would do was loosen up their shirts and ties, then remove their jackets. Why put them on to take them off? I've always appreciated the freedom and comfort of male ballet dancers in their leotards: I figured, if they could wear them, why couldn't I? So I coupled my tights with a chain belt and necklace, and was offered a custom-made chain creation by Hollywood designer Charles Rubin. That shirt ultimately became my signature piece during the *Shaft* period. It's one of my most popular performance costumes. For me it represents freedom and power!

My style is very individual. I've always done my own thing. A makeup artist once told me I could wear any color because my skin tone could carry it. I've been in brights ever since. Some of my clothing is custom-made, sometimes I buy off-the-rack, but, either way, comfort is key. My palette changes with my mood. When I want to relax, my colors are softer.

Early on, my style was southern, a little "country." I lived in Memphis. I wore lots of high-water pants and suits with shorts. My pants were so high I had to put sugar in my shoes to talk them down.

As for my hair, or lack thereof, the redux happened in 1964, long before men began to choose to go bald. At the time, most musicians wore a processed hairstyle called "the 'do" or "the conk." We wore it very short, and in order to keep it in place you had to sleep with a stocking cap on. This I didn't care for, especially in the summer when you'd sweat through the night. It was just unmanageable. So I decided to cut it and grow a "fresh crop." I went to my barber Mr. King and told him, "Cut it all off!" When I stepped out of the shop, I felt a breeze and I thought, "Wow! This feels all right!" Regardless of the ridicule I received, I fell in love with the sensation. Plus, I liked the distinction of looking different. But I never did it for show. I did it for convenience. I never looked back and now, years later, it's become the thing to do.

I've always been inspired by African and Middle Eastern fashions, long before designers like Oleg Cassini reinterpreted ethnic clothing and designed Nehru jackets and such. On the home front, I've been influenced by fellow artists such as Otis Redding, Sam & Dave, James Brown, and Joe Tex. What I loved most about their looks were their mohair suits. They inspired me to have many of my own suits tailor-made. In terms of today's artists, I love the way Babyface dresses. If there's one thing brothers can learn from him, it's the importance of a quality, tailored jacket. I recommend that every man invest in something custom-made for his body.

I can't live without leather. I own a leather shirt, which doubles as a jacket in mild weather and a collection of multicolored leather jackets, which remind me of my days in the seventies, when I was wearing lots of Pucci.

Jeffrey BANKS

MENSWEAR DESIGNER

Award-winning Seventh Avenue menswear designer Jeffrey Banks is a paradigm of classic style. Prior to heading up his own label, Jeffrey Banks Menswear, he honed his skills under the tutelage of designers Ralph Lauren and Calvin Klein. Banks studied at New York City's Parsons School of Design and is a native of Washington D.C.

Banks brings a classicist's concern for quality and simplicity to his designs, then infuses them with color and energy. The crisp, contemporary edge of his clothing line won him a coveted Coty Award for his menswear in 1987. A staunch advocate of well-fitting pants, Banks shares his expertise on the subject.

The PANT

Pants are probably the most active part of a man's wardrobe, so fit, fabric, and durability are key factors in selecting one's britches. While pants have witnessed their share of trends, from hip-hugging flares to sagging jeans, there are basic guidelines for choosing a tailored pant that is both supportive and comfortable.

SELECTION

Banks has very clear ideas about the first and most important step in building a collection: "Brand-recognition is important when shopping for pants. Take the time to visit both large, reputable department stores and smaller, private-label shops. Ask the sales help for explanations and advice. In addition, rely on word-of-mouth. Benefit from the experience of friends, relatives, colleagues, and, of course, a trusted tailor. Conduct an independent survey. The information will prove useful."

CONSTRUCTION

Always look for the best money can buy within a designated budget. Instant indicators of poor quality bottoms include loose threads, lightweight buttons, and uneven stitching. "Look inside the pants and take note of how they are made," Banks advises. "Make sure the waistband has interlining (a lining made from a lesser-quality fabric which finishes the interior edges of the pant fabric)—it adds needed stiffness and structure at the waist." Most men's pants are not fully lined unless they are made of 100 percent wool, and even then they are often only half-lined, from the waist to the knee.

When purchasing pleated pants, be sure to check the finish at the point where the pleat meets the waist. A well-stitched pleat should weight the line of the pant, allowing for a cleaner drape when hands are

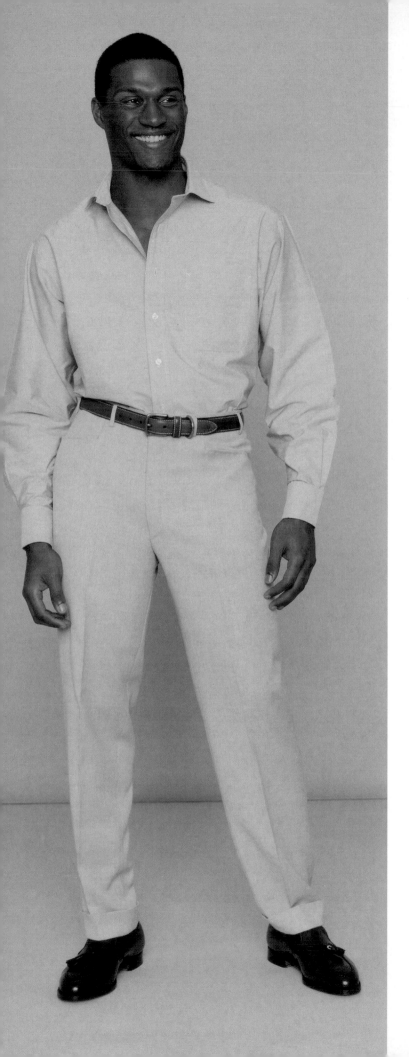

in pockets. Pleats will sometimes be aligned with the waistband's two front belt loops. These seams should close with a clean finish of about a half-inch, to protect the pleat from opening.

Good construction is best judged when pants are on the body. Pay close attention to side pockets: From a side view, they should lie flat to the hip, and their crease should perfectly split the leg's center.

FIT

A proper-fitting pair of pants should sit securely at the waist and drape fluidly on the body, to create the illusion of a clean vertical line, regardless of whether the style is cut full or narrow. Pants should not cinch the waist, ride up in the rear, or fall short of the instep of the shoe. Banks asserts, "The worst sight in the world is that of a man wearing too-tight pants. It can kill a look. It's important not to get caught up in the psychology of size: If you normally take a 44 but in a particular instance a 46 feels better, go with the 46."

COLOR

"Stick to strong basic colors such as black, navy, gray, khaki, and a warm tan," suggests Banks, "especially when just beginning to build a working wardrobe. While color has its place in every man's closet, it can sometimes overpower its wearer—not to mention the problems it can create when it comes to matching shirts and shoes." Men of color have never shied away from bold hues in daily dress. Part of the attraction is the ability of darker skin tones to carry rich colors without washing out. In spite of this advantage, it is important for Black men to carefully consider which trousers are appropriate for the occasion at hand. Pants are the foundation of a well-styled ensemble, and understated colors work best. As Banks prescribes, basic black, navy, and gray are foolproof choices: They stabilize the line of the body and provide contrast for a lighter-colored shirt treatment. Bright-colored bottoms often call for even lighter

tops, which can render an outfit overbearing. Color should be selected according to the environment: Creative fields may be more receptive to color in the workplace, while corporate cultures regard navy blue and charcoal gray as non-negotiable elements of an unspoken uniform.

FABRIC

Movement is an important variable when it comes to choosing a pant fabric. Many men of color appreciate the flair and fluidity that liquidlike bottoms can provide. This preference can cause some problems, however, since luxurious materials such as silk and satin are not always the best choices when it comes to durability. Banks agrees, and adds that "Versatility comes from choosing a material such as wool gabardine, which is a reliable, year-round fabric." "Corduroy also offers a lot of options," he continues, "because it can go from elegant to rustic, depending on what it's paired with."

Seasonal choices, specifically cotton or linen for warmer months, are less durable. These lighter fabrics wrinkle with normal wear, but the distressed look actually adds to the character of the garment, giving it a textured, weathered appearance. Over-pressing linens and casual cotton pants detracts from the true nature of these fabrics.

PLEATS VS. FLAT FRONTS

Pants are made with one of two frontal treatments, pleated (above left) or flat (below left)—also referred to as "plain." Pleats are folds of fabric on either side of the leg at the point where it meets the waist. Contrary to popular opinion, pleated trousers are actually quite flattering to the average Black man's physique. According to Banks, "Black men can wear either style, as long as we choose a pant that fits properly." Pleated bottoms are a bit sportier than flat fronts, and allow for more flexibility in movement. When sitting, the garment gives. Flat fronts, without the visual distraction of pleats, give a longer, cleaner line to the leg. Note that for best results, flat fronts require the wearer to fit the same description.

CUFFS

The Jeffrey Banks rule of thumb: "A gentleman always wears cuffed trousers because they help the pant leg break more gracefully. My own personal preference is for an inch-and-three-quarter cuff." In the forties, zoot-suiters donned drapes with cuffs as wide as four inches. By the seventies, Black men upped the ante to nearly eight inches on dungarees. Today, cuff size is a matter of personal taste. The basic attributes of a good cuff include a tack-stitched finish at the points where it meets the pant's side seams and a hard first pressing, which firms the folds and prevents sagging.

CARE AND MAINTENANCE

Well-constructed pants require minimal cleaning and care: As clichéd as it may sound, pants will take care of you for as long as you take care of them. Herewith Banks's three easy steps to trousers maintenance:

- "Hang your pants upside down from the hem with a clip hanger." This prevents mid-leg creasing.

- "Dry-clean as little as possible." Many men have a tendency to over-dry-clean, thereby overprocessing, fading, and slowly ruining the garments. In most cases, a good steaming from the dry cleaner or at home should suffice.

- "Invest in a quality clothes brush." And use it regularly, instead of dry cleaning.

the shirt

third

television

"You will see that from the start we have tried to dignify our race. If I am condemned for that I am satisfied."

MARCUS GARVEY

THE shirt

NEXT TO A MAN'S SUIT, HIS DRESS

shirts are the second major component of his basic business wardrobe. This integral element of clothing is critical: It acts as an eye-level point of reference for anyone he comes in contact with. When placed against the subdued backdrop offered by a suit jacket and pants, the shirt acts as a billboard, broadcasting its owner's personality. When framed by the classic colors of standard suitings—gray, navy, tan—the shirt can stand out through its cut, hue, or pattern.

In the last half of the twentieth century, an amazing cross-pollination of professional sports, popular music, and Afrocentric fashion has resulted in an eclectic assortment of shirtings. When adopted by a prominent Black figure, each style became emblematic of its wearer. From legendary piano man Bobby

Count Basie proved that there's nothing cleaner than a crisp white shirt *(previous spread, left).* **As "Alexander Scott" on** *I Spy,* **Bill Cosby collared the criminals** *(previous spread, right).* **In a 1918 self-portrait, photographer William VanDerZee wore a two-toned day shirt with contrasting white collar and complementary knit striped tie** *(top).* **Crooner Billy Eckstein was so smooth he had a shirt collar named in his honor, the "Mister B."** *(above).* **Stiffly starched shirts were the standard during the war years** *(right).* **By the fifties, convertible collars spread to nearly shoulder-width** *(opposite, top).* **In 1957, Louis Armstrong "popped" in polka dots** *(opposite, bottom).*

Short's signature dress shirts, created especially for him by designer and personal friend John Weitz, to the fifties' "Mister B."—a fold-over flap-collar treatment named after the smooth shirt style of jazz crooner Billy Eckstein—shirts were, and remain, essential to creating a clean image.

Turnbull & Asser, one of England's legendary custom shirtmakers and official tailors to the monarchy, still celebrates Sammy Davis, Jr.'s infamous visit to its Jermyn Street store in 1968: The "candy man" promptly dropped several hundred pounds sterling on forty-three of Her Majesty's appointed creations. During this decade, London's best weren't the only shirts in Sammy's closet. He also namesaked a collection of dress shirts at retail, and the label was stitched with a silhouette of the diminutive song and dance king.

The years after the 1964 Civil Rights Act marked a major turning point in the evolving identity of African Americans, and we began to focus on fashion as a means of getting in touch with our roots. As a conscious expression of a connection to our ancestry, ethnic clothes had definite political overtones. One popular garment, the dashiki—created from just a few sections of cloth, one for the body and one for each sleeve—was worn by both peace-loving hippies and advocates of Black Power. The dashiki, an anglicization of the Yoruban *dànsíkí*, originated in southwestern Nigeria, where it is sometimes worn underneath a suit jacket. In its cross-cultural co-option, it was occasionally referred to as a "caftan" by Whites. Record- and barrier-breaking tennis star Arthur Ashe often wore authentic versions of the dashiki, embroidered with intricate stitchings. Andrew Young and Reverend Jesse Jackson, as dashiki'd disciples, carried on the dream of Dr. Martin Luther King, Jr. Six-inch Afros, substantial sideburns, and prominent medallions completed the powerful look. In music, James Brown—singer, songwriter, restaurant proprietor, record label owner, and, of course, soul brother number 1—sent a rallying cry to brothers and sisters with his 1969 hit, "Say it Loud, I'm Black and I'm Proud." Taking the lead, Brown

abandoned his processed coif for a neatly trimmed 'fro and took to tunic-topped, two-piece leisure wear. Thousands of fans followed suit, literally.

Black men continued to expand the parameters of shirt styles well into the next decade. In addition to Afrocentric anti-fashions, bold colors, bad prints, and a tight fit all signified sexiness in the seventies. Decaled T-shirts described the pervasive philosophy: "Keep on Truckin'." (The pimplike figure strutting across cotton exemplified the simple sentiment of Eddie Kendrick's 1973 number-one song of the same name.) Disco hustled in jumpsuits, platform boots, and nylon high-roll-collar shirts. Designer brands included Chams de Baron, Nik Nik, and Sassoon. Inspired by street interpretations of seventies trends, Black designers such as Willi Smith and Jon Haggins further urbanized the look with color-blocked cyclist-style jersey knit shirts, high V-neck sweaters, floral short-sleeve knit shirts reminiscent of the forties, and jersey jumpsuits that hugged the torso but flared on the leg.

By shifting to baggier proportions and adding texture and chunky hardware, shirts became almost mechanical in the eighties. The "King of Pop" proved himself the leader of the free nation in such industrial ornamentation: Dancing in simple T-shirts topped with multi-zippered, rhinestone-studded, red leather jackets, pushing up tight sleeves for added tension in a tuxedo, Michael Jackson ignited one craze after another in videos for such hits as "Beat It" and "Billie Jean." Break-dancers piled brightly colored mesh tank tops over white T-shirts. Bill Cosby spiced up the men's sweater business by wearing a different knit every week on his top-rated prime-time sitcom.

An important milestone in the history of Black media took place in 1980 with the founding of Black Entertainment Television by Robert Johnson. Today, BET is the largest Black-owned broadcasting conglomerate in the country. Johnson believes that part of his business success stems from his personal style. His wardrobe includes a collection of black dress shirts. "On any given day," he explains, "a black dress shirt can take me from a daytime meeting in a suit at my headquarters in DC to an evening entertainment dinner in LA, while making it all seem effortless." An avid fan, Johnson considers basketball players to be the most stylish Black men, and cites Michael Jordan, Scottie Pippen, and Patrick Ewing as the best-shirted players off the court.

Major sports stars do seem to dictate shirt fashions for men in the nineties. Many fans don professional team jerseys to proudly display the name and number of their favorite players. On the dressier side of shirtings, status labels convey cost and quality in just one look. Greco-Roman prints and jewel tones in silk by labels such as Versace are the choice evening shirt for many celebs. Andre Harrell, former CEO of Motown Records, defends the conspicuous trend, "As 'Ghetto Fabulous' as it may seem, it's about wearing your wealth on your sleeve, to tell the world you're a 'Big Willie.'" Fashionable Black men know that quality shirt style begins with solid fabric, construction, and design. Once the foundation has been set, the sky's the limit in terms of individual looks.

In the seventies, African dashikis, whether worn with dungarees or underneath a suit, proudly promoted Black Pride; the more color, the better *(opposite, top)*. Miles Davis, meticulous about the details, adjusts the buttons on his form-fitting, western-flavored, nylon, snap-cuff shirt *(opposite, bottom)*. Coolin' in printed banlon Nik Niks, textured muscle-T-shirts, and colorful woven tanks, four brothers take a break *(left)*. The nineties have witnessed a refreshing return to the understated elegance of a crisp white oxford *(above)*.

Ed BRADLEY

"THE SHIRT"

When I lived in Paris in 1971, I worked as a news stringer for CBS News. I didn't make much money, but I used to pass by Charvet, a custom shirt shop, and look in the door at all the bolts of fabric. I promised myself if I ever got to the point where I could afford a tailor-made shirt, that was where it would come from. Today, all of my shirts are made there. I like French-cuff shirts with either a pointed or spread collar, for variety. The first person whose style I can remember admiring is Billy Eckstein. Years later, when I met him, I told him so. I always thought he was the coolest because they named a shirt collar after him.

My style is very collected. I can wear anything, from a custom-made Saville Row suit, to Versace or Armani couture, to a pair of Gap overalls. Likewise, my on-air style is all me. I'm not dressing to play a character—I am what I do, I do who I am. But I do dress to fit the occasion. If I'm going to interview somebody on a farm, I'm not going to wear that Saville Row suit. And I'm not going to interview the president in a pair of overalls. I'm going to wear what's appropriate.

Over the course of my life, my style has evolved, but I've always loved clothes—I just didn't have any growing up. When I was a kid, back in a boarding school for poor children in Philadelphia, you had one pair of pants and one pair of shoes that you wore to class every day. After school you changed into play clothes. And for Sundays you had a pair of Sunday pants and shoes. If those wore out beyond repair, they became your everyday clothes. But my sense as a kid was that you always wanted to be clean, no matter how poor you were. When I was in the seventh grade, I got a new pair of pants for Easter, and I'll always remember a girl named Barbara commenting that they were really cool.

My left ear has been pierced for about ten years now. It was a bit radical at the time, and I heard about it from the network guys: "Are you going to wear an earring on the air? What does that say? What does it mean?" To me it just meant I had a hole in my ear and an earring in it. It wasn't a statement. For work I wear a small gold hoop. It's tasteful and unobtrusive. At play, I wear different studs or a larger hoop. When getting dressed, it's important to pay attention to the details as well as to the overall look of your clothes.

Black Men and THE BOX

BY NICK CHARLES

ONE NIGHT IN 1956, IN WHAT MUST

Cross-dressing Flip Wilson brought plenty of color to the small screen in the seventies: In Kodachrome wigs, floral minidresses, and patent pumps, his alter ego "Geraldine" personified sass *(above)*. **In spite of his conked hair, timeless tuxedos, velvety voice, and winning smile, Nat "King" Cole faced pressure from network sponsors uncomfortable with his race** *(opposite)*.

have been a high point in modern-day Black male iconography, the most elegant Black man in television showcased another sophisticated Black gent. Nat "King" Cole, the thrush-voiced, silky-smooth pianist, singer, and host of his own eponymous variety program, presented Harry Belafonte, he of the faux calypsos and unbuttoned Hawaiian shirts, to the American public. Surely the sight of this dynamic duo must have been too much for some viewers. Cole's program, long the bane of White citizen councils everywhere, was preempted later that year. His wasn't the first variety hour hosted by a Black man: Pop singer Billy Daniels had emceed a show years before. But Cole's popularity rose above racial lines, making his effort an even bet to succeed.

Wishful thinking. Once the show was canceled, with it went the hope that Black performers would find a permanent place in the burgeoning medium. Thanks to Cole's guidance, millions had been introduced to the talents of Belafonte, Sammy Davis, Jr., Johnny Mathis, and others. Now it seemed as if such performers would forever be limited to cameo appearances on White-hosted variety hours and to menial, caricatured roles on family series.

But lo and behold, the next decade brought the explosion of Motown and the civil rights movement. Both helped fuel what is now regarded as a golden age in television for Black performers. The period, which ran from the late sixties through the seventies, gave opportunities to many Black entertainers. Television executives, eager to offset images of Blacks marching for equal rights, protecting themselves from full-throttle fire hoses, or laying waste to inner cities, found creative

ways to program Black folk. Cross-dressing Flip Wilson got his own variety show in 1970. On it, he featured comedians George Kirby, Nipsey Russell, and Bill Cosby—who starred in his own show in 1969, after *I Spy* had ended. Through performers such as Little Richard, Sam Cooke, Marvin Gaye, The Temptations, Jimi Hendrix, and Al Green, television also brought Black music into America's living rooms. Long before the seminal and enduring "Soul Train" hit the air-waves, "American Bandstand" sang rock 'n soul to the heartland. The tube also presented a platform for the emerging Black-athlete-as-style-icon. Who wouldn't be awestruck by the sight of Muhammad Ali, Jim Brown, Lew Alcindor (aka Kareem Abdul-Jabbar), or many of the Black track-and-field titans of the era?

But the most notable Black male character of the period was Cosby's "Alexander Scott" on *I Spy*. Part James Bond, part Stagger Lee, Scott was an equal partner of Robert Culp's "Kelli Robinson." On occa-sion, Scotty even got the girl. Stylish, but not foppish, Scott could go through a tux, a two-button suit, and tennis apparel in a single episode. His success paved the way for other substantive Black characters. Percy Rodrigues played the understated federal agent "Jason Hart" on *The Silent Force*. In the Revolution-ary War series *The Young Rebels*, Louis Gossett, Jr. was "Isak Poole." Hal Frederick appeared as one of five anxious young doctors on *The Interns*. But only

one of these series lasted more than a season. It seemed as if television could not get past racial stereotypes to show virile, sexually attractive Black men who also had some control over their environments.

While the mini-boom of the sixties attempted to unleash a diverse array of Black celebrities, there was severe stereotyping. Some TV roles were nothing more than updated versions of minstrel characters from the early part of the century. For every classy Cosby, intelligent Greg Morris ("Barney" in *Mission Impossible*), or stalwart Clarence Williams III ("Link" in *The Mod Squad*), there was a clowning Fred Berry ("Rerun" in *What's Happening?*), whining Redd Foxx (*Sanford and Son*), or buffoonish Jimmy "J. J." Walker (*Good Times*). Two divergent archetypes were clearly delineated: the cool, colorless professional, or the grinning jokester whose cultural identity was permanently on display. The latter came to predominate.

Of course, there were characters and actors who slipped outside the lines. Demond Wilson, as Redd Foxx's reasonable half, was one, as was Don Mitchell's complex aide-de-camp to Raymond Burr on *Ironside*, Georg Stanford Brown's cop, "Terry Webster," on *The Rookies*, and the entire Black cast of *Room 222*.

But the breakthrough character of the era, who simultaneously promoted and subverted some of the worst racial stereotypes, was Sherman Hemsley's "George Jefferson." In both *All In The Family*, where he debuted, and *The Jeffersons*, his starring vehicle, this diminutive, brash, myopic dry cleaner evinced an upwardly mobile trajectory that was accented by his attire. George Jefferson was always dressed to the nines—as if he had come across the Brooks Brother (sic) catalog and ordered his wife "Weezie" to buy everything in it.

During *The Jeffersons* decade-long run, George was in a class by himself, surrounded by lesser lights: Lawrence-Hilton Jacobs's "sweat hog" student "Freddie 'Boom Boom' Washington" of *Welcome Back, Kotter;* Antonio Fargas's pimpish "Huggy Bear" on *Starsky and Hutch;* Ted Lange's bow-tied barkeep Isaac on *The Love*

A radical Afro, muttonchop sideburns, and aviator shades confirmed the cucumber-cool of Clarence Williams III's "Link" on *The Mod Squad (opposite, top)*. The multi-patterned John Witherspoon, as the father of *The Wayans Bros.*, clearly contradicts his character's sartorial motto, "Coordinate!" *(opposite, middle)*. In three-piece suit, point collar, and tie, "George Jefferson" finally got a piece of the pie *(opposite, bottom)*. With his newsboy cap, righteous 'fro, form-fitting turtleneck, and bell-bottom jeans, *The Cosby Kids'* "Rudy" was by far the most stylish playa on Saturday morning TV *(top)*. On *What's Happening?*, Fred Berry's "Rerun" locked and popped his way into the hearts of millions long before break-dancing became a craze *(above)*.

Boat—all second-class citizens in ensemble pieces. As the unequivocal star and center of attention, George Jefferson's strength demanded respect, if not affection.

If prime time was a stagnant pool for forceful images of Black men, daytime TV provided an interesting petrie dish. James Earl Jones portrayed doctors on both *Guiding Light* and *As the World Turns*. Billy Dee Williams played an assistant D.A. on *Another World*. Others, such as Palmer Deane (*The Doctors*), John Danelle (*All My Children*), and Herb Davis (*The Edge of Night*), had small soap roles. Al Freeman, Jr., as "Detective Ed Hall" on *One Life to Live*, stood out.

Portrayals of professionals aside, there was the sense that these roles were simply White characters in Blackface. Actress Ellen Holly, who played the controversial role of "Carla Gray"—a Black woman light-skinned enough to pass for White—on *One Life to Live*, said in 1972, "Media are like mirrors. . . .You look in a mirror and you see what you are. And for generations the Black man has looked into the mirror of this society, and been thrown back an image so absolutely grotesque that it's a wonder he could even get together the minimum ego necessary to survive."

In the post-*Roots* (1977) years, much changed and much stayed the same. More Black characters were allowed leeway to be risky, even sexy. Avery Brooks's "Hawk" on *Spenser for Hire* was a bold, bald, bad man, whose wardrobe undulated between "Superfly" gear and Afrocentric garb. But the persona was that of the outlaw, the Black man just this side of incarceration. Good examples of three-dimensional characters that resonated beyond caricatures included Tim Reid's "Venus Flytrap" on *WKRP* (a deejay whose smooth on-air persona, when balanced with his off-air regular-guy appeal, poked fun at the stereotype of the lady's man), Michael Warren's and Taurean Blacque's *Hill Street Blues* regulars, and Blair Underwood's well-suited attorney on *L.A. Law*.

The breakthrough program for Blacks was the hugely successful *Cosby Show*, which featured an almost-too-good-to-be-true nuclear family of over-achievers. Scion "Heathcliff Huxtable" ran through a series of multi-fabric sweaters that looked as if they had been designed by Tommy Hilfiger by way of Jackson Pollock. He also had a penchant for braces, and never missed an opportunity to don a tuxedo (a sly wink to Cosby's *I Spy* days). Cliff's only son "Theo" (Malcolm Jamal-Warner), though, was mostly oblivious to fashion.

Youth culture—pioneered by the likes of Jamal-Warner on *Cosby*, Kadeem Hardison on *A Different World*, and Will Smith, the "Fresh Prince" himself—has birthed a breakthrough of Black male substance and style. Through his talk show, Arsenio Hall introduced phat threads and fly gear to the mainstream, even if at times he seemed to be caught in a glitter-filled, epaulet-wearing, seventies zone.

With the advent of cable and the emergence of start-up networks from such outlets as Warner Brothers, Black culture is more American culture than ever. And the trendsetting that once creeped from the streets to the suburbs is now on at eight o'clock. Even LL Cool J, decked in FUBU, has a sitcom. It's certainly a long way from when Harry met Nat.

On *L.A. Law*, Blair Underwood's buppie lawyer stayed on the case in his precision-cut fade and double-breasted Armanis *(opposite)*. In silk jackets and tropical shirts, "Detective Rico Tubbs" apprehended those guilty of a *Miami Vice (above)*. By the eighties, Bill Cosby had become America's father figure, comfortably wrapped in colorful Coogi sweaters *(above, right)*. Arsenio Hall brought new-jack style to his late-night talk show, playing host to a cross-cultural array of patterns and colors *(below, right)*.

Bryant GUMBEL

"TELEVISION"

When I'm on the air, I want the viewers' attention to be focused on the exchange, not on what I'm wearing. I try to dress with a degree of authority that is not distracting—the program should never be about, "Hey everybody, look at Bryant in his purple suit!" I always try to dress with some sensitivity to the topic I'm dealing with on any given day. If the mood is somber, I'm not going to arrive in a loud plaid jacket. Off-camera, I don't give much thought to my ensembles. I spend some time putting them together, but then I never give them a second thought the rest of the day.

I've never put a label on my look. In a fashion sense, it's more "classic" than anything else. I've always dressed first and foremost to please myself. My choices just so happen to fit into the norm. I love clothing by my good friend, Joseph Abboud. His designs are classic in nature, but they're also stylized; they have personality. He adheres to the highest production values and uses wonderful fabric. What more could I ask for?

The most essential item in my wardrobe is a navy-blue blazer. In my mind, it is the basic necessity. If push came to shove, I could go to the White House in a navy-blue blazer and gray slacks. The jacket must be single-breasted, so that you can dress it up or down. You can wear it with shirt and tie, or T-shirt and jeans.

I don't consider myself a particularly good student of style. When I was a kid I sold clothing at a store called Henry P. Lyttons & Company in downtown Chicago. Through that experience I came to realize that *you* should wear clothing, it shouldn't wear you. I watched people make the mistake of thinking they could buy class. The purpose of a good suit is not to walk into a room and get a big reaction. A good suit should subtly convey a certain degree of confidence. It shouldn't be ostentatious. Like a second skin, clothes should be something in which you feel completely comfortable. A man should wear what fits him, both literally and figuratively. That consideration should come before any concerns about trends.

Part of the reason why I think our clothes historically tend to be ahead of the curve is because there was always this desire, this need, to be recognized. We were so invisible to majority Americans for so long that, once we earned the option to choose, we adorned ourselves in a way that would force others to take notice. But I'm not necessarily sure that today's African-American men maintain this approach to fashion. Those breaking through social barriers and overcoming economic obstacles are much more inclined to show that they can be themselves and still dress the part for success.

Tommy HILFIGER

CLOTHING DESIGNER

Since his debut on the fashion scene in 1984, Tommy Hilfiger's signature red, white, and blue logo has come to symbolize the American spirit. From men's and women's collections to home furnishings, Hilfiger's unique take on "classics with a twist" celebrates a melting pot of styles, from conservative-preppy to hip-hop. His objective is to design clothes that reflect the individuality, diversity, and creativity that define America. As a result, his clothes appeal to an enormously wide range of consumers.

Hilfiger started his multimillion-dollar clothing collection with a line of casual but classically inspired oxfords. His first love is music, and his influences range from the colorful eclecticism of Jimi Hendrix to the street-savvy style of Sean "Puffy" Combs. Timeless but never stuffy, Hilfiger offers men of color advice on how to identify the good from the bad when buying a dress shirt.

The SHIRT

Quality shirtings are at the core of better dressing. A wide selection of shirts can nearly quadruple a man's wardrobe when combined with different ties, suits, and accessories. There are countless choices of fabric, color, pattern, and construction to consider when buying shirts. These options should be weighed against personal taste, tradition, and price limitations.

COLLARS

The only constant in fashion is change, and over time collar styles have varied considerably. Hilfiger classifies the five classic styles as follows:

1. "The button-down is of English equestrian descent and was originally designed to prevent the collar from flapping when playing polo." Today, the button-down treatment can be found in the business world, worn by junior executives and Ivy Leaguers. In fact, the style has become synonymous with conservatism, so much so that an uptight type is often described as being "buttoned-down."

2. "The round collar comes in and out of style," Hilfiger admits. "It's a choice traditionally found on bankers, and it is often fashioned with matching white cuffs on contrasting shirt 'bodies.' It projects a very dressy statement, and is often worn beneath a pin-striped suit. Round-collar shirts are also a staple of English schoolboy uniforms."

3. "The spread collar is pretty stodgy, the natural partner to a Windsor-knotted tie. Its opening at the neck is wider than that of most other collars, and should always be worn with a tie—preferably a fuller one."

4. The popular straight, or point, collar is adaptable to several different looks. Hilfiger concurs, "The straight collar is the most basic of collars. It can be worn open with a blazer for a casual look that travels from work to dinner. It can also mean serious busi-

ness: When lightly starched, it holds up amazingly well under a suit, and it gives a clean line to an expertly knotted tie."

5. The tab collar fits high on the neck. A small loop closure connects both collar points, keeping them put. Hilfiger recommends that shorter-necked men avoid this particular treatment: "The higher collar band reduces the neckline." The beauty of the tab collar is its crisp, clean finish, which highlights the tie.

CUFFS

Although only a sliver of cuff may be showing at any given time, cuffs are a defining detail. "There are two types of standard-issue cuffs," Hilfiger explains. "The first, the barrel or button cuff, is the most basic and versatile. It usually closes with one button, unless it's an English make or a trendy model. The second, the French cuff, is a soft double cuff created by folding back half of a wide band of fabric and fastening with cuff links. This option is the dressier of the two and will almost always be found on formal shirtings."

COLOR AND PATTERN

Hilfiger agrees with the adage about never having too many white shirts. "A white shirt conveys trust, confidence, clean business." When prescribing an ideal palette for the man of color, Hilfiger recommends shirts in: a classic French blue; a pale yellow; an assortment of subtle checks and stripes, including a mini-check mixed with white; a fine pinstripe (preferably blue); a tattersall (a fine-lined colored grid usually on a light ground); and, of course, as many crisp whites with different collar treatments as are affordable.

FABRIC

Choice of fabric is critical for many reasons. Number one, fabric largely determines comfort. This is why Hilfiger always recommends 100 percent cotton. Unlike cotton blends, 100 percent cotton allows the skin to breathe. "Besides," Hilfiger adds, "when professionally laundered, cotton looks great!" Cotton is both durable and absorbent, and it ages well, gaining softness with every year of wear. Cotton dress shirts come in many varieties: Broadcloth is a smooth, fine cotton commonly used in dress shirts; end-on-end is a cross-weaved thread pattern that mixes white cotton with a softer color that adds a light shine; chambray, a casual, denimlike cotton, is also produced by a cross-weave, in this case of white and blue threads, resulting in a softened, weathered appearance; Egyptian cotton, used in expensive formal and dress styles, has a silky hand.

PACKAGED VS. CUSTOM-MADE

Well-dressed men in the know always opt for custom-made shirts. Hilfiger admits, "At a certain point in buying dress shirts, a man is sometimes better off having one tailor-made. The cost of a custom-made shirt usually begins at around $100; a pre-packaged shirt maxes out at about $85. So a made-to-order, perfectly fitting shirt, unique in fabric, collar, cuffs, and buttons, can be had for a difference of about $20."

"We used to be 'shiftless and lazy,' now we are 'fearless and awesome.' I think the Black man should take pride in that."

JAMES EARL JONES

attitude

WELL-DRESSED MEN KNOW THAT

attitude is the defining accessory for any eye-catching ensemble. But attitude can't be bought. For many American men, clothes don't merit much consideration. Getting dressed is an unconscious act. This thoughtlessness, when combined with poor fit, bad posture, and nondescript style, is a formula for bland conformity. Conversely, the decision to make a statement through dress requires a keen sense of self. It demands an unflinching acceptance of size, an understanding of fit, and an acknowledgment of what works. An unabashed approach to dress as a means of nonverbal communication, "statement dressing" always makes an impression. Black men, with multiple messages to convey, have mastered this marriage between style and attitude.

First and foremost, it is important to establish that there is not one attitude embraced by all Black men in America. Our attitudes are as dynamic and

With caped coats, top hats, and glittering watch chains, dapper twins from the turn of the century displayed a double dose of attitude *(previous spread, left)*. Spike Lee and Denzel Washington embodied the zany flavor of the forties zootie in Lee's 1992 epic *Malcolm X (previous spread, right)*. Pride was in the details for this 1900s dandy: wing-collared shirt, striped silk cravat, double-breasted waistcoat, patch pocket overcoat *(top)*. In the twenties, the standard American sack suit fit comfortably behind the driver's seat of status vehicles *(above)*. A tilted hat and tightly wrapped ascot exemplified attitude in the thirties *(right)*. Convertible collars and polished cars were cool for cats in the fifties *(opposite, top)*. Nat "King" Cole's effortless confidence inspired millions of fans *(opposite, bottom)*.

diverse as the many fashion trends we've incited. On Wall Street, the spirit is alive in three-piece "six and two" suits. Downtown, clothes are label-driven, but the status is styled with anti-establishment elements that add to the irony.

Attitude is in the way we break our hats, situate our jackets, lace—or not—our shoes, and strut down the street. Fine vines alone have never been enough to achieve Black sartorial cool. It's always been about walking the walk, talking the talk, and backing it up with a closetful of zoot suits, double-knit pants, or Adidas sneakers, as the decade dictated.

Where does our attitude come from? Collectively, under slavery, Blacks in America were conditioned to repress their innermost emotions during intense episodes of abuse, for fear of further punishment. Curiously, this stoicism, initially a survival skill, would years later translate into one of the key attributes of coolness. For many, but not all, African Americans, emotional detachment stemmed from a hatred for and rejection of all that was White America. Added to an unwillingness to define oneself according to "the enemy's" lifestyle, this laid-back demeanor became the defining characteristic of street cool. Attitude is at the foundation of the African-American mystique.

Black male attitude manifests itself in body language. When a clothing ensemble gets "good" to us, we contort our frames with a near-rhythmic dip in our step, as popularized in the seventies by Jimmy Walker on television's *Good Times*. When we're filled with pride, we affect an erect stance that's dignified, but never inaccessible, à la General Colin Powell. When joy takes hold, we might explode into the "Hi-De-Ho" jitter of forties zoot-suiter Cab Calloway.

Attitudinal details are the style appendages to African-American contributions to fashion. It's evident in the spit-shined, two-toned wing tips of the thirties; the flounced, hand-rolled handkerchiefs of the forties; the fat, untied shoelaces of the eighties. In the nineties, our ultra-relaxed attitude was epitomized by the droop of wide-leg jeans, often positioned well below our

exposed underwear waistbands, far south of our actual waistlines. At first, the trend was declared unkempt—until the establishment homogenized the look, deeming it fashionable for the masses.

Willfully oblivious to such validation from mass-market designers and the fashion press, Black male attitude continues to reinvent itself in its own communities—the only place where approval ever matters. For generations of Black men, rites of passage are performed through style. From the distinctive tip of a hat, with a flip of the wrist that's "just like your father's," to a stroll down the avenue in Easter Sunday best, to the ceremonial induction into a college fraternity, "group-profilin'" in matching Greek-lettered jackets—fashion marks some of the most memorable moments in our lives.

As documented in archival photographs, the obvious pride on the faces of noted Black leaders burned a positive impression into the minds of generations of young African Americans. The powerfully pensive abolitionist Frederick Douglass, the self-assured

SNCC leader Stokely Carmichael promoted Black pride with his tapered 'fro and dark sunglasses *(top)*. The early sixties lounge scene was all about slim suits, skinny ties, and smooth poses *(above)*. Michael Jackson's coy sexiness—wide-collar silk shirts open to the navel, ornate belt buckles, studded designer jeans—added to his image as a precocious manchild *(right)*. Equipped with lip balm, an indispensable accessory of any lady's man, a Morehouse Tiger puts the moves on an unsuspecting Spelmanite in the sixties *(opposite)*.

agitator W. E. B. Du Bois, the diverse group of attorneys and specialists chosen to be Franklin Roosevelt's "Black Cabinet" in the late thirties—images of these groundbreakers inspired Black leaders of the late twentieth century, leaders such as congressman Adam Clayton Powell, Jr.: His political prowess went hand-in-hand with his epic stature and style-savvy attitude. Powell worked hard, played hard, and kicked back in style. In *King of Cats: The Life and Times of Adam Clayton Powell, Jr.* (Houghton Mifflin, 1993), biographer Will Haygood describes Powell's presence as he approached the congressional podium in January 1961:

"Neatly dressed in a dark blue suit, yellow shirt, and knitted blue tie, he struck an imposing figure as he laid aside his notes. . . .Tall, six feet three inches, wavy black hair, light-skinned, now suntanned after weeks of fishing on his yacht off the Bahamian island of Bimini, neatly trimmed mustache, he was more the figure of a movie star than any of his congressional colleagues."

Like Powell, who brought a stately image of Black pride to the U.S. political arena, James Earl Jones, legendary star of stage, screen, and television, also broke race barriers in the exclusive world of entertainment. His regal demeanor is a result of a series of character-affirming experiences. Jones recalls the direction he received in 1960 while performing Off-Broadway in a play entitled *The Pretender:* "Act like Cary Grant." Such demeaning suggestions left Jones hungry for more validating roles. Things began to change in 1968 when he starred on Broadway as world champion boxer Jack Johnson in *The Great White Hope*. Jones remembers "approaching acting as I have approached language and speech, upside down and standing on my head to try to listen to my *own* drumbeat." Working out before each performance, wearing gold teeth onstage, shaving his head bald in order to "become" the character, Jones's dramatic interpretation delivered an intense attitude rarely seen on "The Great White Way." In 1970, Jones gave a repeat performance in the film adaptation of the stage play, and maintained his retro, pre-Isaac-Hayes baldness. Jones

was one of the first of a string of movie stars to create a new image of the no-holds-barred Black man. His contemporaries included Richard Roundtree, who played both the take-no-mess private dick "Shaft" (1971) and the eponymous protagonist of Melvin Van Peebles's *Sweet Sweetback's Baadasssss Song* (1971).

The "slap-me-five-on-the-black-hand-side," gangster-leanin', jive-talkin', fist-picked seventies brought Black male attitude to international attention through soul music hits, political luminaries, and Blaxploitation films. Brothers bounced to William DeVaughn's seventies anthem "Be Thankful for What You've Got." Face-forward politicians such as Stokely Carmichael and Huey P. Newton spoke to the people. *Black Caesar* (1973) and *Black Belt Jones* (1974) brought Black male icons to the silver screen. The ideas, stances, and styles of such groups as the Black Panthers trickled down to the 'hood, turning those who were once our neighbors into our "brothers and sisters." Whether decked out in high-shined, two-toned, Stacey Adams lace-up oxfords, stacked patchwork-leather platform boots, or maxi-length fur coats, supporters of the "player chic" aesthetic populated city streets. At the opposite end of the spectrum, motherland-loving brothers proudly donned Afrocentric attire such as dashikis, cowrie shell and leather accessories, and "Jesus" sandals.

In the seventies, although our clothing was mostly the same off-the-rack merchandise available to the average man, our body language and fierce styling made it fresh and exciting. Custom-made clothes worn by celebrities were often glitzier versions of current staples—the sequined zip-front jumpsuits of the soulful Commodores, for example, or the ancient-Egypt-meets-outer-space mix-and-match of Earth, Wind & Fire. High-style stage clothes, syncopated dance steps, and spirited attitude are all part of the legacy of the "me" decade.

Attitude. It's the cool elegance of Nat "King" Cole under the pressure of systemized segregation. It's the soulful interpretation of White hippie style and military regalia by rock and roll pioneer Jimi Hendrix.

It's the ear-shattering screams and sweaty crescendos of a laméd Little Richard. Reggie Dwight, aka Elton John, recalls the first time he witnessed the fabulous fury of the pompadoured piano man: "When I saw Little Richard standing on top of the piano, all lights, sequins, and energy, I decided there and then that I was going to be a rock 'n' roll piano player!"

Smooth, cool, phat, baad—as inherent as it may seem, attitude is a learned trait, the response to centuries of marginalization from mainstream privileges. The sense of self-worth translated through stylish clothes makes us trendsetters, risk-takers, sometimes pariahs. But attitude allows us to break the rules, no apologies. It gets us noticed.

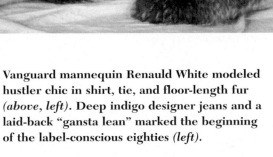

Vanguard mannequin Renauld White modeled hustler chic in shirt, tie, and floor-length fur *(above, left)*. **Deep indigo designer jeans and a laid-back "gansta lean" marked the beginning of the label-conscious eighties** *(left)*.

While clothes don't necessarily give me my attitude, they do help to define it. I can get up in the morning feeling a certain way, then walk into my closet, where something from my wardrobe will jump out at me and, once I put it on, will change my outlook for the entire day.

As an actor, I'm well aware of the benefits of dressing the part. If I'm going to a meeting with independent film producers, I know it's cool for me to wear jeans, a T-shirt, and a sports jacket. But if I'm going to a Hollywood studio meeting with some suits, then I know I need to wear a suit too, and possibly one more powerful than theirs, so that I'll be perceived as being, at the very least, their equal. A friend once told me that a gleaming white shirt worn with a suit is the strongest statement you can make: The message conveyed is that you are so in control you can wear a white shirt and keep it spotless.

Samuel L. JACKSON

"ATTITUDE"

My style is best described as classic with a twist. When I was growing up my mom always dressed me in Ivy League looks—corduroys, classic suits, oxfords. I was also influenced by my uncles, who had an old-school gangster way of dressing. They always wore Kangol hats—the brand is not new, not one that jumped out during the hip-hop era—and consequently, so have I. Because I'm a child of the sixties, I went through a period when I wore a lot of Afrocentric and New Age clothes. I was into Hendrix. Those influences are still with me today, and probably account for the colorful aspect of my wardrobe. For instance, I like classic suits, but I also like suits that have an interesting cut or come in an unexpected color, like a purple so deep it looks black.

When I was in junior high, I wanted to wear the trendy things the other brothers were wearing, but my mom wouldn't buy them for me. Instead, I had monogrammed Gant shirts, tweed trousers with the adjustable side tabs, and narrow-legged pants. My mother was a buyer for a clothing store in our hometown, Chattanooga, Tennessee. She would go to all these trade shows and buy samples, so I would end up with classically designed clothes that were going to be out the following season. In other words, what the White boys were going to be wearing, not the brothers. But by the time I got to high school I realized I was something of a trendsetter and I came to appreciate it, even if the threads were kind of square.

Keeping it REEL

BY DEBORAH GREGORY

AS WE BLAST BLACK TO THE FUTURE

In 1968, James Earl Jones portrayed the Saville-Row-suited "Jack Jefferson" on Broadway: The character was based on boxing champion Jack Johnson *(above)*. **Black men were frequently portrayed as bumbling buffoons in movies from the forties: "Pigmeat Markham" acted out all manner of comic capers; André De Shields landed the title role of Broadway's *The Wiz* when he showed up for his audition wearing silver platform shoes and matching silver earrings; Jack Benny's sidekick and chauffeur "Rochester" stepped out of uniform and shook a leg in a plaid three-piece suit; Cab Calloway hit all the high notes in white tux with tails *(opposite, clockwise from top left)*.**

into the twenty-first century, we're transporting the daring and deftly defining images of Black men's style from the stage and screen over the past 100 years. With the invention of motion pictures at the turn of the twentieth century, and of television in the fifties, performing arts archives are proof positive of the indelible legacy of Black men's style—despite the crushing odds against getting their wing-tipped oxfords in Hollywood doors.

The depiction of Black men during the early part of the century primarily lent itself to comedic, dim-witted Negroes in overalls or rough burlap, a stereotype parlayed to the hilt by Hollywood's first Black star, Stepin' Fetchit. More provocative were the startling images of White actors in Blackface, costumed in plantation-issue beige, brown, or blue linen or cotton, fabrics which came to be known as "Negro cloth." Of course, these marginal characters—usually stripped down to a torn shirt and bare feet by the end of the film—were always on the run, from either the Ku Klux Klan, plantation masters, or post-Reconstruction carpetbaggers. Best example of this genre: the controversial 1915 blockbuster film, *Birth of A Nation.*

Black men's self-created style came into sharp focus during the Jazz Age. From Harlem down to the Delta, Black men were looking clean, sharp, dressed to the nines. Legendary stage and screen actor Paul Robeson bestowed his proud presence on American cinema. Powerful, virile, intolerably charismatic, Robeson transformed himself from a member of the Black bourgeoisie to a shifty preacher with the flick of a top hat and tails in his first film, *Body and Soul* (1924). During the Harlem Renaissance, all that finger-poppin', foot-stompin' jazz was synonymous with spit-

PIGMEAT "Alamo" Markham in "Fight that Ghost"

RELEASED BY TODDY PICTURES CO.

COUNTRY OF ORIGIN U. S. A.

JACK BENNY

BUCK BENNY RIDES AGAIN

with
ELLEN DREW
ANDY DEVINE
PHIL HARRIS
VIRGINIA DALE
LILLIAN CORNELL
DENNIS DAY
and
ROCHESTER

Produced and Directed by
MARK SANDRICH

A Paramount Picture

Copyright 1940 by Paramount Pictures Inc. All Rights Reserved. Country of Origin U.S.A.

and-polish glamour in the Black community, and Robeson was the most widely respected role model on the scene. In such films as *The Emperor Jones* (1933), in which he played "Brutus," a flamboyant character who rises from Pullman car porter to autocrat of an island, Robeson's command of the medium captured audiences. Thanks to him, the world was finally made aware of the undeniable virility of the Black man, be he tuxed down and bow-tied or laced up in high leather boots, riding pants, and elaborately embroidered jackets.

The glamour intrinsic to Black jazz clubs was caught on-screen in films galore, from *Harlem is Heaven*

(1932) to *St. Louis Blues* (1958). Entertainers such as Bill "Bojangles" Robinson and legendary bandleaders Louis Armstrong, Duke Ellington, and Cab Calloway set the precedent by wearing dapper, loose-fitting, wide-shouldered jackets with baggy pants pleated at the waist. Such suits were usually topped with fedoras or brimmed hats. Black performers gradually exaggerated the silhouette, creating the look now known as the zoot suit. The height of zoot hype resulted in a jacket knee-length or longer, with broad, manly shoulders and flashy wide lapels that sliced into the slenderest waist. Ferociously baggy pants in corresponding or contrasting colors were tapered and cuffed. Through the flamboyant fashion statement of the zoot suit, brothers announced to America, "I'm lean, clean, and working for the green. You can't stop me now!"

The central role the zoot suit played in Black life is documented in films such as *Stormy Weather* (1943), starring Lena Horne and Cab Calloway. Calloway knew how to work an image and was perhaps the most widely photographed zoot-suiter, preferring white suits adorned with gold pocket chains that glistened brighter than his flashy smile. Spike Lee's adaption of Malcolm X's autobiography in 1992 offered a celluloid reincarnation of another great, zoot-suited, conked-hair, brimmed-hat,

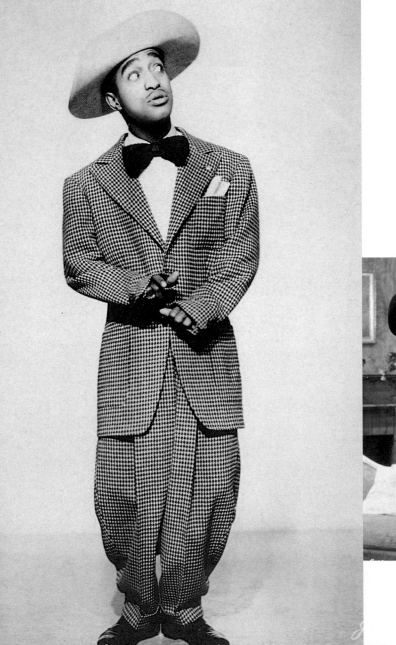

contemporary cat of Calloway's. Portrayed by Denzel Washington, the young Malcolm is shown relishing the ritual of donning his first—powder-blue—zoot suit and struttin' proudly down the avenue.

Despite the Harlem Renaissance, Hollywood's persistence in stereotyping Black performers as frightened slaves, big-eyed Sambos, shirtless bucks, or toothy comics severely limited the style images of many talented performers. Lorenzo Tucker, for example, the protégé of independent film producer Oscar Micheaux, was sophisticated and debonair and down, the "Black Valentino" in such films as *Wages of Sin* (1927) and *Underworld* (1947). Had he not been colored, Tucker would have claimed his rightful place as a leading man, alongside the Gary Coopers and Jimmy Stewarts of the day.

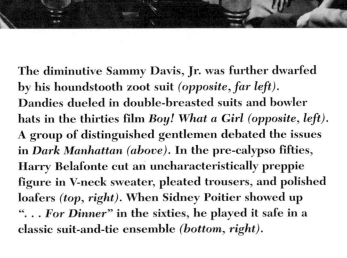

The diminutive Sammy Davis, Jr. was further dwarfed by his houndstooth zoot suit *(opposite, far left)*. Dandies dueled in double-breasted suits and bowler hats in the thirties film *Boy! What a Girl (opposite, left)*. A group of distinguished gentlemen debated the issues in *Dark Manhattan (above)*. In the pre-calypso fifties, Harry Belafonte cut an uncharacteristically preppie figure in V-neck sweater, pleated trousers, and polished loafers *(top, right)*. When Sidney Poitier showed up "*. . . For Dinner*" in the sixties, he played it safe in a classic suit-and-tie ensemble *(bottom, right)*.

Nat Cole, Sidney Poitier, Harry Belafonte: These three kings broke new ground in the fifties. Poitier in particular shattered the stereotypes every which way but loose. Partial to the slim gray or black suits and white shirts that were the order of the day, Poitier was so sought after that he became the first Black actor in American history to achieve box-office superstardom. But Poitier and Belafonte would remain the exceptions to the rule for quite some time, until comedians such as Richard Pryor and Eddie Murphy achieved celebrity on their own terms in the seventies and eighties.

The arrival on the scene of Little Richard, Frankie Lymon, Chubby Checker, and Jimi Hendrix gave birth to a brand-new bag: Black men wore their hair conked, then slicked back into proud pompadours; suits were suddenly scandalously tight; ties lost their bulge; shoes got right to the two-toned point. Although the rock and roll style was quickly copied by Elvis Presley and other White entertainers, screen idols such as Sammy Davis, Jr. captured the look on-screen.

Surging through the sixties, Poitier continued to personify the dignified rising Black bourgeoisie—getting the job done in clean, understated suits and crisp white shirts à la *The Heat of the Night* (1967). Meanwhile, alongside the civil rights movement, a more defiant, anti-establishment style emerged, as personified by muscle-man Jim Brown, the first Black action hero. With the founding of Motown Records, Berry Gordy turned Detroit into a veritable style factory, concocting sugar-coated glam and suave sounds for kids around the globe. On the funky end, Jimi Hendrix set a style precedent that has been revisited by scores of new funkmeisters for decades, right down to his princely purple majesty, The Artist. Hendrix's uncut funk personified the freedom of self-creation. Pushing the androgynous envelope to the max, he favored skinny velvet pants, ruffled shirts, embroidered vests, colorful beads, and an exotic crown of unruly hair. The influence of his flamboyant fashions was apparent in Blaxploitation films.

In the seventies Blaxploitation flick *Shaft*, Richard Roundtree settled the score in slick leather coats, form-fitting turtlenecks, flared pants, and platform shoes *(opposite, far left)*. Billy Dee Williams resurrected the styles of the Harlem Renaissance in *Lady Sings the Blues* *(opposite, left)*. Ron O'Neal, aka "Superfly," stood tough in head-to-toe white; a status watch, chunky jewelry, and silver pistol were his accessories of choice *(above)*.

Street style—a term bandied about in the nineties as if it were nouvelle cuisine—actually got its first screen creds back in the seventies. The street style of the day was a look that usually consisted of an Afro, turtlenecks, platform shoes, knee-high boots, wide-lapelled jackets, maxicoats, and furs. Real furs. Blaxploitation flicks picked up on the street style of the Black community, packaged its nuances, and served it as cinema. Many of the male stars of these films became style icons—Richard Roundtree, of *Shaft* (1971) fame, being the most notable example. Whether they were swaggering as defiant antiheroes, like Fred Williamson in a slew of films, including *The Legend of Nigger Charley* (1972); dipping "Mack-Daddy"-style, like Ron O'Neal in *Superfly* (1972); running from "the man," like Melvin Van Peebles in *Sweet Sweetback's Baadasssss Song* (1971); hot on the detective trail, like Raymond St. Jacques in *Cotton Comes to Harlem* (1970); achieving hoop dreams, like Bernie Casey in *Maurie* (1973); karate-chopping enemies, like Jim Kelly in *Black Belt Jones* (1974); or wooing a ladylove à la Billy Dee Williams in *Mahogany* (1975), Black men brought a provocative style to the screen that reverberated around the world.

After Blaxploitation films played themselves out—killing off a vital segment of the film industry for many Black performers—almost twenty years would pass before another Black film renaissance blossomed. In the interim, a few funny men figured out how to laugh all the way to the bank. Black comedians began to tell it like it is—"it" being, of course, the Black experience. Bill Cosby and Richard Pryor were leaders of the pack. Yin and yang, Cosby played the consummate gentleman to Pryor's bad brother, the former a spokesman for family-brand products and a future sitcom star, the latter a stand-up who straddled the fence between minstrel show and raw mockery in such films as *Car Wash* (1976) and the semi-autobiographical *Jo Jo Dancer, Your Life Is Calling* (1986).

Although Black stars were not as visible in the "Gettin' Paid" eighties as the "Mack-Daddy" seventies,

a whole new breed of brothers—Louis Gossett, Jr. as the drill sergeant in *An Officer and a Gentleman* (1982), Denzel Washington as a militant young soldier in *A Soldier's Story* (1984), and Howard E. Rollins's memorable movie debut as "Coalhouse Walker" in *Ragtime* (1981)—kept busy by honing their craft, until the third renaissance firmly put Black talent on top again. With a brand-new attitude and point of view, Black style was back in business by 1990. And this time, everybody from Harlem to Holland wanted a piece of the box-office action.

Thanks to the success of indie efforts by Robert Townsend (*Hollywood Shuffle*, 1987) and Spike Lee (*School Daze,* 1987 and *Do The Right Thing*, 1989), audiences were exposed to all the nuances that made up Black male style. From buppies to homeboys, the range of our fashions was brought into view. It was on full display in four ground-breaking Black films: *New Jack City* (1991), *Boyz 'N the Hood* (1991), *Jungle Fever* (1991), and *Straight Out of Brooklyn* (1991). With these commercially successful movies, new style icons were born: Wesley Snipes became the new Black action hero/sex symbol/film god; Sam Jackson was anointed character-actor connoisseur; Laurence Fishburne portrayed the dignified street brother; Ice Cube represented the rap star as all-around pop cultural ambassador. Steppin' to the hip-hop philosophy of "keeping it real," the everyday brother became a cinema star: movies such as *Juice* (1992) and *Menace II Society* (1993) cast unknowns in lead roles and reaped considerable rewards. Gone were the larger-than-life athletic Adonises like Jim Brown and Fred Williamson, gone were the romantic, crossover types like Danny Glover, Lou Gossett, Jr., Sidney Poitier, and Billy Dee Williams. The brothers of the hip-hop generation looked more like Ice Cube's "Doughboy" from "around the way." On East Coast or West, clad in baggy pants, fly sneakers, baseball caps, and Starter jackets or sweats, the rising Black star represents the lower- and middle-class strata that populates the contemporary urban landscape. A broader range of films reflects our lifestyles. The result: dignified diversity. Old-school stars such as Morgan Freeman and James Earl Jones join with new-school brothers such as Larenz Tate, Omar Epps, and Mekhi Phifer to portray all the flavors that we savor. In its efforts to reflect the real world, Black cinema continues to break new ground in the reel world.

Denzel Washington has made it his métier to portray a wide range of African-American characters, most notably Malcolm X (1992) *(above)*. Thespian Morgan Freeman was nominated for an Oscar for his role in *Driving Miss Daisy* (1989) *(top, right)*. Comedian-turned-actor Eddie Murphy mocked society's stereotypes of Blacks in such films as *Trading Places* (1983) and *Coming to America* (1988) *(bottom, right)*.

André DE SHIELDS

"STAGE"

I've been in the theater for thirty years, so, not surprisingly, much of what I know about style I've gleaned from show business. The quintessential example of this was an epiphany I had when I was nine years old. I saw the Vincent Minelli film *Cabin in the Sky*, which starred some of the greatest Black talent in the history of show business: Lena Horne, Eddie "Rochester" Anderson, Ethel Waters, Mantan Moreland, and Louis Armstrong, to name a few. But the actor who influenced me the most was John Bubbles. There's a scene where he enters a tavern, resplendent in white from head to toe. He initiates an exquisite jitterbug with Ethel Waters, then proceeds to dance up to the bar, across it, up a flight of stairs, onto the roof, and finally into the air. He seemed to take flight. At that moment I knew I wanted to be equally miraculous, and I've carried that image with me throughout my career.

On Broadway in the seventies, I set a style precedent myself by starring in the hit musical *The Wiz*. It was an Afrocentric stage version of the classic film *The Wizard of Oz*. I played "The Wiz" himself, in all his extravagant splendor. But the funny part is, initially I wasn't even considered for the role. I'd gone through a series of auditions for the "Scarecrow," "Tin Man," and "Lion" characters, and I didn't get any of them. I had to convince the producers to allow me to audition for the role of "The Wiz." They'd envisioned an older, wizened person for the part, but I had something different in mind. I went home and picked my hair out into the biggest Jimi Hendrix bubble I could get, slipped on some silver platform shoes, and even wore silver earrings to match. There are still people today who say I was the first man they ever saw wearing an earring in each ear. When I returned to the audition it was as if the martians had landed! The late Charlie Smalls, the show's composer, said that when I walked into the room he knew right away I would be "Mr. Wiz." With a change of attire, I changed the mind of the producer, and won the chance to create a title role.

As an actor, I have to be a chameleon. I have to fit into different situations and still be comfortable. I don't know of any one designer who can serve me for every occasion, so I mix and match. But when I have to do the executive thing, I have three classically designed suits—one by Giorgio Armani, one by Yves St. Laurent, one by Pierre Cardin—that have served me well for fifteen years. I've also held on to some favorite piece from each decade of my life. Fashion does tend to repeat itself! Now, in the nineties, when a young friend mentions, "I wish I had a pair of platforms," I can say, "Borrow mine from the seventies." I still get complimented on one of my father's sports coats—a box-cut, black wool jacket flecked with red and white—and it's more than fifty years old!

Billy Dee WILLIAMS

"SCREEN"

Lady Sings the Blues made me into a matinee idol, partially because of my own persona, but also because of what I was wearing and how I wore it. Clothes are like collectibles to me. I tend to buy them the same way I'd buy a painting: I shop for great individual pieces according to how they make me feel. I don't adhere to a rigid agenda in order to round out my wardrobe, and I don't necessarily believe you need a lot of money to purchase nice things. As a kid in New York, I loved buying suits and other clothing from thrift shops. Some of the best buys, some of the best quality stuff I've ever owned, have come from those places. Today, I also like pieces by Armani, Brioni, and some Ralph Lauren.

I have an affinity for the menswear of the thirties and forties. Back then, men, and Black men in particular, seemed to be a lot smoother than they are today. They were gentlemen. Some might argue that, at the time, we were merely copying White culture, but Whites borrowed ideas from us as well. It was an exchange. Black Americans have always had such an original way of reinterpreting the standards, although I think White people benefited from it more than we did.

Styles from the seventies, however, I never want to revisit! When I think of the things I used to wear back then, I cringe. And I never liked natural hair on me. It just didn't look right, and it was hard to comb. It's interesting how people think that straightening your hair is somehow the equivalent of rejecting your racial origin. I disagree. African culture is filled with examples of Africans using natural elements to straighten hair. It's not unusual in any culture for people to use various methods of adornment to make themselves attractive. It's not a question of trying to assimilate, but of finding things that work for you.

I have a reputation for possessing a smooth style, but it's not as premeditated as some may think. Much of my demeanor, personality, and idiosyncrasies comes from the men in my family. My father and uncles have a slow grace and softness about them that I've acquired by unconscious imitation—a style inheritance, if you like. It's not just in the way that I dress, it's influenced the whole package: my smile, my hair, my walk.

White actors dominated the silver screen when I was young: I especially liked the way Fred Astaire wore those wonderful suits, and I wanted to be like Rudolph Valentino, because he had an air of old-fashioned romance. I admired Black actors like Ossie Davis and Roscoe Lee Brown. Roscoe in particular embodies a kind of eclecticism, a charm, and an ambiance that makes his appeal universal. He's a brilliant man. And Geoffrey Holder is another interesting, extraordinary person—certainly one of the most creative men I've ever known.

Shaka KING

MENSWEAR DESIGNER

Shaka King Menswear New York opened its doors in 1991. Since then, King's custom-tailored designs have been featured in *The New York Times*, *Vibe*, and *DNR*, which hailed him as "The King of Chic." King was honored in 1993 with the Fashion Association's *Playboy* New Talent Showcase Award. For his inspired Fall 1994 "Harlem Renaissance" collection, *Essence* magazine dubbed him the "Menswear Monarch." A native of Miami, King received his BFA in Fashion Design from New York's Pratt Institute in 1982.

King has a reputation for creating tailored clothing for Black men whose style sensibility projects intense attitude. He counts director Spike Lee, jazz visionary Branford Marsalis, actor Lou Gossett, Jr., R&B musicians Boyz II Men, and NBA standout Alonzo Mourning among his hipster clientele. Based on his experience, King reviews some signature style nuances and suggests new ways to pump up the volume.

ATTITUDE

Attitude is an intrinsic part of how an ensemble comes together. Climate, occasion, culture, cost—all the externals aside, it's mood that is often at the heart of a seemingly subconscious selection of clothes. Are there rules on how to incorporate attitude into a wardrobe? King offers a few hints, but emphasizes that attitude comes from within and is translated in our daily choice of threads.

DEFINING ATTITUDE

According to King, attitude is beyond definition, but not recognition. "It's in the way we adjust our belts and knot our ties—or choose not to wear one when tradition says we should," states King. He adds that Black men, rarely afraid of taking risks, have created edgy, emotionally raw styles: "Our daring nature guides our independent fashion spirit." A man of discerning taste hates to see his same outfit worn by some other guy on the street. King gives an example: "If we're corporate executives, we may opt for a dark pinstriped suit. But our version usually incorporates a wider chalk stripe and a broader lapel. Many of my Wall Street clients have asked me to line their suit jackets with brightly colored silks. Outsiders may never witness this nuance, but it's a detail that affects posture and pride in the workplace."

PANTS

"When brothers take the time to have their trousers professionally tailored, many of us choose to add cuffs," King says. "We tend to exceed the American standard of an inch-and-a-half cuff. Since the apex of cuff altitudes, the six-to-eight-inch cuffs of the seventies, we've settled somewhere around the two- to two-and-a-half-inch range." In the tradition of sixties groups such as "The Temps" or "The Tops," stylish men can opt to have standard bottoms tapered. A

recent trend for lax-waisted pants has swept both casual and tailored clothing lines. This often beltless style choice began with inner-city Black youth. King also considers "paper-bagging" a pair of high-waisted pants or jeans a chic statement. To achieve the look, tightly fasten a belt around the waist of a pair of oversized bottoms in order to create a gather in the front.

SHIRTS

"Button-down collars don't always need to be buttoned." King suggests shirt attitude can be easily accomplished by leaving cuffs unbuttoned or even by removing collars to convert an old dress shirt into a well-worn, band-collar, summer favorite. Unconventional fit also provides an avenue to fashion attitude. From the dramatic layering of finger-brushing, lace-trimmed, poet's shirt cuffs under tight-sleeved military jackets in the sixties, to the slim or "painted-on" stretch shirts of the seventies, to the elongated dress shirt sleeve cuff that exceeds the jacket of the corresponding suit in the nineties, tweaking traditional fit is a sure sign of attitude. Try a ribbed, high V-neck or plain T-shirt underneath a suit instead of the traditional shirt-and-tie combination. Turtlenecks and long-sleeve pullovers in merino wool or cashmere make great "waist-wraps," and provide a unexpected jolt of color when exposed through the cut of a jacket's vents (just be careful not to choose a sweater that's too bulky in texture, or it will disrupt the line of the suit).

HATS

Admittedly a "mad hatter" himself, King believes that your hat is truly your sky: "It's all in the way you tilt that brim! Whether it's a knit cap high on your head, tilted to the side, or pulled over an eye, most hats are very moldable. Black men have made the fedora legendary with their own particular break in the brim." Much of the Black man's "hattitude" was born of necessity. King recalls, "If a hand-me-down from dad or an uncle didn't quite fit, we still had to make it work." Be it a one-size-fits-all variety or a custom-fitted chapeau, explore the possibilities by flipping a brim in reverse, back-combing a furry surface to add texture, or changing the color, pattern, or width of the hatband.

ACCESSORIES

Black men have no bones about wearing jewelry above and beyond cuff links and tie tacks. In the eighties, hip-hop's obsession with oversized, solid-gold status symbols and chunky chains provided a pointed commentary on the decade's compulsive consumerism. The Paris-based House of Chanel double-backed the irony factor by replicating the look a few seasons later with its own massive, interlocking Cs, stamped on everything from earrings to belt buckles to medallions. By the global nineties, rustic fabrics and ethnic elements —from kuba scarves to handcrafted metal ankhs— conveyed the end-of-millennium universal vibe.

Switching the buckle on a belt to an ethnic, artisanal, or vintage piece conveys an appreciation of culture and craftsmanship. Richly colored silk scarves take a day suit to night. King suggests, "Ascots add finesse to a suit or a simple dress shirt. Compared to the typical bow tie or necktie, they make an unexpected statement." When it comes to jewelry, King advises, "It should be worn against one's skin, or with sportswear." Some brothers choose to display necklaces on top of shirt collars and tie knots, but this registers as busy, and can detract from a beautiful tie.

FOOTWEAR

Shoe attitude, according to King, is obvious in the way Black men "personally treat the surface of a common shoe style." Adding a super-high, patent-leather-like shine to a basic, cap-toe oxford gives an unexpected gleam to a work suit. Intentionally scuffing or scratching the surface of a rugged, lug-sole work boot, on the other hand, creates a weathered, rough-hewn effect. Either way, the lesson to be learned is that opposites make for intriguing combinations.

elegance

sports

"If you don't have confidence, you'll always find a way not to win."

CARL LEWIS

RELAXED elegance

IT CAN BE HOT AND COOL ALL AT ONCE.

An easy grace that floats around the body like smoke. It's relaxed elegance, an understated dazzle practically patented by silky-smooth Black music icons in the forties and fifties. Tuxedo-clad Nat "King" Cole wore it like a second skin. Louis "Pops" Armstrong said it all in the way he'd wipe his brow. "The Duke" Ellington had it down, his choice of suit per performance carefully selected from a stable of twenty or so in his dressing room.

Relaxed elegance is the ability to take a fastidiously contrived clothing ensemble and make it appear effortlessly assembled, by choosing garments that fit perfectly, convey sophistication, but never register as constricting or dandy-overdone. Quality fabrics express the high level of taste, as does the casual, fluid drape of the cloth. Relaxed elegance goes beyond a garment's face value. It comes to life through personality. From the limplike gait of the first hip-hop kids in the eighties,

Tyson Beckford personifies relaxed elegance in a casual cable-knit sweater *(previous spread, left)*. **In 1936, Jesse Owens greeted the press wearing a chalk-striped, double-breasted suit** *(previous spread, right)*. **A duo in the twenties accented their informal attire with shawl-collared sweaters, dimpled homburgs, and sharply creased pants** *(above)*. **Even in lounge settings, the tuxedo remained de rigueur for turn-of-the-century entertainers** *(right)*. **In the heyday of the zany zoot, "respectable" gentlemen wore a more subdued suit, complete with pipe** *(opposite, top)*. **Pre-bebop, beret, and goatee, Dizzy Gillespie unwound with a smoke** *(opposite, bottom)*.

back to its forebear, the long-legged strut of the Harlem zootie in the forties, attitude was as much a part of the outfit as the foot-long feather bobbing in rhythm atop a wide-brimmed hat.

Although our American journey has been anything but relaxed, our style has served as both a survival skill and a means of celebration. Relaxed elegance was born from our collective desire to be seen not just as dissatisfied second-class citizens, but as proud members of a separate, self-contained culture—a culture rich in its own heritage. From boxer Jack Johnson, sporting his hefty-sized take on the traditionally slim dandy look, to tailored politician Adam Clayton Powell, Jr., turned out in pinstriped suits and crisp white shirts, Black men have made public style statements about the comfort inherent in refined clothing. For Black men, relaxed elegance has never been an oxymoron.

Nowhere was this independent style spirit more obvious than in the culturally fertile streets of Harlem USA in the twenties and thirties. Regarded as the "Harlem Renaissance," this period in Black American history marked the beginning of successful Black communal living. There was something magical about Harlem. A functional society of businessmen and -women, home-owners, artists, writers, and musicians creatively coexisted. The positive vibe produced by the community resonated throughout the city and around the world. After the First World War, Harlem became a proud enclave of mainly middle-class Blacks who supported each other's businesses and cultural endeavors. Harlem's favorites sons, whether born and bred or honorary adoptees, were style leaders: actor Paul Robeson, poet Langston Hughes, Pan-Africanist Marcus Garvey.

A mecca for entertainers, Harlem was home to some of the most legendary nightspots of the thirties and forties, such as The Cotton Club and Small's Paradise. The Negro was in vogue. Jazz artist Louis Armstrong would roll into town and draw Black Harlemites and midtown Manhattan Whites together to witness his revues, billed under such saucy headings as "Hot Chocolates."

Armstrong's all-encompassing style ranged from the whimsical to the natty. While other jazz musicians would pass off high-shined police shoes or hard-pressed secondhand attire as stagewear, Armstrong insisted upon marimba-gray overcoats and fitted velour hats (the homburg being the most popular style among jazz cats of the day). White jazz saxophonist Milton "Mezz" Mezzrow was a huge fan of both Armstrong's playing and his clothing. He clearly recalled how the trumpeter's slightest style move invariably caused a frenzy. During his performances, Armstrong would wipe his brow with a bleached white handkerchief, then proceed to wave it about while playing. This style signature was quickly copied by Harlem's cool young cats, who could be seen on the streets clutching white "hankies" in their hands. Mezzrow remembered how "all the raggedy kids . . . were so inspired with self-respect after digging how neat and natty Louis was, they started to dress up real good, and took pride in it, too, because if Louis did it, it must be right."

Louis Armstrong's stage and style persona was truly original. He was known to change his outfits three or four times during a performance. His obvious

In a 1957 snapshot, lounge singer Bobby Short proved that a pair of flat-front chinos could be just as stylish as tuxedo trousers *(opposite)*. On a boating excursion in the sixties, Adam Clayton Powell, Jr. effortlessly adopted New England chic, sporting such all-American staples as a light cotton jacket and a weathered bandanna *(left)*. Nat "King" Cole never let them see him sweat: A double-breasted cardigan kept him comfortable yet crisp *(above)*.

onstage comfort in fine clothing made up a major part of his image and inspired other artists, notably Nat Cole. The unforgettable "King" Cole's elegance came across as more than casual. On-screen, he melted the hearts of millions of fans, Black and White alike, with his honey-dripping renditions of such American popular classics as "Mona Lisa" and "Nature Boy." And although his stage manner was that of calm confidence and tasteful refinement, behind the scenes he had to cope with the pressure of the show's sponsors trying their best to pull the plug.

In the face of fifties segregation, Nat Cole's image served to elevate him. With elegant style counterparts such as Sammy Davis, Jr. and Harry Belafonte in his hip pockets, the tall, slim Cole was known for his dashing appearances in custom-made lace tuxedo shirts and mohair suits. His signature tuxedo had no satin stripes down the sides—very clean and modern for the day. (Cole admitted that his wife Maria, who supervised his clothes shopping, had a lot to do with these idiosyncratic specifications, such as file-top shoes and

In suede car coat, mohair pants, and chain-link bracelet, Miles Davis modeled the comfort of a relaxed silhouette *(above)*. Velvet smoking jacket, silk ascot, Scotch on the rocks—Black men in the seventies enjoyed the finer things in life *(right)*. End-of-the-millennium minimalism meant tone-on-tone dressing, T-shirts with suit jackets, and comfortable ethnic slides in place of lace-up shoes *(opposite, top)*. Actor Danny Glover showcased the power of color in a pale yellow suit and two-toned spectators *(opposite, bottom)*.

narrow-brimmed tweed hats.) Fastidious about details, Cole would take up to twenty minutes just to knot his bow tie. This king had an air of dignity, apparent in his literal and lyrical haberdashery. Sometimes, he topped it all off with his trademark cigarette holder.

Nat "King" Cole's barrier-breaking style influence was so powerful that it resonated throughout more areas of Black male culture than just music: The reality of a Black man whose lifestyle was equal to that of any other mainstream public figure was incredibly inspiring.

Historically, Black men have had a love-hate relationship with the rigid dictates of European clothing standards. The typical Black man's body is physically different than that of a man of European descent. In general, the Black man has fuller thighs and buttocks, a broader chest, and more developed arms. These differences have forced us to either reinterpret mainstream styles or abandon them altogether for authentic Afrocentric fashions, which epitomize relaxed elegance through their fit and functionality. Black star athletes, with their larger-than-life bodies and money to burn, have been at the forefront of casual elegance in clothing. The tradition of sports style, sometimes flashy but always confident, dates back to men like "Sugar" Ray Robinson, and is kept alive by such paragons as Michael Jordan. For example, Hakeem Olajuwon is a walking hybrid of a motherland physique married to a classically European style sensibility. The Nigerian native is known for wearing well-draped suits over Nehruesque band-collar dress shirts, and favors custom-made designs by Ermenegildo Zegna and Giorgio Armani. Olajuwon's motto sums up the essence of relaxed elegance: "Never let people see you look as if you're trying too hard . . . dressing is fun. . . it's expressing yourself without saying a word."

For Black men, part of the appeal of style is that it lifts us above the dreariness of dressing as necessity. The farthest contrast to mere body-covering is luxury apparel. Who needs it? No one, but Black men have made it clear that it needs us to come to life. Relaxed elegance proves the power of understatement.

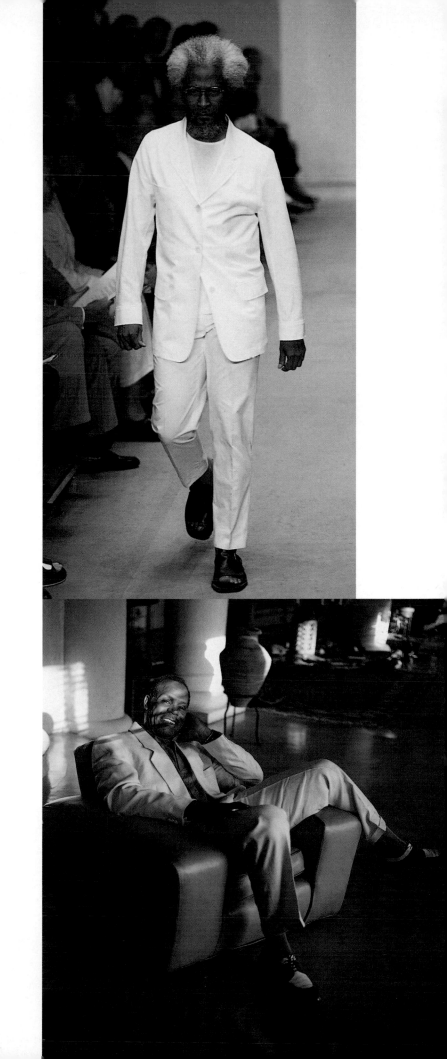

Ahmad RASHAD

"RELAXED ELEGANCE"

I learned about the importance of relaxed elegance from my father. My mother told me that when she first met him, she thought he was one of the cleanest guys in town. When he went to dances, he would drape a handkerchief over his shoulder so that the girls he danced with wouldn't stain his suit with their hair oil. And when it was time to go to church, it wasn't my mother we had to wait on. He spent a lot of time getting himself right.

My father taught me the importance of quality. He had no tolerance for anything that was trendy or cheap. His motto was, "If you can't buy a quality piece now, save up until you can." For him, it was all about long-lasting fabrics, drape, and fit. And then there were the details, the things that set you apart, like a good pair of shoes. In his opinion, you could look "bummy" with the wrong shoes or elegant with the right ones. His attention to clothes was all about how he wanted to be perceived. Being well-dressed made him Mr. Moore, not just Joe. He told me that one of the ways White men used to demean a well-dressed Black man was to ask him if he was preaching. That would piss off Black men of the day.

When I was growing up, there were certain Black sports stars I revered, not only for their style on the field, but off the field as well. In my eyes, these athletes were like artists, because they were geniuses at expressing what they did, and that expression was so strong it came to be known as their signature. You recognized Jack Johnson style, or Satchel Paige style, or Muhammad Ali style. Unique traits set them apart, and their dress was an extension of their individuality. In terms of today's players, Michael Jordan is very fashionable, and incredibly talented as an athlete. The overall package offers a positive image to Black youth. Even in my career as a sports anchor, it's important that young Black men see me in a suit and realize through my personality that you can wear one and still be cool.

Style says a lot about who you are. My style reflects my persona: easy-going and confident. I'm a stickler for a nice shirt. A custom-made shirt can work wonders, and it doesn't necessarily cost more than a quality off-the-rack shirt. You can be wearing the most wonderful suit that money can buy, but if your shirt doesn't fit properly, the whole look suffers.

The MVP

BY CRAIG ROSE

A LASTING IMPRESSION WAS MADE

that summer afternoon. What I remember more vividly than the cheers of the crowd, the fiercely heated competition rising between each team, and the pounding of my heart, was a remarkably stylish player named Jamal. Despite his lazy dribble and apparent lack of overall skill, Jamal was a walking, talking creation of head-to-toe hype. He looked and sounded the part of a seasoned professional well beyond his years. By this measure, Jamal was the most valuable player of the game. Even the painstaking effort he put into styling his "kicks" was something to be admired.

Jamal's sneakers were a work of art: soles so white from liquid polish you'd swear they never touched the ground; leather so clean it looked as if it was patent; and laces so wide and colorful they needed room to breathe, open and untied.

These loud and boastful laces, commonly referred to as "New Yorkers," immediately won the respect of a generation of grade-schoolers nationwide.

Boxer Sugar Ray Robinson tweaked the classics in the forties with his plaid-print tuxedo jacket *(top)*. Satchel Paige, the legendary baseball player, was impeccably styled on and off the field *(above)*. Muhammad Ali's colorful personality couldn't be contained by a standard shirt and tie *(right)*. Joe Louis delivered a knockout punch in herringbone suit and rakishly tilted fedora *(opposite)*.

As was often the case with trends, they met with much disapproval from educators, who regarded them as an ominous sign of self-endangerment and sloth. Soon thereafter, much to the dismay of our superiors, posses of young Black boys could be spotted pimping down the halls in their outlawed footwear, emulating the style that had earned Jamal his superstardom.

Every Black boy in America, from the inner cities to the suburbs, learns at an early age one of life's most valuable truths: It's not how well you play the game, but how well you look playing the game, that scores you the most points. Win or lose, the most stylish player always comes out on top.

Today's star players are revered as much for their fashion sense as for their athletic prowess. The two often work hand-in-hand. It's practically impossible to conceive of Chicago Bull Michael Jordan taking flight in anything but his namesake sneakers, or of Olympic-gold-medalist Michael Johnson moving at the speed of light without his gilded Nike running shoes. Likewise, the one-two combination of black-tie good looks and a round-the-world sucker punch gave boxing middleweight champion "Sugar" Ray Leonard his edge, and it was Tiger Woods's loud-red Nike sweatshirt, worn at the 1997 Masters Tournament, that announced the dawning of a new day in pro golf.

Given the real or perceived lack of opportunities for Black Americans in other areas of the economy, sports have become an arena for upward mobility. Thanks to the impact of a few extraordinarily successful players, many young Black males regard sports as a way of gaining respect. So great is the influence of superstar athletes that corporations can't get enough of them, using their image to market everything from cars to cologne. And the stars willingly sell themselves, promoting their ideas and idiosyncrasies to adoring fans through movies, books, video games.

But sports has not been without its genuine heroes: It was boxing legend Joe Louis and track-and-field hero Jesse Owens who used their celebrity appeal to persuade Negro men to enlist in the armed forces during the Second World War. Many followed "suit," donning their patriotism by way of military uniform. Bringing the cycle full-circle, Hall-of-Famer Jackie Robinson traded his army getups for a baseball uniform, and went on to become one of the game's greatest players.

The power and privilege to affect social, economic, and political gains for African Americans did not belong exclusively to professional athletes. The sixties gave rise to two virtually unknown track-and-

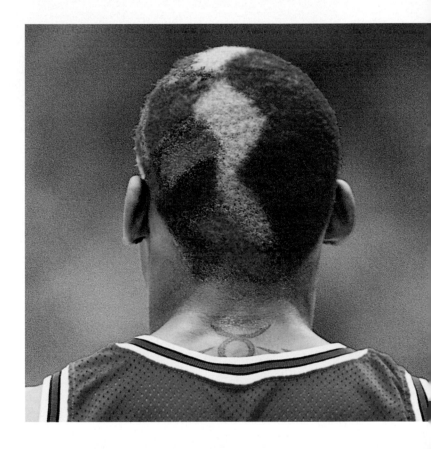

Arthur Ashe preferred comfortable separates and professed to own only five suits and five pairs of shoes; Houston Rocket Hakeem Olajuwon has clothes custom-tailored to fit his seven-foot-plus frame; "Magic" Johnson, retired from the game and focused on entrepreneurial endeavors, dresses for success in pinstriped suit, polka-dot tie, and pocket square; the incomparable Michael Jordan used his athletic prowess to establish a business empire, which includes licenses for everything from sneakers to cologne *(opposite, clockwise from top left)*. Extensive tattooing, numerous piercings, and multicolored hair all add to shock jock Dennis Rodman's rebel image *(above)*.

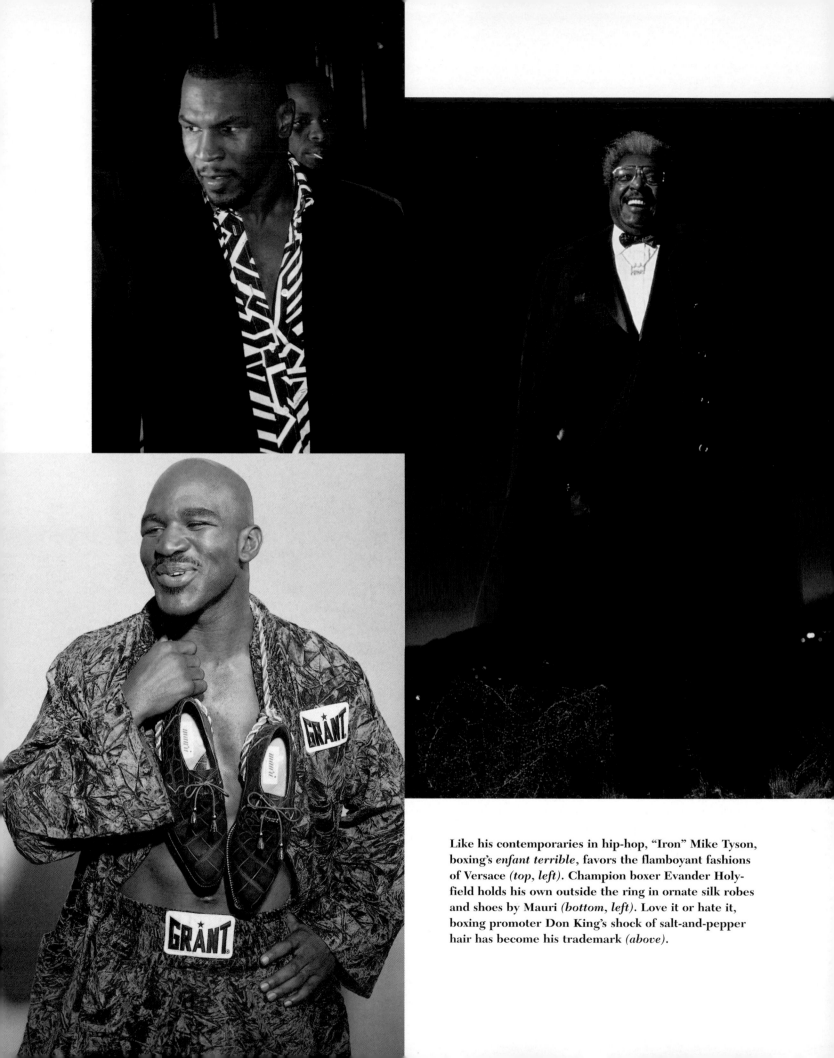

Like his contemporaries in hip-hop, "Iron" Mike Tyson, boxing's *enfant terrible*, favors the flamboyant fashions of Versace *(top, left)*. Champion boxer Evander Holyfield holds his own outside the ring in ornate silk robes and shoes by Mauri *(bottom, left)*. Love it or hate it, boxing promoter Don King's shock of salt-and-pepper hair has become his trademark *(above)*.

field Olympians—Tommie Smith and John Carlos—who each used his winning platform to cry out for "Black Power" with a raised fist. Whether clad in army fatigues or Olympic sweats, Black men have overcome challenges in both the battlefields of war and the playing fields of these United States.

Through the years, the public lifestyles of professional Black athletes have led to greater social and spiritual changes for the Black community. Retired NBA all-star Kareem Abdul-Jabbar first embraced the teachings of Allah as practiced by the Hanafi Muslims in the seventies. Today, he strives to achieve the good life not through material excess but spiritual richness. Of like mind was the late, great tennis champion Arthur Ashe, who wrote in his memoir *Days of Grace* (Alfred A. Knopf, 1993), "I spend very little on clothing. I own only four sport coats, five suits, and five pairs of shoes." Ashe's modest choice of wardrobe, the explosive impact of his two consecutive Wimbledon wins, and the fierceness of his fight against the racial injustices suffered by minority athletes made him something of a god among men, the antithesis of the athlete-as-marketing-tool. Both Ashe and Abdul-Jabbar exemplify the quiet fire for justice and peace that burns deep in the souls of African-American brothers.

With his flagrant showmanship, former boxing heavyweight champion Muhammad Ali was a great deal less conservative. The "float like a butterfly, sting like a bee" Ali dominated professional boxing, and looked every bit as "pretty" outside the ring as he did in it. Ali's impeccable taste ran the gamut, from slim-fitted, custom-tailored suits worn in solidarity with his Muslim brothers to the easy, Afrocentric elegance of short-sleeve linen camp shirts or authentic dashikis. The pimp aesthetic—wide-brimmed hats, velvet suits, fur coats—belonged to another boxing great, Walt "Clyde" Frazier. Together, Frazier and Ali introduced the world to the more entertaining, if not always fashionable, side of the sport, while upping the ante for future athletes itching to be considered world-class.

The seventies gave way to a more sophisticated side of cool. In his classic suits, Julius "Dr. J" Erving marked the start of something big for Black men in sports, whose images were becoming increasingly more palatable (read: marketable) to middle America. In the ensuing years, sports heroes such as Magic Johnson, Walter Payton, and Michael Jordan catapulted to the top of their games with multimillion-dollar contracts complete with product endorsements and grand-scale promotion schemes.

Professional athletes of the eighties and nineties undeniably work hard, and they play pretty tough, too. Dennis Rodman, Shaquille O'Neal, and Eric Davis—when it comes to fashion, their respective styles often say as much about them as their game stats. The blasphemous ensembles of Bulls power forward Dennis Rodman range from the exotic in men's underwear (leaving little to the imagination) to a virgin-white wedding gown that would cause any mother of the bride to sob uncontrollably. Laker Shaquille O'Neal fancies the forties silhouette—constructed shoulder, longer coat, baggier pant—of Beverly Hills designer Dion Lattimore. Lattimore also dresses Baltimore Oriole Eric Davis, arguably one of the most stylish players in the National Baseball League. A tailor's dream, Davis opts for fashion-forward designs—an eight-button, double-breasted coat that cuts away at the bottom, for example—many of his colleagues wouldn't dare try.

Whether wearing an outfit that would be regarded by most as risqué or setting a new world record, the phenomenal success of African-American men in sports is a testament to their strength, will, and courage. In the face of insurmountable obstacles, Owens's mad dash, Ali's thunder, Robinson's runs home, and Ashe's ace all left an indelible mark on the American landscape. This legacy of triumph shows its true colors today in Jordan's flight, Tiger's eye, Holyfield's spirit, and Griffey's smile. Generations of African-American men in sports have proved to be some of life's most valuable players.

Reggie MILLER

"SPORTS"

On the court, I follow a simple rule: I keep my uniforms clean, my shirts tucked in, and my socks low to my shoes. I don't mind the baggy shorts look, just not past my knees—that's a little too sloppy for my taste.

Off the court, my style is smooth, but confident. There's no substitute for a tailor-made suit. Because I'm 6',7" I can't just buy clothes off the rack. There was a time when I had to look to Brooks Brothers for my suits, and the results were sometimes painful. In those years, I learned the art of accessorizing to hide flaws. By adding cool shoes, scarves, hats, and overcoats, I could spice up a $200 suit, make it look like it cost a thousand. Luckily, I can now afford to have all my suits and shirts custom-made. It's a wonderful privilege to be able to order everything to my liking—the fabric, the length, and especially the fit.

My siblings were my earliest style inspirations. My sister Cheryl, who is an Olympic gold medalist and coach of the WNBA's Phoenix Mercury, taught me a lot about how to dress when we were growing up. Various sports stars have also had an impact on my style. I clearly remember being influenced by the stylish presence of the legendary Clyde Frazier. His oversized brimmed hats, funkadelic shirts, and fur coats were outrageous. He was known for walking into Madison Square Garden like a big ol' pimp. And speaking of entrances, I cannot forget Muhammad Ali. His fashion evolution from the suited Cassius Clay to the exotic Muslim Ali was incredible.

While I don't believe there is a definitive Black basketball style—like all Black men, we have individual tastes—many players do have a certain flair

that gets them noticed. Dennis Rodman likes to show a lot of flesh, while many of the Generation-X players—Stephon Marbury, for example—sport casual hip-hop gear along the lines of Karl Kani. On the flip, there is the regal elegance of Hakeem Olajuwon, who, at 7'-plus, is one of the best-dressed men in the NBA.

As for favorite style era, it has to be the forties, with the rise of the zoot. There is something so smooth about the shape of that suit! The baggy pants, the tapered leg, the pocket chain. It exudes self-confidence, especially when it's pin-striped, like the ones Cab Calloway used to wear. The look was somewhat menacing, yet very businesslike.

Anthony McINTOSH

FOUNDER, DUENDE

Since its premiere at the 1993 *Playboy* New Talent Showcase, Anthony McIntosh's Duende collection has drawn rave reviews from such outlets as *Essence* and *Ebony Man*. The company's name comes from the Spanish word used to describe the indescribable, the irresistibly, inexplicably attractive. McIntosh defines his objective: "It is important for men today to find their own tradition, to use the past only as a reference point."

McIntosh attended Fordham on a basketball scholarship and earned an undergraduate degree in Quantitative Methods. In 1987, he received his Master's in Business Merchandising from New York University. But during his years at school, he also completed courses on weekends and evenings at the Fashion Institute of Technology and Parsons School of Design, preparing himself for his eventual career in the fashion industry.

Relaxed ELEGANCE

By combining the classic elements of traditional men's clothing with the forward aspects of contemporary sportswear, McIntosh has created a line that epitomizes the spirit of relaxed elegance. With his design philosophy in mind, he describes the finer points of refined, casual dressing.

RELAXED ELEGANCE

"Relaxed elegance is a more comfortable way of dressing," explains McIntosh. "It's less buttoned-up than a suit, but not as casual as jeans and sneakers. It means you still dress appropriately for an occasion, but in a way that is less constricting." The phenomenon of casual Fridays in the workplace has given men many options to expand their wardrobes.

JACKETS

McIntosh follows a basic rule of thumb when choosing a jacket: "Casual suit jackets and blazers usually have a relaxed, more natural shoulder, and are made from a softer fabric, such as brushed tweed or linen crepe." Even with this in mind, brothers, it is still important to ensure proper fit. Pay attention to such key areas as: the shoulder, the fit of which should allow the fabric of the jacket to drape smoothly down the arm; the waist button closure, which, with a single-button jacket, should fall approximately a half inch below the natural waistline; and the jacket length—in general, the bottom of the jacket should align with the base of the pinkie finger.

PANTS

Bottoms can range from well-worn khakis on the weekends to velvet drawstring lounge pants for the

McIntosh's translation: "If in a more formal setting the shirt would typically be undone by a single button, in a more relaxed environment, two or three will do."

Fabrics such as satin, rayon, and matte jersey create a loose, gauzy effect—just note that finer materials such as these typically have shorter life spans, and are especially sensitive to perspiration. Fine-gauge sweaters in cotton, merino wool, linen, and cashmere are the epitome of comfort. And variety in necklines (V-necks, boatnecks, turtlenecks) allows for versatility when layering.

SHOES

Loafers, driving shoes, or sandals without socks are perfectly comfortable footwear options, but, when exposing feet, it's common courtesy to keep them pedi-

holidays. The most important feature of relaxed pants is just that. According to McIntosh, "They should allow comfortable movement, but still appear sophisticated. The thirties high-waist pant is a prime example." Relaxed elegance in pants is also conveyed via fit. If a pant is slightly larger in the waist, it should be allowed to hug the hip, and should not be constricted by a fitted belt. Hectic pocket incidentals, such as wallets, keys, beepers, and cellular phones, add unnecessary bulk to an otherwise smooth line.

SHIRTS

Attitude can make almost any shirt or sweater register as relaxed. The fit should be generous, but not sloppy. Buttoning should always take a backseat to flair.

"Men today have the opportunity to expand their wardrobe," McIntosh explains, "and to add some personal flair in the process. The key to achieving casual style is to select pieces that are a little less constructed than suits, but that are made with the same attention to fit. Relaxed doesn't mean oversized. Softly constructed blazers, cardigan sweaters, merino wool polo shirts and crewnecks, cotton or corduroy trousers—all are good choices when going for this look."

cured and lotioned. A pair of chukka boots in suede or leather, some of today's trendier, thicker-soled shoes, and just about any footwear in suede, be it a loafer or an oxford, are all nice finishes. But remember, when it comes to elegance, McIntosh asserts, "Sneakers are not an option."

ACCESSORIES

No rules, no limits. Relaxed elegance means ascots, decoded of their stuffy connotations when coupled with a dress shirt and a favorite pair of jeans. Ties can work as belts or pocket squares after five. Casual occasions offer the chance to try those patterned socks, or a watch with an interesting face—accessories that wouldn't typically be paired with a tailored suit.

dance

"It is the 'man farthest down' who is most active in getting up."

ALAIN LOCKE

THE shoe

IN NINETEENTH-CENTURY AMERICA,
the average annual clothing allotment for a slave consisted of two pairs of pants, one coat, and one pair of shoes. This single set of shoes had to serve him in all his labors, regardless of weather. The fit of the shoe was haphazard, the material rough-grade rawhide. Stylishness was hardly a priority. But one former slave named Mollie Dawson recalled the men in her family preparing their shoes for a church meeting: "You could see dem all gittin' soot otten de chimney and mixin' it wid water der polish, and dis is what dey all polish der shoes wid. It didn't look nice and slick like it does now, but it made dem ole buckskin shoes look a lot bettah though."[1] Tallow, a tough white animal fat, was sometimes used to bring up a shine. While such

In high-shine, two-tone wing tips, Marcus Garvey personified Harlem Renaissance haberdashery *(previous spread, left; Garvey right)*. In the thirties, dancer John Bubbles wore a velvet-lapelled jacket, crisp bowler, French cuffs, and pinkie ring *(previous spread, right)*. Button- and lace-up leather gaiter boots formed the foundation of business attire at the turn of the century *(above)*. Young Louis Armstrong was one of jazz's earliest style-setters: His white leather oxfords with contrasting black sole and heel made for a witty match with his cream-colored suit *(right)*. Two brothers in the forties sported bold two-tones *(opposite)*.

early attempts at stylish self-definition might seem almost nonsensical when considered within the context of a slave's existence, it's important to acknowledge that personal adornment was one source of private dignity for an otherwise powerless man.

The shoe is the foundation of the complex visual equation that is Black male style. Not always having been in a position to purchase expensive shoes, Black men have long understood the value and visual impact of well-made, well-maintained footwear. The predecessor of pre-packaged "kwik-shine" was aptly dubbed "spit-shine" by Black men who earned their living detailing the soles and uppers of passers-by on city street corners in the early 1900s. Similar to the Black barbershop for its folkloric significance, the shoe-shine station and its brief exchange of services became a forum for local news and stories.

About fifty years after Blacks walked free from slavery, shoes began to be manufactured by machines. Mass-production allowed for a greater variety of styles at a cheaper cost. High-buttoned and high-laced shoes, typically reaching up over the ankle, were the footwear of choice as the American Negro cakewalked and juba'd into the early twentieth century. But as former slaves and sons thereof, life in the South or the industrial North wasn't just a song and dance. Whether toiling in fields, building railroads, or mending fences, intense labor was the norm. To accommodate any kind of lifestyle outside the trenches, work clothes had to transcend their intended use. Basic work boots were once again shined up for Saturday-night socializing and Sunday worship.

It wasn't until the twenties that urbane Black men began brandishing the stylish two-tone lace-ups made famous by legends Louis Armstrong and Bill "Bojangles" Robinson. Worn with the double-breasted suit of the day, the extremely popular, softly pointed, staple shoes just about became our feet. Superstars such as the notoriously stylish heavyweight boxing champion Jack Johnson were known to own numerous handmade editions of these factory-produced favorites,

Blues master Muddy Waters had no fear of soiling his shoes while tuning up in the sixties; his white lace-up oxfords with black piping were a force to be reckoned with *(opposite)*. Front and center in this forties family portrait is the youngest brother, all the better to spotlight his contrasting cap-toe oxfords *(above)*.

often cut from doeskin or crocodile. But the most common color combinations of these so-called "spectators" were black and white for winter, tan and cream for summer.

Inspired by the duke of Windsor and various entertainers, tastes expanded in the years preceding the Second World War. Solid Irish brogues were the shoe of choice for the masses, and can be seen in many of the images of Black men photographed by William VanDerZee. A predecessor of the wing tip, the round-toed brogue laced up or buckled on the side, and was designed with holes to allow for quick draining of water accumulated while walking in drenched Irish bogs. Such a staunch, hardworking shoe gave its owner an aura of respectability and responsibility.

The shoe was a literal focal point in fashions of the forties. The swing era, and its resident jazz artists Lionel Hampton, Cab Calloway, and Count Basie, embraced a silhouette that was notable for its extremes. A true zootie wasn't complete without his

"keen-toed" shoes—pointed, lace-up oxfords which served to firmly punctuate the penguinlike pant taper. Still soft enough to hop till the club closed, "keen-toeds" expressed the kind of stark contradiction that Black men were already familiar with: sharp on the outside, soft on the inside, and always ready to shift from styling to surviving.

In the decades to follow, Black men began to embrace the leisure shoe. Laces took a backseat to Latin-chic Cuban heels and Ivy-League-inspired penny loafers. (Although the loafer—a square-toed slip-on furnished with beef-roll closures and a "saddle" on top—had been introduced some twenty years earlier by G. H. Bass & Company, it didn't begin to take on its preppy connotations until much later.) Chubby Checker, Little Richard, and The Isley Brothers provided the fifties soundtrack. Beyond the world of entertainment, Black men needed a more dependable shoe to see them through civil rights marches in the South. Sturdy cap-toe lace-ups got the job done. In the

Motor City, color barriers were broken by nattily clad singing groups, such as The Temptations, The Miracles, and The Four Tops, that spun, kicked, and slid in syncopation while wearing impeccably polished two-tones.

By the sixties and seventies, a militant atmosphere affected fashion trends, as evidenced by the army boot's entrance onto the scene. In their leather lace-ups, Black Power leaders Huey P. Newton and Bobby Seale stood firm in the face of adversity. On the hippie flip side, artists such as Jimi Hendrix elevated the approach to footwear with stacked, pimp-famed platforms made from exotic skins. Often customized for celebrities, off-the-rack versions featured leather uppers stitched with side-seam zippers that ran as high as the knee, set on top of a layered sole made from wood or compressed cork. The average height of the heel was four inches. Such shoes were not about comfort. Harlem resident Neal Jones recalls one passionate brother whose stylish stilts nearly grounded him: "I once went to a dance back in the seventies in Harlem and saw a brother in a pair of stacked platforms which made him nearly a foot taller. He started to dance, tried this turn, and broke his leg in two places. I saw him on the avenue after his leg healed, up in the same exact shoes."

Fitness and agility mattered the most in the sportswear-dominated eighties and nineties. Endorsement partnerships, such as the one created fifty years earlier between Olympic-gold-medalist Jesse Owens and the Adidas corporation and carried on into the eighties by fat-laced rappers RUN-DMC, are now the norm. Many Black men today choose to wear the star-validated sneakers of Michael Jordan, with Nike, or Shaquille O'Neal, with Reebok—shoes that are closer to industrial-designed sculptures than traditional active wear. In the professional world, Black businessmen display contemporary dress shoes designed by Ferragamo, Bally, Gucci, and the like. But it is America's Black teens, with best feet forward, who will continue to set the course of what's cool, drawing their inspiration from music, movies, and sports.

Ankle-hugging sixties slacks pointed to the freshly polished oxfords and loafers of an astutely styled group of Morehouse College students *(opposite)*. **Actor/model Gary Dourdan brought city and country sensibilities together on the runway, kickin' it in chocolate-suede, lug-soled work boots strung with rescue-red laces; the eighties and nineties have been marked by the use of rugged, all-purpose shoes in urban settings** *(above)*.

Gregory HINES

"THE SHOE"

When it comes to shoes, comfort is very important to me. I can *see* the comfort in a shoe. That's probably because, having been a child dancer, my feet received special attention from my parents. They didn't have a lot of money to spend on clothes for my brother and me, but when it came to shoes, they didn't skimp. Oftentimes, they would spend more on our shoes than they would on our clothes. If our suits cost twenty dollars, then our shoes were thirty. And it wasn't enough just to try on a shoe for fit. My parents used to have us wear the shoes in the store for, like, twenty minutes! "Walk around," they'd instruct us. If my mother could have had her way, we probably would have taken the shoes outside for a run around the block. My parents taught me that my feet should always be comfortable. To this day, I've never been plagued by corns or any of the other problems that come from wearing ill-fitting shoes.

In general, I prefer loafers over lace-ups, because I like to be able to just slip them on.

My tap shoes are, of course, a different matter. They have to lace up. In fact, I have my own signature shoe that Capezio makes. I like to wear them until they almost break up. I usually get about two to three years of wear out of them—that's about the amount of time it takes for them to respond—and then they're finished.

Nat "King" Cole and Billy Eckstein are two of the stylish men I admired when I was young. There was also a time when I idolized Sammy Davis, Jr. I wanted to dance, sing, and dress like him. I even wore my hair like his. I figured I'd just *be* him! And then there was my Uncle Ly: In the summer he wore camp shirts. He owned several, and they were always crisply ironed. He looked so good in them that, when I was about thirteen, I'd wear the same type of shirt. Of my contemporaries, I've always been impressed with Bobby Short's style, and I like the way Luther Vandross is able to pull off those bold pieces by Versace.

But of all the Black men whose styles I've admired, it's my father who has had the most impact on me. He never had a lot of money to buy designer clothes, but with what money he did have, he always managed to look good. He placed much more emphasis on fit than fabric, because he couldn't afford expensive suits. I've always been influenced by the care he took in his clothes.

Reborn in FREEDOM

BY GEORGE FAISON

WHEN THE FRAMERS OF THE CONSTITUTION

contemplated the forming of a new republic, their goal of freedom and democracy did not include us. Since slavery, our challenge has been to make something out of nothing. When life offered us little resolve, we resorted to making the best of a bad situation. When we emerged from the Black-and-White, civil rights days of the turbulent sixties, we came out with a new-found freedom. Freedom to be, do, and wear anything we wanted. Finally, we were able to turn in those tap shoes, leave the chorus lines, and start dancing in the streets. Art belonged to everyone, from the jazz abstractions of Miles Davis to the syncopated beats of Motown crooners; from the glittering rhinestone dreams of Sly and The Family Stone to the revolutionary wails of Gil Scott-Heron. We went from au naturel to slick and glamorous. We went from polite cheek-to-cheek dancing to stomping with reckless abandon. Sammy Davis was on Broadway, The Temptations were on Ed Sullivan, and the *Ebony* Fashion Fair toured the world, showing us how beautiful we were. Gone were the head rags and coveralls of our fathers. A new and personal freedom of creativity had emerged. When you talk about what dancers wear, from warm-ups to suits, beneath these fine threads there is a body that speaks louder than clothes.

Dancers break the bounds of the ordinary and allow us to see the ideal. Louis Johnson and Arthur Mitchell changed the face of the New York City Ballet with their classically well-groomed good looks. They showed us that we made a difference in tights. Lester Wilson, taut and dramatic with his all-showbiz style and signature gold hoop earring, took us to cabarets and nightclubs from Las Vegas to Paris wearing everything

Bill "Bojangles" Robinson, featured in a promotional advertisement by The Cotton Club, kept his feet happy in tap shoes, tuxedo, and top hat *(above)*. Buck and Bubbles outfitted their song-and-dance act with zany, zigzag suits; a trio from the turn of the century stepped lightly in straw boaters, sports jackets, creased white trousers, and walking canes; a young tap duo from the twenties put on the ritz in tailed tuxes, top hats, and kid gloves; a hint of the zoot is visible in the fuller-cut trousers of The Nicholas Brothers dance team, sharp as a tack in window-pane plaid and three-point pocket squares *(opposite, clockwise from top left)*.

from bell-bottoms to feather boas, and was known to dance in six-inch-high platforms. The men Alvin Ailey told stories about in his dances were deep, sensitive, strong, and proud. Instead of puttin' clothes on, they were taking theirs off. Ailey performed barefoot.

In hip-hugging, thigh-grabbing, double knits, we took on the world, telling our stories. We danced out our lives, felt the sorrow, pain, happiness, and joy of being Black and male and telling the world our story.

Whether we were in leotards and tights, tap shoes or bare feet, we put on clothes and danced like men as we traveled the world, buying suits in Milan, dashikis in Kinshar, tie-dyed T-shirts in San Francisco. You can tell where we've been and where we're going by what you see on our backs, 'cause we do it with style.

"Hi-De-Hi-De-Hi-De-Ho!" Cab Calloway jumped jive in his pearly white zoot suit and matching "keen-toed" shoes *(opposite)*. Back in the thirties, cool cats could swing; a jitterbug duo demonstrated the need for comfort in dance clothes *(left)*. Sammy Davis, Jr. high-stepped it in the fifties in a slim, pinstriped suit and pointed-toe boots *(above)*.

Black style: reborn in freedom and dressed up in
hand-me-downs:

> We've been bought and sold,
> Lynched and laughed at.
> Got to keep on movin',
> No time to look back.

> We gave the world bebop,
> Made dances, invented hip-hop.
> Our dreams took us to the top,
> And all night long we sang doo-wop.

> It's something special to see a Black man dance.
> What looks so easy did not happen by chance.
> It all got started way back in the day
> With men like Bill Robinson and Cab Calloway.

> From Stepin' Fetchit and his buck and wing,
> To Bojangles dancing on the silver screen.
> Cab Calloway truckin' with his "Hi-De-Ho!"
> Or the Nicholas Brothers goin' toe-to-toe.
> It's the same old thing just done up new,
> And it's all in the rhythm of that old tap shoe.

> Dance is the spirit that lives in the drum,
> The heartbeat of life where we come from.
> The earth, air, fire, and wind,
> The vamp starts and the dance begins.

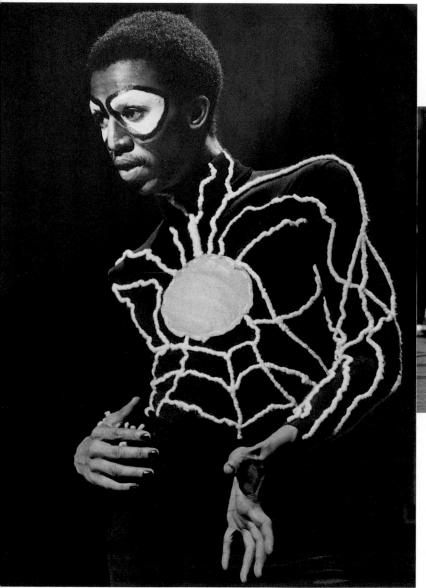

**George Faison, a principal dancer with the Alvin
Ailey American Dance Theater, won awards for his
experimental choreography for such Broadway plays
as *The Wiz* and *Porgy and Bess* (left). An eighties
break-dancer rocked and popped in primary color
sportswear: graffiti-sprayed hat, hot-red mesh tank,
T-shirt, jeans, and sneakers (above). On his feet,
a hip-hop dancer got busy in color-blocked pants,
multi-zippered jacket, and tap shoes (opposite).**

Savion GLOVER

"DANCE"

Just loose. When I'm dancing, mine is a straight, free style, a total free form. It's whatever I find comfortable. I am not into fashion at all. My look comes from my way of life. My brothers, my music—which is hip-hop—R&B, jazz. Like it's been for Black men historically, my style is my way of life. It's time that we take credit for what is ours.

When I started on Broadway, as the title character in *The Tap Dance Kid*, I wore the traditional costume, which was usually a tuxedo. I was ten years old. But I got to the point where I decided I wasn't going to wear that stuff anymore. I often leave my boots or tap shoes untied, for comfort. If it's a quick dress change and I need to be onstage, I just slip them on and go.

I'd be lost without my "skullies." Any kind of skullcap. Ski-inspired skullcaps, short-hair skullies, whatever—I spare no expense. What I love most about them is the fact that you can create your own design. There is no brim, there are no limits. You can roll them, mold them, or shape them according to your mood at that moment.

All men should have tap shoes! Besides that, a good pair of durable boots, several pairs of jeans, and an assortment of comfortable T-shirts. That's it.

I dig the hippie style of the late sixties and seventies. The culture seemed so free. But in terms of dancers I've admired, on the legendary tip it would have to be Mr. Jimmy Slyde. And nowadays I have to say Gregory Hines, of course. He's just smooth!

STAR

VETERAN SHOE-SHINE MAN

Star is a professional shiner with well over three decades of experience in his trade. A native New Yorker now based in Harlem, Star has shined the shoes of many high-profile Black men, including Bill Cosby, Arthur Davis, Walt Frazier, and Redd Foxx.

Star lives by a maxim that he passes on to all of his clients: "Buy good shoes, and keep 'em shined!" Well-kept shoes are the foundation of a great outfit. At right, the veteran craftsman defines the four essential types any man of style should have in his wardrobe, and offers a few tips to keep the kicks in high-steppin' shape.

The SHOE

In addition to the obvious importance of support and comfort, appearance is also a primary consideration when it comes to evaluating shoes. In general, a man's shoes should be discreet, solidly anchoring his suits, not competing with them for the viewer's attention. The best accessory for a shoe is not an ornate buckle or garishly colored shoelace, but a simple high shine.

LACE-UPS

A classic of traditional menswear, lace-ups (page 152, left) can make or break an ensemble. The best lace-ups are handmade, but a standard-issue lace-up can have a high-end appearance if properly maintained. Avoid heavy or trendy ornamentation that may date the shoe—the only dramatically designed lace-up worth investing in is the perforated wing tip.

Cap-toe oxfords make a great partner for the classic business suit. Pair black oxfords with dark suits (navy, gray, and black), and brown with earth-toned suits. A brown wing tip wears well with checked or tweed pants, and can also complement gray wool.

LOAFERS

Loafers (page 152, right) can be found in a variety of styles, depending on personal taste. Trendy details such as defined square toes, chunky heels, or logoed metal plates will pass. A classically shaped loafer has a more rounded toe, and is designed with as few distracting details as possible. The penny loafer is distinguished by the leather slot atop the upper, which welcomes a penny (for brown or oxblood leather) or a dime (for black leather). Whatever its guise, the loafer is a casual alternative to the stately lace-up, and should be worn with khakis, jeans, or relaxed twill pants.

FORMAL SLIP-ONS

Formal slip-ons (page 153, left) are reserved for wear with tuxedos. Signature details may include a wider opening, an ornate finishing trim, a subtle tonal bow, or a patent-leather finish. Due to the shoe's low, flat structure, befitting its lounge-wear intention, socks can provide additional support and comfort.

DRESS BOOTS

Although variety in boots is abundant, one style has always outshined the new jacks—the Chelsea, or jodhpur (page 153, right). In Star's opinion, such a dress boot is a necessity, because it provides better ankle support. This English staple is ideal: It doubles as a dress and casual shoe, working with both tapered jeans or a dark suit. Its streamlined stance is enhanced by a smoothly polished, nondescript finish.

Classic versions of the Chelsea have a slightly pointed toe and black elastic side tabs for slipping on with ease. The boots are traditionally designed without zippers.

CARE AND MAINTENANCE

Storage: Shoes should be stored as a pair on a flat surface in a cool, dry environment. Be sure to keep cedar shoe trees inside shoes whenever they are not being worn. Star agrees: "A cedar shoe tree absorbs the moisture that accumulates in leather with regular wear. Cedar shoe trees also keep the shape of the shoes over time, and help to lessen wrinkles and lines caused by walking and squatting." An ounce of prevention is worth a pound of cure: When buying new shoes, also budget for the cost of a corresponding pair of quality cedar shoe trees.

Cleaning: When cleaning shoes at home, Star recommends the following five easy steps:

1. Using a soft, natural-bristle shoe brush, gently remove all surface dirt.
2. Apply a good, solid coat of canned shoe polish in the appropriate color, and follow up with a thorough brushing.
3. Apply a second coat of polish, and completely brush it in.
4. With a soft, slightly damp cloth, rub the shoe very gently until a shine appears.
5. For a high shine, spray a small amount of water on the shoe surface and follow with an intense buffing using the same cloth until the desired glow results. Note: This final step can transform a nondescript black slip-on into a formal flat, with the comfort already built in.

Reinforcement: Any shoes sold with a soft leather bottom require an additional layer of resistance against concrete and other hard surfaces. As with the cedar shoe trees, the cost of such rubber grips should be calculated into the price of a pair of shoes upon purchase, and the protective soles should be attached immediately thereafter, prior to first wear. Star agrees, "Rubber grips will save your soles, because, without them, the shoe will wear down, lose its form, and ultimately fall apart. Have a professional shoe repairer adhere a thin layer of rubber to the original sole. When it wears out, the shoe's bottom will still be intact, and you can just apply another protective grip."

Inclement weather: A myth dispelled: "Rubber shoe covers don't work," states Star. Many men opt to cover their dress shoes with soft rubber "overshoes" to protect against rain and snow. But Star swears that "a good shine should almost always do the trick. Rubber, by storing moisture in and around the leather, defeats its own purpose. All that excess moisture will rub the life out of the skin and eventually destroy the shoe."

Just above MY HEAD

the hat

hip-hop

"Your crown has been bought and paid for. All you must do is put it on your head."

JAMES BALDWIN

THE hat

THE WORLD'S GREATEST LEADERS

have traditionally used distinctive head dressings as a way to distinguish themselves. From Shaka Zulu's feathered headpiece to Marcus Garvey's plumed military tricorne, iconic images of historical figures frequently include a hat.

There was a time when it was considered indecent and insulting for a man to appear hatless in public. For working-class Black men at the turn of the century, a hat was often part of the uniform: Pullman porters wore red caps, elevator attendants were topped with the bellhop's standard pillbox, chauffeurs maintained their air of discretion with a subtle visored lid. Out in the fields, sharecroppers and migrant workers made do with a simple straw hat. At around the same time, the traditional top hat, also referred to as the "Jim Crow" due to its use by wandering minstrel shows,

Black men make a hat their home by "breakin' it down," shaping the brim and crown according to personal preference *(previous spread, left)*. Hip-hop style often includes hats—in this case, furry Kangol-style berets *(previous spread, right)*. Due to its warmth and comfort, the newsboy has retained its popularity for decades *(top)*. At the turn of the century, a stiff felt derby made the perfect topper *(above)*. In 1938, boxer Henry Armstrong considered his hat options in a Harlem haberdashery *(right)*. A chip off the old block: Paul Robeson sports a homburg, his son wears an "applejack" *(opposite, top)*. Top hats distinguished officers from non-ranking members in a group photo of Elks men from the twenties *(opposite, center)*. In the fifties, Coretta Scott King sent Martin on his way wearing a standard-model fedora *(opposite, bottom)*.

began to diminish in popularity. Although the silken cylinders were favored by entertainers such as blues founder W. C. Handy, they fell out of fashion as styles evolved. Replaced by the sportier English bowler, top hats were reserved for formal events.

The homburg, made of brushed felt, with a stiff, curled brim and a high crown creased lengthwise, was the hat of choice in the twenties. Narrower in build than a bowler, and notable for its pronounced center crease, it meant business. Of the same era, the trilby was similar to the homburg in shape, but was constructed from softer felt, and with a lower crown. And although the fedora debuted in the late 1800s, it didn't fully take on its "gangster" connotations until the Jazz Age.

Black jazz artists in the forties were fastidious about their smooth brims. Although many a bebopper donned a hat or two throughout his career, it was pianist Thelonious Monk who claimed the chapeau as the symbol of his style. From the funky Moroccan fez to the classic French beret, Monk collected hats like souvenirs. Stingy-brimmed porkpie hats, brushed-felt fedoras, a black silk skullcap picked up while performing in Hong Kong—he owned them all. Legend has it that, on his downtime, Monk played basketball wearing a pointed straw Asian fieldworker's hat pejoratively referred to as a "rice patty."

The celebrity cool cats of the fifties were unquestionably well-capped: Sammy Davis, Jr. hit the Vegas stage in a creased Borsalino; Dizzy Gillespie's chic tam-o'-shanter inspired a nation of White beatniks. But it was the Black man on the street who took pride in personally styling his own individual creations. "No one can 'break down' a hat like a Black man," declared legendary New York fashion-show producer Audrey Smaltz when asked about the mystique behind Black male style. Growing up in the forties, she recalls the daily hat ritual her father, Mr. Raymond Bailey Smaltz, Sr. would partake in prior to departing from their Harlem hearth:

"In the forties, men never left their home without a hat on their head. My father was a fastidious

dresser who hand-rolled his own handkerchiefs from raw yards of linen, pressed his own shirts, organized his dresser drawers to be completely accessible in the pitch dark, built his own shoe-shine box in order to shine the entire family's shoes, and even polished his belt buckles. I clearly remember watching him leave for work each morning, wearing either a pale gray fedora with a thick grosgrain hatband or a taupe 'stingy brim.' First he would remove the hat, which he stored by the front door, upside down in its box from Knox Hats, the sharpest hat shop in New York. After carefully placing it on his head, he would play with the brim, pinch it sharply down the center of the crown with his thumb and center finger, and cock it firmly to his right side. Then out the door he went."

"Breakin' down" or "breakin' in" a hat is what makes it a home for a Black man's head. The process begins with the purchase: A hat that doesn't respond to shaping in the store is often left on the shelf. The broken down, or "broke-down," hat is artfully bent and shaped by its owner to exaggerate the standard curve of its brim. Breakin' down can also involve denting the cap's crown according to personal taste. The makeover, coupled with a comfortably secure fit and contrived positioning on the head, completed what in the superfly seventies was called "my sky."

At ease: In the sixties, structured, short-brimmed straw hats detailed with madras bands were warm-weather favorites of many stylish gents *(left)*. A funky dude and his foxy lady showed off seventies hustler chic: His wide-brimmed fedora was reminiscent of styles featured in such Blaxploitation films as *Superfly (above)*. In the early days of hip-hop, rappers such as LL Cool J helped popularize hats for a new generation of fashion-conscious MCs and Mack-Daddies *(opposite, top)*. He's gotta have hat: Spike Lee singlehandedly made the baseball cap the American equivalent of the French beret for modern-day film directors *(opposite, bottom)*.

When the anti-fashion sixties and seventies demanded a Black-Power-based, progressive, youthful identity, some brothers still held on to the family tradition of a hat a day, but personalized the look, with preppy coconut straw "stingy brims" trimmed with striped or madras ribbons, or soft, moldable newsboy caps in solids or checks. The industry standard of a two-and-three-quarter-inch brim was in for a rude awakening as soul brothers embraced big-daddy proportions. The look was popularized by films starring the irreverent comedian Rudy Ray Moore and by such Blaxploitation flicks as *The Mack* (1973) and *Superfly* (1972)—a character that lives on in the memories of many Black men as the archetype of seventies hustler chic. In an over-the-top attempt to attain status and wealth through ostentatious attire, "Superfly" outfitted himsef in outrageously wide-brimmed felt hats hued in peacock colors, wrapped with thick patterned bands, and plumed with foot-long exotic feathers.

The eighties and nineties have witnessed a whole new generation of mad hatters. A nation of sports fanatics has bowed to the sportswear revolution, looking to its leaders for directions in style. Film auteur Spike Lee, actor Denzel Washington, media-mogul Russell Simmons, and golf maverick Tiger Woods are rarely seen without their baseball caps. Hip-hop style-setters RUN-DMC and LL Cool J brought back the porkpie, breaking it down in the crown to create a halolike effect. Nouveau soulsters such as Terence Trent D'Arby reclaimed the newsboy, while urban Rastafarians stuffed their natty dreadlocks into expansive knit "tams." More recently, the logoed stretch-nylon skullcap—a refined version of old-school stocking caps once used to make waves—has made its mark on the street. The Black man has long understood the visual impact of the hat and its function as an attitude-extending accessory. As he moves into the next millennium, he'll continue to command attention as the undisputed crowned champion of style.

LL COOL J &
Russell SIMMONS

"THE HAT"

LL COOL J: Ain't nothing like a nice, comfortable baseball cap. You can dress it up or down. I own a tremendous amount of hats, a couple of thousand, in fact. I'm known for sporting hats. Earlier in my career, I had a complex about my head, I just thought it looked twisted, so I started wearing Kangols and it became a fashion statement. I'm over the head thing now, but I still like wearing hats because I like the way they frame my face.

RUSSELL SIMMONS: I like to wear hats that are somewhere between baseball and polo caps. Just the other day I had on this khaki hunting cap, a little bit loose, kind of rugged, kind of outdoors. Every hat that my company, Phat Farm, makes is based on my taste. If I wouldn't wear it, I don't sell it. My style is understated and simple, yet full of character. My hats reveal this character.

LL COOL J: Hip-hop and street culture dressed me. Whether I was riding around with the guys who were gettin' money uptown, or checkin' out what some of the better-dressed cats in high school were wearing, I took it all in. My earrings and the other jewelry I wear bring a little more flavor to it. Those big, gold dookey chains I used to wear back in the day are a case in point.

RUSSELL SIMMONS: LL changed the way people all over the world viewed urban American culture. He put the rope chains on. Throughout my own career, I've been a big advocate of keeping it real. Even back in my earliest days at Def Jam, I wore exactly what I wear today. Baggy jeans, argyle sweaters, oxford shirts, shell-toe sneakers. Hip-hop style conveys honesty and a "get-the-job-done" attitude. It's a street thing. Nowadays, the urban *is* the traditional American, and that style has evolved from the brothers, who are constantly reaffirming and recreating it.

LL COOL J: No matter what's going on in our community, African Americans in general find a way to look decent. Even when we have no money, we still manage to get the kinds of clothes we want. I don't know if that's always a good thing, I don't know what it says about our priorities. But it's interesting how important it is to Black men to look right. It says a lot about the image we want to project.

And it DON'T STOP

BY JULIA CHANCE

I'D LIKE TO GIVE A BIG SHOUT OUT

to all the brothers of the hip-hop nation: the deejays, MCs, b-boys, and graffiti artists; the dancers and new jacks; the gangstas, playas, and stone-cold hustlers; all of the posses and the crews; alumni of the old school, students of the new school, and enrollees of schools still in session. They said hip-hop was just a trend that would never last—"Them boys don't even play instruments!" But you showed 'em, kid. Not only has the culture prevailed for nearly three decades, becoming an ever-prospering part of the music industry, but hip-hop, probably more than any other musical movement, has sparked some of the most exciting style trends around. From baseball caps and sneakers-of-the-moment to relaxed-cut jeans, work boots, and team sports jerseys, one would be hard-pressed not to find your influence in the wardrobes of today's man.

Sky-high fades made rap duo Kid-n-Play hard to miss: In keeping with their onstage personas, the comical Kid gave new meaning to the phrase "shock of hair," while straight-man Play maintained a more level look *(above)*. **Regardless of his ability to flip like an acrobat in glittery genie pants, MC Hammer's credibility in the rap community was always questionable** *(right)*. **Artful fades in the eighties incorporated everything from ethnic prints to corporate logos** *(opposite)*.

From the Black mecca of Harlem's 125th Street to the studios of Seventh Avenue designers, from dressed-down Hollywood power powwows to the courts of the NBA, and all around the globe, you have left an undeniable, indelible mark on the way men dress.

Your style began as humbly as the culture itself, at the end of the Carter-era seventies. Back then, you were just a Bronx kid searchin' for the perfect beat. You took to the streets armed with self-styled sound systems—dual turntables and gigantic speakers—powerful enough to rock the nation. Your outdoor jams spawned not just a new noise, but an entire movement with an aesthetic all its own. Donned in the styles of the day, a jazzy mix of casual and athletic sportswear indigenous to you and your Black and Latino home-

Leaders of the New School fronted in urban gear: basketball sneakers, work boots, track suits, duffel jackets, and an assortment of hats (top, left). Born to some degree from funk, rap initially oufitted itself in flashy red leather and Jheri curls, but, even at the beginning, Kangol hats and chunky gold chains were in the house (bottom, left). Rap's Holy Trinity, RUN-DMC, kept it real in Kangols and fedoras, denim and leather, dookey chains and shell-toe Adidas (above).

boys, you body-rocked in brands like Le Tigre, Playboy, Sergio Valente, Lee (the more colors the better), Chams de Baron, and Members Only. You wore your quarter-fields, polyester mock necks, double knits, and tube socks, then topped it all off with flippets or Kangols, borrowed from older heads. You adorned yourselves with stupid-fat rope chains, name rings that spanned the hand like brass knuckles, and brass-name belt buckles. You performed your fanciest footwork in a fresh pair of kicks—shell-toe leather Adidas, suede Puma and Converse, British Knights, and "referees" heading the list. Even an element as essential as sneakers received mad flava when you either threaded them with fat laces, left untied, or, in the case of some style rebels, when there were no laces at all.

As your music spread, to club gigs and record contracts, the media raced to cover your sound, giving many of us our first glimpse of who you were. What we saw in terms of style was an amalgamation of looks, from everyday casual to showbiz glitz. The party-hardy Sugar Hill Gang, the threesome who first put rap on the national map with their 1979 hit "Rapper's Delight," took on the look of average joes, while Kurtis Blow

Public Enemy frontman Flavor Flav kept time with an oversized alarm clock that served to remind the country of the late state of race relations; Flav's clock, capped gold teeth, and white wayfarers became emblematic of eighties rap style *(top)*. Hip-hop hosts of "Yo! MTV Raps" Ed Lover and Dr. Dre, flanking Tone-Lōc, mug for the camera in two-toned fades, leather medallions, and paisley prints *(above)*. In top-stitched denim overalls and biker's cap, designer Patrick Kelly brought the street to the catwalk *(left)*.

gave us "The Breaks" in funky-fresh sweatsuits worn with shiny gold chains—all the better to accent his perfectly coiffed Jheri-curl Afro, neatly trimmed mustache, and sideburns. "The Message" from Grand Master Flash and The Furious Five was one of pure flamboyance, reminiscent of seventies funk bands. They hit the stage sporting skintight leather ensembles over bare chests and soft swashbuckler boots in matching colors. They accessorized with feathers and fur pelts, studded belts, wristbands, and fingerless gloves. They wore their hair Jheri-curled, relaxed, or braided. And taking all that to another dimension still was deejay Afrika "Planet Rock" Bambaataa. As leader of the hip-hop crew Zulu Nation, Bambaataa's mystical, Afrocentric style, mixed with some space-age nuances, was no doubt gleaned from P-Funk-meister George Clinton himself, if not from jazz's own outer-space traveler, the eccentric Sun Ra.

Then RUN-DMC exploded straight outta Hollis, Queens, in 1983, heralding a new era in hip-hop, taking it from the streets of New York to the world stage. With their loud, raw sound and defiant posturing, MCs RUN and DMC and their deejay Jam Master Jay became the international icons of b-boy style. They were keeping it real long before it became a phrase. Sure, they wore the leather, sweats, sneakers, and jeans of the day, but it was the no-nonsense way in which they put it all together that gave them their edge: Color was kept to a minimum, black was the shade of choice, jeans were straight, never too tight, shirts stayed on and were mostly pullovers. RUN-DMC's devotion to their beloved Adidas, about which they waxed poetic, resulted in the trio becoming the first hip-hop act to sign an endorsement contract with a sneaker company. But what *really* made their look fly was their knack for mixing unlikely elements, such as nylon Adidas warmups worn under black leather jackets, paired with matching leather pants, unlaced Adidas, and staunch fedoras. Sneakers with fedoras? 'Nuff said.

By the mid-eighties your hip-hop party was in

Naughty By Nature's Treach represented the sportier side of hip-hop style in a colorful New York Knicks team jersey: The padlocked chain was worn in solidarity with "the brothers on lock-down"; dubbing himself "The Overweight Lover," Heavy D never compromised style for girth; West Coast rapper Coolio, modeling for Tommy Hilfiger, demonstrated the symbiotic rapport between fashion and music (*opposite, clockwise from top left*). As quintessential b-boy "Mookie" in *Do The Right Thing*, Spike Lee dressed his character in a straight-outta-Brooklyn Dodgers jersey, razor-lined fade, and motherland medallion (*above*).

full swing, and the line waiting to get in swelled with brothers dressed to impress. The teenage LL Cool J, on the heels of RUN-DMC, boastfully rocked the bells sporting sweatsuits, Kangol caps, a dookey chain, and a signature gold ring that spelled out his name from index to pinkie finger. The Fat Boys offered comic relief in colorful duds accented with crazy-thick Cazell glasses. Heavy D showed you how to be a fly overweight lover in drapey suits. Big Daddy Kane gave us a taste of sensuality in dapper suits accessorized with walking sticks. And who could forget the gilded jewelry statements of Slick Rick, whose only rival in the race for the most gold was Mr. T.

Meanwhile, his royal airness Michael Jordan slam-dunked us with his eponymous Nike joints, leading many of you to trade in your Adidas and Pumas for a pair. Operation swoosh was in full effect. But bedazzlement was still your credo, and the true style mavericks stayed one step ahead, blowing up the spot in

Tupac Shakur promoted "Thug Life," his high-low take on the gangsta aesthetic, in denim, leather, diamond nose ring, and bandanna tied rabbit-ear style *(opposite)*. As an outgrowth of the nouveau Afrocentrism of the nineties, cornrows brought an ethnic flava to the traditionally urban hip-hop sensibility *(left)*. In the final days of his career, Big Poppa himself, The Notorious B.I.G., traded in ghetto-wear for upscale, old-school gangster gear: shirt, tie, three-piece suit, camel-hair coat, and walking cane *(above)*.

gear emblazoned with the initials of luxe fashion houses such as Gucci, Louis Vuitton, and MCM. Passing on the authentic offerings along Fifth Avenue, you dropped your dough at custom shops like Dapper Dan on 125th Street. There you could have designer cachet, your way, for less. These were the indulgent Reaganomic eighties, after all, and appearance mattered, whether or not you had loot for the real deal.

You've always partied till the break of dawn, but it never made you immune to the bleakness of the times. When the nightly news reported that Black employment was woefully low, Black-on-Black crime was at an all-time high, crack cocaine was the drug of choice, or cops were wielding their sticks in your direction far too frequently, you responded in rhyme and in style, making sure you were heard and seen. Some of you prepared for the worst, cloaking yourselves in authentic army-navy surplus gear once reserved for outdoorsmen and construction workers. Public Enemy said it would take a nation of millions to fight the power, so rugged clothes for rugged times just made sense. Others saw this period as proof positive that the struggle continues, and went neo-Nubian in Afrocentric garb that helped to keep pride intact. Following robed members of the X Clan, who instructed you to look "to the east, my brother, to the east," you replaced your gold chains with leather medallions and African beads, chose kente and mudcloth as your coverings of choice, sported baseball caps embroidered with the letter "X" in homage to Brother Malcolm, and slipped on T-shirts that proclaimed pro-Black politics across the chest. "It's a Black thing, you wouldn't understand" became your rallying cry. Out on the left coast, groups such as NWA made gang-related antics real: You dressed in Cholo-style flannel shirts buttoned all the way up, loose-fitting chinos, and bandannas that, depending on their color, could mean life or death.

These were bleak times indeed, but many of you kept your heads up through it all and never let the more sinister looks bumrush your wardrobes. You found delight in a new breed of rappers, such as De La Soul, A Tribe Called Quest, and The Jungle Brothers, whose boho style spoke—but didn't shout—to your sense of Black nationalism and to your artsy intellect. Serving up raps on the ultra-light side were Kid-n-Play or Kwame, prince of polka dots, who let the good times roll in fluid, colorful ensembles made for fun times and dancing.

In recent years you've relaxed considerably, in oversized styles that get blamed for everything from the romanticization of prison life to the demoralization of society, but you take it in stride because your true goal is to gain a little bit of comfort in an uncomfortable world. One purveyor in particular, White rapper Marky Mark, made a mint off your slouchy-jeans look by offering the masses a watered-down version in ads meant to sell his skivvies. Starting with Calvin, big-name designers flocked like vultures to prey on your style. For a while we saw almost as many baseball caps, jerseys, baggy jeans, and heavy jewelry parading down runways as we did on the street. But whatever, man. You never needed the sartorial affirmation before, and you hardly needed it now. In fact, you've always flipped the script on popular brands, mixing Versace, Gucci, and Armani with Kani, FUBU, and The Gap, wearing Polo nowhere near equestrian grounds, and sporting mad logos as if your life depended on it.

And through it all you've known that hip-hop style is about much more than what you wear. It's about how you wear it. It's the gangsta haberdashery of Too $hort, the Hilfiger top gear Grand Puba boasts about. It's LL Cool J spewing out rhymes with one pant leg rolled up, Tupac proudly displaying his "Thug Life" chest tattoo, Naughty By Nature's Treach wearing industrial-strength chains in homage to the brothers on lock-down, and Jay-Z rhyming in a slickly coordinated ensemble. Hip-hop style reflects the common spirit of a group of young brothers striving to get theirs despite the grim odds. And it don't stop, because like rap music itself, hip-hop style is forever evolving.

Menswear designer Shaka King updated the "hoodie" duffel coat in whip-stitched melton wool *(top, left)*. The influence of both seventies hustlers and eighties rappers is evident in Nautica's single-breasted plaid suit, complete with matching "fisherman's" hat *(bottom, left)*. Donna Karan is just one of the American designers to tap into street style: This example from her DKNY men's collection draws heavily from bike messenger duds *(above)*.

Sean "Puffy" COMBS

"HIP-HOP"

I'm a part of what I like to refer to as the "hip-hop nation" or "generation." Hip-hop style comes out of New York. The best way to describe it is Black Generation-X going against the grain of what's acceptable on the fashion scene and creating a visual definition of what we're feeling. It can clearly be seen in the styles of artists like the late Notorious B.I.G., Busta Rhymes, and Heavy D. It's a youth-take on the diversity of Black culture. My style is a true reflection of that, as well as of the wide range of experiences I had growing up during the seventies and eighties in the suburbs of Mount Vernon, New York, the streets of Harlem, USA, and on the campus of the historically Black Howard University in Washington D.C.

The eighties had to be the most stylish era for Black men. The decade was so dynamic, kind of crazy. It seemed as though styles were changing every day. It's when hip-hop style took off, when we wore the big gold chains, the shell-toe leather or suede Adidas with the fat laces, Lee twill pants in all colors, mock-neck shirts, and our British Knights.

Today, like back then, brothers can wear just about anything and pull it off. I'm no exception. I can go from Calvin Klein to newer, Black-owned brands like FUBU. I don't look to designer labels primarily for status—it's the quality that draws me to Gucci, Versace, Armani, Karl Kani. It's all about the fabric, texture, and production values. And although I love European designer clothes, it's unfortunate that many of their garments don't seem to be cut for us. They don't seem to take our proportions into consideration. It's unfortunate because we spend a lot of money on luxury items.

You'll never catch me in tight clothing, but you'll almost always catch me wearing my dark shades, especially those by Mossimo. I used to watch celebrities parade up and down that status strip called Fifth Avenue, and they'd have dark sunglasses on at all times. I picked up on that, and I must admit I enjoy being able to look at people without them knowing it.

Black male style is incredible. We style ourselves in every direction, and it works! I love the way Seal and Maxwell put it down, and then there are artists like NAS who do the same flavor with a hip-hop flair. Black men haven't always had the means to purchase clothing made of fine fabrics. Since our arrival here from Africa, we've had to face the challenge of working with what we had. So maybe we couldn't buy that brand-new suit. Our mothers would make a similar style. Chances are it was a bit too baggy, or lopsided, or too long, or had "high-water" pants. But we rocked it with pride and dignity. At the end of the day, it wasn't about the suit itself, it was about the flavor and the man who gave it life. This trendsetting attitude is at the core of hip-hop style today, and it's why Black male style is worthy of celebration.

Rod SPRINGER

J. J. HAT CENTER

"Hats are like the icing on the cake of a well-put-together ensemble," states Rod Springer, and he should know. Springer has a long and extensive background in men's apparel, having worked at leading haberdasheries such as F. R. Tippler, Inc., Paul Stuart, and Brooks Brothers. Springer is currently head salesman at New York City's J. J. Hat Center on Fifth Avenue, where he has assisted fly-skied brothers such as Bill Cosby, Smokey Robinson, and Aaron Neville.

Hat styles vary, and in recent years there has been an influx of fashions that are more casual and sports-influenced, but the classics endure. Springer rests his own hat for a moment to classify the preferred "lids" of the man of color.

The HAT

THE FEDORA

Remembered by many as the signature hat of gangsters, the fedora (page 176, top) became one of the Black man's hats of choice in the forties. It is traditionally made from fur felt, with a two-to-three-inch brim and a grosgrain band. According to Springer, "A hat's crown is where we leave our own unique fingerprint, by blocking (or pinching) it in a way no one else can." A fedora's pointed crown welcomes personal adjustment. Although its popularity made it the "everyman's" hat, distinguished style-celebs such as Paul Robeson and Satchel Paige were known for wearing pinched fedoras. Springer recalls, "The eighties was another decade that celebrated the fedora, mainly in corporate circles such as on Wall Street, where the pinstriped power suit made a comeback."

THE DERBY AND THE HOMBURG

The derby (or bowler, page 177, top) was originally the working-class hat of the late 1800s, but by the early twentieth century it had taken on elitist tones, at which point it was replaced with the homburg (page 176, bottom) by the average Black man. It remained the hat of the moment through the early twenties. With its trademark pencil-curled brim, wide hatband, and creased crown, the homburg was a casual favorite that took on some flair when accessorized with a colored feather. Springer adds, "Well-dressed Black men in the nineties are once again embracing this tradition, but in a range of colors, not just black and gray." Rap stars such as Heavy D have led the way.

THE BASEBALL CAP

A more recent phenomenon, propelled by style luminaries such as director and acknowledged sports fanatic Spike Lee and rap mega-star LL Cool J, is the

fitted baseball cap. The style has transcended its intended use as protective headgear and now makes a casual statement of control and comfort when paired with sweats or even a tux. In the late eighties and nineties, designers across the board began to cash in on the Black man's penchant for the baseball cap, labeling it with everything from authentic team logos to corporate icons, political messages, and status symbols. Worn backwards, forwards, or somewhere in between, the ball cap is indisputably the everyman's hat of choice at the end of the millennium.

THE PORKPIE

Springer recalls the fifties as being "the style apex for the classic porkpie, as a direct result of Black jazz legends such as the always-hatted Lester Young. The fact that the hot jazz artists of the day chose this style, yet never broke the brim, set a trend among fans both Black and White." Because of the porkpie's compact, telescopic shape and its two-inch brim, it offers a concise fit, ready off-the-rack.

THE BORSALINO

A forerunner to the gangster favorite, the fedora (left), the felt Borsalino hit the scene just after the First World War. With a wider, side-bowed hatband, a larger, three-inch brim, and a creased crown, the Borsalino was also the beginning point for the floppy, parodic version worn with the zoot suit. The style enjoyed a strong resurgence in the fifties, when it was worn by such prominent Black men as the always-impeccable Adam Clayton Powell, Jr.

THE NEWSBOY OR APPLEJACK

The "cappy" (page 177, bottom), as Springer endearingly remembers it, "was the biggest thing since sliced bread back in the twenties. We wore this hat out of necessity; it kept us warm when working outdoors—which many of us did in those days. And because of its heavyweight wool, we could place many pins in the hats, to show our club affiliations." An overstated version of the newsboy, made of polyester and available in a wide range of colors and plaids, resurfaced in the seventies. On television and in film, these hats became a style stamp of actor Bill Cosby.

THE BERET

From Dizzy Gillespie to James Baldwin, men of color in artistic and literary circles have long favored this collapsible felt cap. "A beret is timeless," asserts Springer. "My customers will buy several at once, in a range of colors." The classic felt beret travels well, and is like clay for the molding, allowing Black men to add their own individual touch to this popular style.

THE MATERIAL

A hat's material determines how well it will stand up to the elements. Better hats are made from animal hair, either beaver or rabbit. Springer explains, "The natural oils in rabbit and beaver fur make hats made from these materials more water-repellent. The fur also holds dyes better than other fabrics, so the color is richer." Second in terms of quality are hats made of plush wool velour, a material which Springer notes is a favorite among Black men: "The velour is not quite as thick as long-haired beaver fur, but you can still see its texture, and when velour is dyed, the result is a deeper dimension of color. A black hat is going to be a very deep shade of black." Finally, there are wool-felt varieties, which may be combined with a percentage of fur for repellency.

THE FIT

Regardless of what a hat is made of, if it doesn't fit, the style statement is lost. "A proper-fitting hat allows you to slide a finger between the top of the ear and the brim," says Springer. And then there's proportion: The brim and crown should strike a balance with your face. For example, if your face is small or narrow, the crown should not be too big nor the brim too wide, or the hat will look overwhelming. By contrast, Springer continues, "A man with a full face needs a wider brim and taller crown, to keep the hat from looking too small."

Hats are measured in increments of one-eighth an inch, with sizes ranging from six-and-three-quarter inches to eight inches in circumference. To determine hat size, wrap a soft tape measure around the head, looping it at the fullest part of the back of the head and bringing the ends together at the center of the forehead, approximately one inch above the eyebrows. Professional sizing can also be done on the premise of specialty hat boutiques, where the staff is knowledgeable and custom designs are available—all advantages over the average department store.

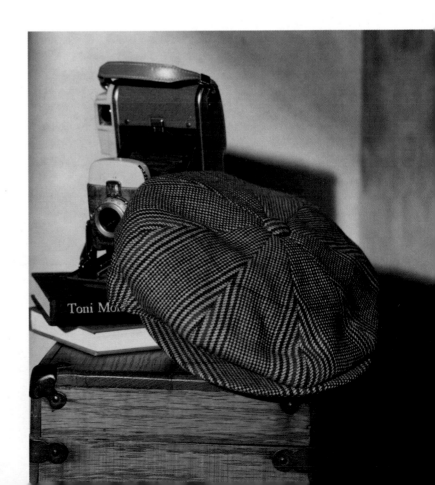

hair

rock'n'roll

"If you love 'em in the morning with their eyes full of crust,
if you love 'em at night with their hair full of rollers, chances
are, you're in love."

MILES DAVIS

hair

MOST AFRICAN-AMERICAN MEN BEGIN

their hair affair in that *other* pillar of the Black community, the neighborhood barbershop. A childhood rite of passage, when a boy is about three or four, his mother decides "it's time." At the barbershop, he's placed in the grown-up's chair, stacked with telephone books or maybe a homemade, C-shaped, wooden-horse booster seat or, more recently, a plastic model, custom-molded to fit the chair and the tiny behind inhabiting it. Maybe he cries like there's no tomorrow as the barber, unfazed, gently tries to coax him into good behavior, telling him "It ain't gonna hurt" as he scales his scalp with buzzing clippers. Or maybe he's a "big boy," letting the barber palm his head and edge him up in the back,

In the early part of the twentieth century, Black men styled temporary curls using combs and pomades *(previous spread, left)*. Fats Domino effected an owl-cut congalene along with his engraved, six-point star-shaped diamond wrist-watch and matching pinkie ring *(previous spread, right)*. A gentleman at the turn of the century counterbalanced his closely cropped hair with a full mustache and beard *(top)*. Natural waves could be further emphasized by setting the entire head with cloth rags *(above)*. A short length and pronounced part conformed to the norm *(right)*. In 1915, a dapper quartet took the short cut to looking neat and clean *(opposite)*.

as if he were an old pro, all the while anticipating his reward, the lollipop. From that fateful day forward, what we as Black men do to our hair has as much to do with the age or place we live in, our politics, education, social standing, and self-perceived sex appeal as it does with our actual need for a trim. Like our skin, our hair is an instant indicator of our race, and like our clothes, it is often used to send a message.

Natural hair, untreated by texture-altering chemicals, was the norm for most Black men in America up until the early twenties. Former slaves and their sons styled their hair with the help of tonics and pomades incapable of permanently altering the state of their tresses. Varied lengths, pronounced parts, and "grease-and-water" or "cold-soap" waves were achieved with common combs and brushes and old cloth rags— tied over the entire head to produce pressurized wave

patterns, temporary modifications of the natural curl. But in popular depictions for decades to follow, such conservative hairstyles took a secure backseat to stereotypical images of the hair-raised "pickaninny," a figure that was unapologetically promoted on product labels and in print advertising and motion pictures.

With the success of the straightening comb, invented in 1905 by Madame C. J. Walker for Black women intent on hot-pressing their hair into a flaxen texture, came the inevitable crossover of such style options for men. It wasn't until the twenties that a home-mixed concoction called "congalene" provided Black men with their own method of achieving bone-straight hair. The intense scratch-recipe solution was made from over-the-counter lye, fresh potatoes, and raw eggs. By far the most famous account of the process is recorded in the revealing autobiography of

Malcolm X. The young Malcolm Little recalls the moment when he was first "conked."

"The congolene just felt warm when Shorty started combing it in. But then my head caught fire. I gritted my teeth and tried to pull the sides of the kitchen table together. The comb felt as if it were raking my skin off. . . . He lathered and spray rinsed, lathered and spray rinsed, maybe ten or twelve times. . . . When Shorty let me stand up and see in the mirror . . . on top of my head was this thick, smooth sheen of smiling red hair . . . as straight as any White man's. . . . I vowed that I'd never again be without a conk. . . ."[2]

This vow was a subconscious one taken by legions of well-groomed Black men who shared the same belief that straight hair was more manageable, offered more styling possibilities, and was simply more attractive than their natural texture. The initial craze for straightened hair became the sanctioned norm through the sixties, validated by such stylish cats and celebrated performers as legendary "conk-heads" Cab Calloway, who maintained a poker-straight, slick-vinyl-like 'do, Nat "King" Cole, whose sculpted coif closely resembled those of crooners Frank Sinatra and Dean Martin, and Little Richard, whose hot-curled ringlets shook, rattled, and rolled into a wiry frenzy by the end of each piano-banging performance.

Kinky hair was "conked" with a caustic mixture of lye, potatoes, and eggs *(opposite)*. **Little Richard's waved bouffant, glamour brows, lined eyes, and stenciled mustache blurred gender lines in the fifties** *(left)*. **In the forties, even a vigorous jitterbug couldn't shake Cab Calloway's slicked-back coif out of place** *(above)*.

In 1965, a Black Power activist spread the word in a tapered 'fro and trim goatee (above). During the soulful seventies, angelic teenage heartthrobs The Jackson 5—Jackie, Marlon, Michael, Tito, and Jermaine—wore their 'fros like halos; the funky bubble blow-outs were a far cry from the Jheri-curl 'do Michael would adopt in the eighties (opposite).

As the pride-reclaiming Black Power movement came to the fore in the mid-sixties, the popularity of the once near-obligatory conk began fading fast. A revolution in Black hair was the natural result of a movement that stood for self-awareness. Leaders of such activist groups as the California-based Black Panther party embraced a return to untreated hair, viewing it as a proud symbol of their ethnicity. Starting with students, then spreading to community leaders, popular entertainers, and ultimately the brother-next-door, the Afro swept Black America like a burning bush. In recalling his "'fro" days, Reverend Jesse Jackson admits, "When we started wearing dashikis and our Afros, we made a huge political statement. I feel that the way I wore my hair was an expression of the rebellion of the time. It was our statement which was not easy to imitate. The tragedy was that most of the Afro picks were made by White manufacturers."

Reverend Jackson's attitude was not uncommon. The seventies saw the conscious mission of power-reclamation sustained by show-business luminaries. The Afro and braided hairstyles got bigger by the act. Formerly conked James Brown performed his smoothest turnaround when he went natural, topping it off with his "Say It Loud, I'm Black and I'm Proud" hit anthem. Singer Stevie Wonder sported shoulder-length cornrows embellished with ornate beads, shells, and accessories. "Blown-out" hair was worn by world-famous Black acts such as The Jackson 5, Sly and The Family Stone, The Commodores, and Earth, Wind & Fire. Afro wigs in natural and candy colors could be seen as far afield as Japan, and the "Jafro," the nickname for the Jewish version of the Afro, showed up on the heads of Barbra Streisand and *Welcome Back, Kotter*'s Gabe Kaplan.

At the end of the seventies, aided by both the mainstream commodification of the haloed hairstyle and the fall from grace of many of the Black Power leaders behind its initial political potency, the Afro became a parody of itself. Grooming products were packaged with the express purpose of making hair stand at its tallest by straightening it—a sad contradiction of the Afro's original intention.

Inspired as always by trusted celebrities, Black men embarked on a long and winding road of post-Afro hair experimentation. One detour some may wish to forget is that of the "Jheri-curl" trend, which once again promoted processed, or "relaxed," hair, this time cloaked in an eternally moist facade. The supposedly low-maintenance, high-style treatment was de rigueur for any man who wished to have natural-looking curly hair from root to tip. The "curl," as it was commonly known, was personified in the mid-eighties by pop megastar Michael Jackson, only to burn out—as did his own hair on the tragi-comic set of his 1984 Pepsi Cola television commercial. The unfortunate event, and spoofs of the look in such films as Eddie Murphy's *Coming to America* (1988), left Black men to wonder what wet impression the curl was leaving behind.

Regardless of the general ambivalence of the Black community towards processed hair, many stylish men of color have stayed loyal to the look. By lengthening and straightening the curls into wiry tresses, such stars as Little Richard have made the style their trademark. Singer/songwriter Nick Ashford of the hit

R&B duo Ashford & Simpson makes no excuses for his elaborate flaxen 'do: "My style signature is probably my hair. People recognize me for it. I call it 'lion hair'—I want to look like I'm king of the jungle!"

The Reagan-Bush years, complete with power suits and corporate budgets, witnessed the advent of close-cropped styles. Metaphorically speaking, Black men traded in their Afro picks for wave caps and set

Word up: Cameo frontman Larry Blackmon favored a texturized high-top fade in the eighties; the style was favored by everyone from Arsenio Hall to Will Smith *(above)*. When he began shaving his balding dome, Michael Jordan revived the clean pate club first started by the likes of Isaac Hayes and Geoffrey Holder *(opposite)*.

out to "get theirs," be it at a prestigious law firm, financial establishment, or Fortune 500 company. Ironically, during the last days of the Cold War, the military "fade" popularized by Black soldiers in the forties emerged once again. Only this time, the "troops" were fighting a more subliminal form of racism than that which faced their fathers.

The standard-issue fade was shaved close on the sides and graduated to a higher finish on the crown, but, of course, Black men never stop at standard-issue anything. Accentuated with colors, shaved scalp designs, and asymmetrical angles, the once-"safe" style evolved into a veritable canvas for self-expression. History on top of the head, the fade even incorporated elements of many past hair treatments, including "twists" (budding, groomed dreadlocks), braids, and "texturizer" (mild relaxant).

The eclectic nineties have heralded a slew of hairstyling options for Black men. Dreadlocks, once the domain of Jamaican Rastafarians, have become more mainstream, even stylized, with "lockticians" working alongside barbers. The Afro, in low, precision-cut specials and larger, freestyle versions, has made a healthy comeback. And "as Black as you can get" baldness, as Isaac Hayes once put it, might well be the most memorable hair trend of the decade. Pioneered by basketball phenomenon Michael Jordan, the hairless 'do symbolizes strength and simple, clean style. Part of its appeal, outside of its obvious convenience, is its removal of any direct reference to a man's age. Gone are indications of gray, or of a receding hairline. In fact, thinning hair is often the catalyst that prompts a Black man to go bald. Finally, on the opposite end of the spectrum, cornrows and braids have been redefined by such personalities as nouveau soul-crooner D'Angelo and new-jack basketball star Allen Iverson. Truly, whoever declared that hair was a woman's crowning glory did not know the twentieth-century brother.

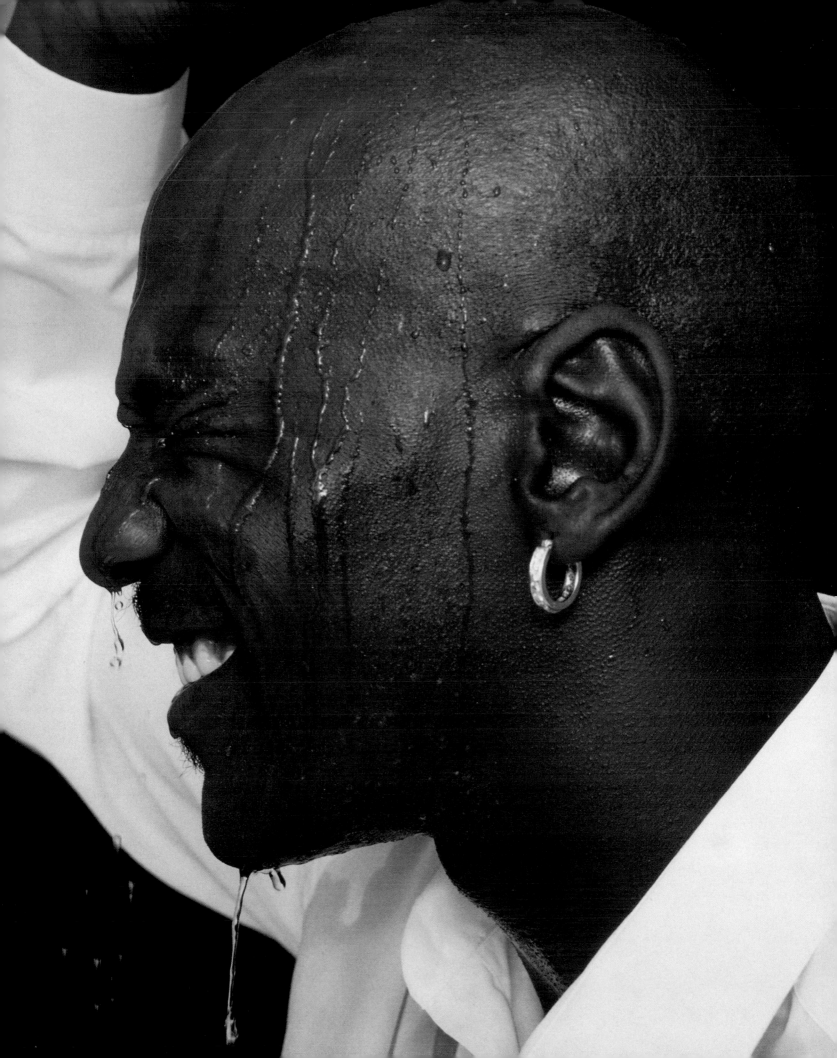

MAXWELL

"HAIR"

I always used to wrap my hair up. People thought it was receding or something. My girlfriend was the only person who would see it out, and she would try to convince me to wear it out. One day at a photo shoot I decided not to use the head wrap, and I got a positive reaction. Of course, it ended up being a blow-drying nightmare. Now I just braid it. I think a lot of African Americans have this whole thing about good hair and bad hair and all that weirdness, so there's never any positivity about what hair can be. There are so many ways you can represent yourself as far as hair is concerned.

Style for me is an ever-changing thing. I think I thrive on the idea of going against what's accepted. In high school, I cut off all my hair and, believe it or not, people thought I was a skinhead. When I grew it back longer than what everyone else was wearing, then I was labeled "Buckwheat." And all I was doing was simply expressing where I was at the moment.

When I was growing up, developing my own style was difficult for me. My parents, who were from the Caribbean, had very definite ideas about how a young man should look. Meanwhile, I wanted to be down with my friends, rocking Lee jeans and Adidas. I was initially kept from expressing myself through clothes. Maybe that's why I strive to exercise the right as much as I can now.

Bob Marley's style was always inspirational to me. He exemplified ease, confidence, and self-awareness. Style is not about a label, it's not about what's in season. It's an attitude. Aside from my admiration for Bob Marley, I've always paid close attention to whatever my girlfriends would say about men's fashion. I soak it all up.

As for essentials, I can't do without tank tops. They're timeless, and they work. The ones I really like are the straight-up Fruit of the Looms, but if it's about being snazzy or wearing something that's extra extra, I go for Helmut Lang. My accessory of choice is sunglasses with tinted lenses.

Style is about self-awareness and being in tune with who you are. Fashions will come and go and come again, but they will never mean as much as the energy that is conveyed from within. Black male style, at its core, is the celebration of ourselves and our culture.

Screams of FASHION

BY MICHAEL A. GONZALES

VIEWED AS A BLARING FREAKY-DEKE

darktown follies kaleidoscope of Black folks' sound and vision since the early seventies, the roaring "Soul Train" has often served as a magical window to the boogie wonderland universe that defines the musical voices and personal styles of young (Black) America. Swaggering superfly guys of the seventies, clad in flared pants, marshmallow shoes, and wide Willie Dynamite feathered hats, are now corny adults, as easily offended by the hip-hop "gangsta gear" dangling in their teenagers' closets as their own parents were by their funky attire. Rather than remain mute, these blokes fondly reminisce about the days when their

Duck-walkin' guitar king Chuck Berry *(above)* **created sounds, moves, and styles that would inspire the British pop invasion; his double-jointed stage scoot, slim suits, and straightened, slicked-back pompadour set the standard for many of his successors, including Little Richard and The Artist Formerly Known as Prince. Crooner Sam Cooke played it straight in 1954; his conked pomp was requested at barbershops across the country** *(right)*. **The electric Little Richard chose fabrics that reflected his every move: satin, sharkskin, sequins** *(opposite)*.

rebel styles were viewed as a form of televised revolution, hi-fi blasting its own sonic-sampled James Brown/Curtis Mayfield/Prince loops and wah-wah-driven soundtracks.

From Stevie Wonder, dressed in a motherland dashiki, his "Living for the City" wild-child electric Afro resembling a nappy angel halo, to Blue Magic, falsetto-crooning "Side Show" in their flashy aqua-colored knit suits, to The Jackson 5, looking like underage rejects from a groovy Grateful Dead commune in their multi-hued cosmic hippie gear, the outrageous fashions that "Soul Train" broadcast into our living rooms could be considered a visual continuum of the Black Power movement. Although cultural critic Maxine Craig once wrote, "To reduce fashion at all times to any one meaning is to close one's eyes to much of the language of fashion," the wild styles that our noir musical heroes draped themselves in were fiery designs that spoke as loud and proud as Malcolm X. Clothes elevated racial consciousness. When the dapper, dandy, crisp-suit-wearing Sam Cooke proclaimed in 1965 that "Change is Gonna Come," who

The Temptations shuffled through the fifties with carefully choreographed steps, high-shined shoes, and structured harmonies *(left)*. Jimi Hendrix, the forefather of hippie funk, masterfully mixed Afrocentric dashikis, psychedelic prints, military regalia, tie-dyed fabrics, and buttoned flares to create fashions that were as exuberant and explosive as his guitar playing *(above)*.

would have thought he was singing about threads?

In his typically conservative manner, the wack Black essayist Shelby Steele states in "The Recomposed Self: More on Vulnerability" (*The Content of Our Character*, HarperPerennial, 1990) that the flamboyant fashions of the Black community serve to disguise "inner fears of inferiority." Besides being a simplistic response to the bugged fashions of any musical generation, from Cab Calloway's zoot suit to George Clinton's bizarro Parliament Funkadelic Mothership gear, Steele's opinion doesn't seem to take into account the fact that "inferiority" is rarely an issue. As Sly Stone once sang on television's "Midnight Special" in 1974, style was all about "different strokes for different folks." Since at the time he was wearing a pink and purple glitter outfit complete with matching applejack cap—an ornate assemblage of sequins so loud one could hear its piercing screams through the screen—one should safely assume his words were gospel.

Although the orchestral voodoo papa of electric guitar, Jimi Hendrix, was already dead when "Soul Train" debuted in 1970, his untimely demise only made it that much easier for America's original atomic dawg to be voted the patron superspade saint of Black fashion. As a guitarist, Hendrix attacked his instrument with the same wild abandon he applied to his extensive wardrobe. Unlike his Black pop peers from the more traditional Motown and Stax schools, where the boys (i.e., Marvin Gaye or Sam & Dave) often dressed in dark suits resembling the threads in their fathers' closets, Hendrix's radical style revolt was as booming as a bomb, as brutally shockadelic as his amplified sounds. Unlike the nameless, faceless protagonist of Ralph Ellison's brilliant novel, Jimi refused to be just another *Invisible Man* sowing the cultural landscape. In fact, Jimi's body became a canvas and his clothes his "art," ranging from explosive surrealism to eye-candy pop.

Having worked in the early sixties as a sideman for The Isley Brothers and Little Richard (who may have passed on a few of his own flavorful fashion secrets), brother Jimi was discovered in the depths

of clubland New York, jamming before being shipped off to England to record his first album, *Are You Experienced?* It wasn't until his American debut at the historic 1967 Monterey Pop Festival that Hendrix —looking like a stardust acid cowboy in a ruffled yellow shirt, tight red pants, embroidered waistcoat, psychedelic jacket, and pink feather boa—became a cracked-rainbow vision of a new musical apocalypse. Burning his guitar at the end of "Wild Thing," Hendrix's finale flames symbolically extinguished any remnants of sharskin-suit style. It's a touch surreal, in retrospect, to view photos from his teenage days: Wearing a white shirt, bow tie, and tight jacket, Jimi looked more like a member of those Chicago doo-wop cliques than the future of the funk.

Although his madcap sense of style wasn't immediately accepted by the Black community, which perhaps viewed this nappy-haired sonic peacock as more of a circus freak than an innovative fashion trendsetter, Hendrix's Blaxadelic genius was embraced by an unknown Bay Area musician who called himself Sly Stone, and by a brilliant jazz trumpeter named Miles Davis. As British professor Paul Gilroy, interviewed by bell hooks in *Outlaw Culture: Revisiting Representations* (Routledge, 1994), stated, "Let's not forget that Sly, Miles, and Jimi were all rejected by the African Americans to some degree. It's a different story now, but how long did it take people to catch up with them?"

In the nineties, the retro Black Velveteen rock movement was officially launched in 1989 with the release of Lenny Kravitz's debut disc *Let Love Rule*. Looking like a thrift-shop version of Hendrix, the boy who would be Jimi, styled in four-color magazine spreads with electric guitar, ranted on about his love of old music, old equipment, old instruments, and old clothes. Ancient became his middle name, aged like cherished wine. Though entertaining, Kravitz's entire persona walked a thin line between sonic coolness and derivative trash. In her essay "Fragments of a Fashionable Discourse" (*On Fashion*, Rutgers University Press, 1994), Kaja Silverman explained, "vintage clothing makes it possible for certain of those images 'to live' on in a different form, much as postmodern architecture does with earlier architectural styles and even with the material fragments of extinct buildings." Unlike Prince, who was more influenced by Hendrix's designs than by his guitar playing (check Carlos Santana in them riffs), Kravitz wasn't always able to take his borrowed styles to the next level. Like his music, Lenny Kravitz's clothes were simply on loan.

As for Miles Davis, his stylistic, stereo-vision switch from sharp-as-a-tack, cool Brooks Brothers suits to exotic fabrics and wild-haired bohemia happened in the late sixties, around the time he tired of playing soothing soundtracks for supper clubs. Searching for a bigger sound through electric instrumentation, Miles began observing the hardcore jollies of those other two squeaking midnight birds soaring over the heads of the progressive masses. In his informative 1983 essay "The Electric Miles," music critic Greg Tate wrote, "Visual evidence of Sly's and Jimi's impact on Miles can be seen in the dress styles he adapted from them: the multi-hued fabrics and talismanic flow of attire." Years later, toward the end of his life, Miles admitted to his biographer Quincy Troupe, "I started wearing African dashikis and robes and looser clothes plus a lot of Indian tops by this guy Hernando, who was from Argentina and who had a place in Greenwich Village. That's where Jimi Hendrix bought most of his clothes. So I started buying wraparound Indian shirts from him. . . ."

Miles Davis wasn't the only cat who caught a contact high from the potent funky fashions of Jimi and Sly. A young producer, Norman Whitfield, who reinvented the Motown sound in the late sixties and early seventies with The Temptations' "Cloud Nine," "Psychedelic Shack," "Ball of Confusion," and "Papa was a Rollin' Stone," was also inspired. In *Where Did Our Love Go: The Rise and Fall of the Motown Sound* (St. Martin's Press, 1985), his definitive account of the history of soul music, Nelson George wrote: "As much as [Norman

Whitfield] admired the music of Sly and Hendrix, he was also moved by their striking visual presence. It was one thing for The Temps—now looking fashionably funky in suede vests, granny glasses, and multicolored pants, but quite another for the Whitfield-sponsored group The Undisputed Truth [to wear] white facial makeup, blond Afros, and silvery metallic outfits—what Whitfield called 'the cosmic thing.' "

Shifting our gaze from the hallucinatory hedonism of sixties styles back to the so-called happy daze of the fifties, old photographs of such artists as Fats Domino and Chubby Checker reveal a conservative image that seemed to fade with the arrival of the civil rights movement, LSD, and the Vietnam War.

On the cover of his album *Here Stands Fats Domino,* the resident king of "Blueberry Hill" does indeed stand, erect as a keyboard warrior, dressed in two-tone shoes—that's as wild as he ever got—and a suit with pleated pants, their starched crease so sharp it could cut glass. In fact, in any photo of this piano-playing pioneer, Fats's hair is always freshly conked and his suits freshly pressed. In the eyes of White America, who had never socialized with Negroes before, perhaps such tailored suits presented the Black man as a gentleman, one that wouldn't frighten weary parents. With the exception of the camp "crazy coon" antics and wardrobe of Esquerita (who was flamboyant when Little Richard was still gospel-wailing), Little Richard (who even wore mascara!), and Screaming Jay Hawkins ("a fiendish dandy in polka-dot shoes and zebra coattails," leaping out of a custom-made zebra-striped coffin), most of the early Black rockers looked as though they'd stopped to sing on their way to church.

Thrill-daddy James Brown was once one of 'em Baptist-church-singing, tailored-suit-wearing mofos, shining bright as the North Star on Sunday morning. In an advertisement for his first single, 1954's "Please, Please, Please," brother James looked like an Augusta undertaker in his funeral-parlor-black suit. Yet, unlike his soul-sonic peers, Brown was able to hang on like

Sloopy, not only as a personality but as a legitimate artist. Taking his own fashion sense as seriously as a heart attack, it was not uncommon for the future God-father of Soul to fine his band twenty bills for wearing wrinkled clothes. A layman might call it crazy, but what does one expect from a brother who draped himself in a velvet cape for his finales?

Fast-forward to the present. Gather in a funky style-council powwow and allow your gaze to drift over the crystal ball. See the black lace, purple paisley, Versace couture of The Artist's wardrobe room. Hangers overflow with the fabrics of his various personas. Flip through them, and hear hundreds of Black rock designs bellow. "Wear me," they say. "Wear me now, wear me out." Tomorrow, these are the threads that will be swinging body-electric style on the "Soul Train" line.

His name was Prince, and he was funky; in the early nineties, The Artist cloaked his royal frame in high-waisted hip-hugging flares and appliquéd bolero jackets (at one awards ceremony, he exposed more than his art in bright-yellow, but-tock-revealing, cut-out pants) *(above)*. Inspired by the grunge finery favored by such contemporary artists as Lenny Kravitz, French designer Jean Paul Gaultier mixed the foppish with the femi-nine with the secondhand: Jason Olive modeled a taupe felt bowler with leopard-print hatband, a butter-yellow maxicoat, musketeer gloves, and various leopard-print accessories *(left)*.

Rock and roll style represents pure freedom of expression, a license to be as freaky as you want to be, no limits. Although some may feel that my ensembles are on the edge, they're normal to me. My free spirit has always kept my clothing way ahead of the curve. I began bringing back styles from the seventies more than ten years ago, and I was laughed at for it, but look at how many R&B artists are wearing the stuff now. Feathered boas, fleece maxicoats, wild prints. It's become commonplace.

I like to mix it up. I learned how to dress from my mom, television actress Roxie Roker (of *The Jeffersons* fame). When I was around seven or eight years old, I used to play in her closet. She had all these really groovy clothes and a very eclectic style. It was the seventies, and I used to dress up like the rock stars of the day—cool blazers and scarves, great prints, feather boas, knee-high platform boots. My mom had all that stuff.

Lenny KRAVITZ

"ROCK N' ROLL"

Besides my mom, my style inspirations were The Jackson 5, back when Michael was young and the group had a real funky flair. They were the first men of color to turn me on, clothingwise. I remember seeing them at Madison Square Garden when I was eight. They had on these bad knickers, knee-high patent-leather lace-up boots, and vests over poofy-sleeved shirts. They dressed as well as James Brown and Sly and The Family Stone, who also inspired me, but were older. On the lesser-known front, I liked the eclecticism of Arthur Lee, who was the leader of the San Francisco-based band Love, and Jimi Hendrix, of course, and Janice Joplin, and old soul cats like Bootsy Collins, Parliament Funkadelic, and Al Green—who, believe it or not, used to dress really slick when he was young, donning fur hats and leather lace-up pants. He was bad! In general, I was heavily influenced by the soul and rock and roll clothing of the late sixties and early seventies.

Besides myself, unfortunately, there are not many Black musicians playing true rock and roll. But, then again, what is "rock and roll"? Many rappers and R&B cats are now taking on that type of persona. Rock and roll has changed, it's merged with all these other types of music. Hip-hop, alternative, techno—it's becoming one big ball of eclectic music, and the styles seem to follow suit. Rock and roll audiences have always been primarily White, which is strange to me. But the same thing was true for groups like Sly and The Family Stone and even Bob Marley and The Wailers. The sudden surge of hip-hop in America has its artists experiencing the same crossover. As Whites begin to live it, Blacks are also becoming more progressive, accepting artists like The Artist, whose style sometimes blurs the lines of femininity and masculinity in its glam flamboyance.

On that note, I personally recommend velvet pants: They are just sexy.

Mandella & SAUNDERS

LOCKS N' CHOPS NATURAL HAIR SALON

Creative director Ademola Mandella (left) and general manager Orin Saunders (right), founders of the Locks n' Chops Natural Hair Salon and Art Gallery, are acknowledged innovators in the hair-care industry. Internationally recognized for modernizing natural haircutting with his revolutionary Brooklyn-style "Fade Away" and "Line Design" techniques, Mandella was responsible for and co-author of the first natural hair enhancement legislation to be approved in the United States.

Since 1993, Locks n' Chops has serviced the New York metropolitan area. Mandella's and Saunders's commitment to developing the natural hair-care industry, their creative hair-care techniques, and their world-class customer service are the foundations of their success. Celebrity clients include Laurence Fishburne, Wesley Snipes, KRS-1, Malcolm Jamal-Warner, Vernon Reid, and Spike Lee.

HAIR

Well-groomed hair is about more than regular trims and state-of-the-art styling products. Mandella and Saunders offer their expert advice on keeping hair in tip-top condition, and outline the cut and care of four classic styles:

THE BALD HEAD

Cut: There are many ways to achieve the "baldy" (opposite, top right), as it is referred to by the Locks n' Chops duo. Black men frequently suffer from *Pseudofolliculitis barbae*—commonly known as razor bumps—caused by ingrown hairs. With this in mind, it's critical to choose the shaving technique that is most appropriate for individual hair texture and scalp sensitivity. Mandella and Saunders recommend the following:

"For soft hair, use an electric razor to completely shave the hair to the scalp. Many men wonder whether shaving with or against the natural direction of hair growth matters. With softer hair textures it doesn't make a difference. You can cut in any direction and as close as you want. Electric razors always leave a very light shadow of hair, which is good because it lessens the chance of sharp stubble, which can curl back into the scalp, causing ingrown hair bumps.

"If hair is thick, an electric razor is not going to cut it. We recommend either a depilatory cream, a straight razor, or a disposable razor. For sanitary reasons, a disposable razor is preferable. For men unaccustomed to wielding a traditional straight edge, a disposable is often simply much easier to handle."

Care: A well-moisturized scalp is essential to healthy hair. When asked about "scalp-savers" for men who choose to go bald, or for men who are bald, Mandella and Saunders recommend "a light product that will

thoroughly moisturize the scalp." If you have a naturally oily scalp, opt for a water-based moisturizer. If your scalp is inherently dry, reach for an oil-based grooming product. Water will only further dry the scalp.

THE BRUSH CUT

Cut: Plain and simple: For professional results in a short "brush cut" (previous page, top left), go to a professional. Whether the damage was self-inflicted or just witnessed firsthand, most Black men have learned the hard way that home haircuts can be brutal on the hair, the head, and, consequently, the social calendar. Unless you are a trained professional, licensed to practice haircutting in your state of residence, Mandella and Saunders agree, "Leave it to the pros!"

Care: "After considering how you plan to style it," Mandella continues, "know that brushing your hair in its natural hair growth pattern is highly recommended. Brush from the top of your head downward, around the head in the shape of an umbrella." When moisturizing the scalp for a brush cut, follow the same rules as outlined for the "baldy"—there is not much difference in the amount of hair on the scalp.

THE PROCESSED 'DO

Care: Although Mandella and Saunders do not advocate the process (pardon the pun), they offer some practical advice to brothers who still choose to relax or texturize their hair (previous page, bottom right). Cleansing is of the utmost importance. "A mild shampoo will be gentle on hair that has already been broken down by chemicals, regardless of whether it's bone-straight or slightly texturized." Due to its fragile state, processed hair shouldn't be washed more than once every five days. After shampooing, thoroughly moisturize hair and scalp with a conditioner formulated for dry hair. Such conditioners will contain plenty of glycerine, a moisturizing substance. When it comes to styling processed hair, Mandella and Saunders suggest the use of a light almond oil: "It's natural, and you can use it liberally without accumulating a lot of build-up." Avoid using mousse or gels, which usually have high alcohol contents and tend to dry out hair.

DREADLOCKS

Cut: Or lack thereof. Traditional dreadlocks (page 199, bottom left) are thick sections of hair twisted together to create braidlike cords. The locking process is permanent, and begins with about an inch of hair growth, grouped and twisted in a natural curl pattern, then held in place overnight for several months. The Locks n' Chops team applaud dreadlocks as "one of the best hairstyles for African-American men today. The only tools required are hands." Combs and brushes are what break and damage hair. Dreadlocks, in comparison, are completely healthy.

Care: In the first stages of growth, locks are merely "buds" and should be disturbed as little as possible. Ideally, a freshly locked head should be treated by a professional, who will be able to clean the scalp and reinforce the "twists." If professional care is not an option, apply a mild astringent such as witch hazel to the exposed parts of the scalp using cotton swabs.

Locks can safely be considered fully bound when the sections measure three inches in length. The weakest point of each section is at the scalp. To wash, soak hair thoroughly with warm water. Using a mild shampoo, massage the individual sections gently, and squeeze out the excess suds. Rinse hair completely, using low water pressure so as not to blast the locks, and apply an oil-based leave-in conditioner. Most hair can air-dry, but for particularly thick dreadlocks, a dryer cap or hand-held blowdryer set on low will do the job. Wash hair as infrequently as possible. New growth at the roots should be twisted once a month.

TOOLS AND SHOPTALK

Purchase quality products, even if they are more expensive. The Locks n' Chops duo advises, "Anything harder than a natural bristle brush will pull the hair and cause breakage. Choose one with soft natural bristles, and use plastic or rubber combs with widely spaced teeth." When selecting a barber, "Make sure the shop is clean. Hair should be swept up regularly, and all utensils should be properly sanitized. The barber himself should be neat and presentable." If you are not comfortable with the conditions, don't patronize the shop—it's not worth the risk of contracting a scalp infection. Of course, consider the way a barber cuts hair.

Facing the RISING SUN

luminaries

"Black men are not going to cringe before anyone but God."

MARCUS GARVEY

ethnicity

BOOKER T. WASHINGTON ONCE

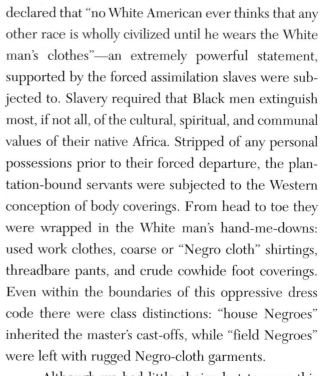

declared that "no White American ever thinks that any other race is wholly civilized until he wears the White man's clothes"—an extremely powerful statement, supported by the forced assimilation slaves were subjected to. Slavery required that Black men extinguish most, if not all, of the cultural, spiritual, and communal values of their native Africa. Stripped of any personal possessions prior to their forced departure, the plantation-bound servants were subjected to the Western conception of body coverings. From head to toe they were wrapped in the White man's hand-me-downs: used work clothes, coarse or "Negro cloth" shirtings, threadbare pants, and crude cowhide foot coverings. Even within the boundaries of this oppressive dress code there were class distinctions: "house Negroes" inherited the master's cast-offs, while "field Negroes" were left with rugged Negro-cloth garments.

Although we had little choice but to wear this new American apparel, many of us never lost our African style sensibility. For example, excess fabric was oftentimes made into headdresses for men and women, to protect them from the sun when working in the fields. The practice of head-wrapping for both functional and decorative purposes is common in many African countries.

As families were separated and tribes were integrated by slave masters, small yet significant efforts were made by slaves to retain cultural and tribal pride. A documented interview with a former slave describes how certain Negro men interpreted their daily workwear by accenting it with European shirtwaists, Arab head wraps, African-inspired handwoven textiles, and precious, smuggled cowrie shells. Statements about tribal affiliation were also made sartorially. As the for-

Quincy Jones made a multicultural statement in the seventies with his fringed, basket-weave tunic (*previous spread, left*). In 1930, "the Negro Poet Laureate" Langston Hughes lounged in double-breasted suit and crisp handkerchief (*previous spread, right*). Head wraps, indigenous to African dress, were used by slaves in the United States for practical and decorative purposes (*above*). In the turbulent sixties, Black Panther Stokely Carmichael mixed the militant with the multiethnic, pairing a dashiki with a dark leather jacket (*opposite*).

mer slave recalled, "(some) weah eahring in duh eah. Some weas it in duh leg and dose from annuduh tribe weahs it in duh right eah."3

Studied assimilation became increasingly important at the turn of the century, as the era of slavery came to a close and freedom slowly filtered through all of the states. For Black men this meant obtaining, through observation but little or no instruction, a clear understanding of the purpose of tailored daywear and its role in daily life.

The learning process took place as we were trained as coachmen, cooks, and paid servants in the homes of the community's most prominent citizens: doctors, bankers, businessmen, and the like. In these domestic positions, we were privy to the closets, clotheslines, and washtubs which held the quality clothing worn by White gentlemen. As multi-tasked valets, we mended, washed, pressed, folded, suited, and served. This taught us about the fit, function, and value of better clothing.

Back in our own homes, we could affect the manners and customs of our employers, along with their way of dress. Setting tables, preparing meals, and maintaining a home were duties we sometimes knew better than the employers themselves. With this conditioning came a greater desire to be seen as equal men. As we attempted to match mainstream society's way of living, we momentarily loosened our grip on the nuances of African dress that we once clung to so tightly.

For the first half of the twentieth century, most Black men made strides to secure homes, jobs, and respect from majority America. Through the First World War and subsequent stock-market crash, we found ourselves eye-to-eye with all people in a near-crippling depression that leveled many Americans. An equalizer for better or worse, this critical state of the union was based on economics, and not color.

Uncle Sam sent more than one million Black men to defend its shores in the Second World War. Hungry for respect upon our return, Black men fought for integration in America, with church and commu-

nity leaders heading up the battle. In these lean post-war years, it behooved us to conform on certain levels and react on others. Clothing, a visual signifier of equality, was an obvious candidate for conformity.

The sixties proved a pivotal decade for Blacks. Seemingly unified on the civil rights front, Blacks individually chose several different roads towards equality. Some joined Martin Luther King, Jr. in his nonviolent quest, while others, often urban youths and collegiate grass-roots activists, leaned towards the more aggressive approaches of Malcolm X or the Black Panthers. From "We Shall Overcome" to "Black Power," we embraced liberating battle cries and reclaimed symbols of our heritage. Our clothing took the lead in this civil and visual transformation.

Afrocentric clothing was popularized in the mid-sixties by such mavericks as Huey P. Newton, leader of the Black Panther party. Known for his Afro, beret, and urban-guerrilla uniform of combat boots,

A kunga player in the Black-is-Beautiful seventies showed his pride in a printed, ankle-grazing tunic, handcrafted beads, and striped knit kufi cap *(above)*. Football legend Jim Brown traded in his helmet for a kufi, knit in the traditional African palette of red, green, and black *(right)*. In the multiculti nineties, diversity rules: tonal, layered linens, knit skullcaps, and prayer beads bring a flavor of the East to Western fashion *(opposite)*.

Actor Laurence Fishburne incorporates ethnic elements into his everyday dress: He wears a loose-fitting, white linen tunic with prayer beads and loop-buttoned vest *(above)*. Head wraps house dreadlocks and frame earrings and pendants *(top, right)*. Actor Djimon Hounsou modeled Industria's equestrian ensemble, Afrocentricized with layers of glittering silver cuffs and rings *(bottom, right)*. Comedian Bill Bellamy goes to great lengths for style: His black and white robes are reminiscent of a clergyman's *(opposite)*.

tight leather jacket, dark sunglasses, and occasional dashiki, Newton personified the toughest translation of Black Power style. Other men chose more traditional interpretations of African attire, including the popular, tuniclike dashiki, leather sandals, and native jewelry, to affirm their cultural identity.

The early seventies introduced style leaders who didn't always set out for sartorial stardom. But intentionally or not, Jesse Jackson, Stokely Carmichael, and Eldridge Cleaver all laid claim to true Afrocentric chic through their supernatural 'fros. Black pride medallions and an aggressive posture gave the bold urban look an authentic air of regality.

African-inspired fashions reflected the general air of social unrest in the sixties and seventies. Protests were a physical manifestation of these frustrations; ethnic clothing made its own statement about racial pride. As political and social barriers slowly crumbled under the pressure of affirmative action and civil rights legislation, assimilation once again took priority. In spite of its richness, Afrocentric clothing began to filter out of our wardrobes, replaced by the funky, farcical side of Black Power as showcased on big screens and city street corners. Afros were relaxed to look smooth. Free-flowing drawstring pants were swapped for crotch-binding double-knit bell-bottoms. Impossibly high platforms took precedence over comfortable leather sandals.

It wasn't until the late eighties that ethnic style experienced a resurgence. Influenced by an increased awareness of apartheid in South Africa, politically active Black Americans began to wear their concerns on their sleeves. The redux was soon noticeable among college students eager to embrace all elements of their long-suppressed cultural identity, and among entertainers in search of creative and artistic links back to the motherland. Medallions resurfaced, this time in leather and embellished with red, black, and green insets cut in the shape of the African continent. Kente cloth cloaked the body. The head was covered with kufi hats.

Black equality is born from more than a century of political struggle. True ethnic style is not something

that can just be pulled out of the closet and thrown on—such a cavalier attitude disrespects our history. To truly pay homage to such a powerful movement, Black men today subtly incorporate ethnicity into their wardrobes, adding color, texture, and simple Afrocentric accessories. This careful balance between American and African traditions has forced Black men to establish a unique identity, one that validates our present-day existence, yet honors our ancestors and their struggles.

My style serves as a uniform of a certain kind of intellectual soldier, one trying to be a force for good. It proclaims my presence on America's cultural battlefields. Same old uniform, a suit, fighting the same old struggle, for freedom. Same old uniform, inhabited by a profoundly humble spirit, a solid, fighting spirit.

My way of dressing is influenced by two iconic figures in Black history: the jazz musician and the preacher. It's in the tradition of such towering figures as Charlie Parker, Dizzy Gillespie, J. C. Austin, Gardner Taylor, and my grandfather, the Reverend C. L. West. They wore clothes that reflected their sense of what it meant to be, and that accented their courage *to* be, living in White America. Our clothes have their roots in traditional European dress, but because a Black body has a different way of stylizing space and time in such garments, we also subvert those traditions. Think of the twist Duke Ellington put on a French suit: On his person, the suit became symbolic of Black elegance and excellence. This sartorial reappropriation reflects to some extent the creative response of people of African descent to various European musical instruments—jazzman John Coltrane's reclamation of the Belgian-invented saxophone, for example.

In the sixties and seventies, I enjoyed watching the styles of soul groups such as The Delfonics and The Temptations evolve to incorporate Afrocentric elements. Struggle is about gaining the right to choose, and style is a critical part of this process. It allows us an opportunity to select clothes that reflect and affirm our African origins. A man who wears ethnic clothing is making the statement that he perceives himself and other people of color with the dignity we deserve. Personally, I reserve African clothing for my annual visits to Addis Ababa; customary Ethiopian dress for men includes white, cotton or linen pant-and-shirt sets that are embroidered along the edges of the cuffs and collar.

Black style comes in many different guises, and one should never try to imitate, emulate, or simply conform to certain dominant ways of dressing. Although it might sound ironic, I suggest that brothers adhere to the Shakespearean dictum "to thine own self be true." It takes tremendous courage; and garments, personalized in distinctive ways, can be an extension of this courage, born of and built on the history of Black struggle. That's ethnic style.

Nineteenth-century British essayist Thomas Carlyle, author of *Sartor Resartus*, argues that clothes symbolize a certain conception of one's self. I agree: Black male elegance is an essential element of our complex humanity. You see it at Black funerals, you see it at Black churches, and you still see it Friday nights at Black clubs. By celebrating the legacy of our style, we acknowledge a crucial aesthetic dimension of our identity. In a society so deeply shaped by White supremacy that it regards Black bodies with disgust and degradation, Black style acts as a type of aesthetic resistance to the various racist myths.

Cornel WEST

"ETHNICITY"

LUMINARIES

BY CONSTANCE C. R. WHITE

IN AMERICA, A SUIT ON A WHITE MAN

and a suit on a Black man do not always mean the same thing. The three-piece suit is the quintessential dress of America's Black luminaries and it has, for as long as grass has been growing under trees, been the armor that our great orators, agitators, and seducers went to battle in. The bulk of a suit shoulder and the sharp peak of a lapel spoke of their seriousness of purpose. The depth of a rich wool declared their station and to some degree their intent. Black men of letters and of the cloth, from Frederick Douglass to Cornel West, from Marcus Garvey to Floyd Flake, have chosen the suit as their cloak.

The suit arose as a unifying element in society, a signifier of both conformity and power. On a White man, the suit, with its iconic accoutrements of shirt and tie, faithfully adheres to this traditional role. But on a Black man, the suit's standard posture is upended.

Booker T. Washington made educating disenfranchised Blacks his mission during the early part of the century *(above)*. Congressman Adam Clayton Powell, Jr. and civil rights leader Malcolm X joined in a rare moment of political and religious unity *(right)*. Literary expatriate James Baldwin favored a European style sensibility *(opposite)*.

History shows the many ways Black men have stylishly subverted it. The suit takes on layers of nuance as complex as the roles of Black leaders in our society. On some, it has become the armor of revolution. On others, it has been made into a flamboyant statement of style, and has been manipulated to be party to an Afrocentrism in dress.

The commonality of style of many of our greatest leaders and thinkers has been their adherence to the suit: a jacket, matching pants, a shirt, and a tie. The suit is clearly the preference of contemporary men of color in visible positions: intellectuals such as Cornel West and Henry Louis Gates; politicians and activists such as Kwesi Mfume and the Reverend Al Sharpton; journalists such as Ed Bradley and Bryant Gumbel; spiritual leaders such as the Reverend Jesse Jackson and the Reverend Calvin Butts. It is interesting how these Black men, more so than their White counterparts, bend the tradition of the suit by adding their own personal insignia, always giving the traditionally staid look heaping spoons of flair. Mr. West's French cuffs and wide, colorful ties add an element of flamboyance, Mr. Mfume's kofis or kente-print scarves imbue his thoroughly Western suit with a dramatic sweep of African style, and Mr. Bradley's earring is a quietly blaring declaration of individuality and artistry that most surely overrides his tailored message of hidebound traditionalism.

In their choice of dress, today's Black power brokers are carrying on a long lineage of sartorial clothing that dates back to amelioration at the end of the nineteenth century, when Blacks began to gain their liberation from slavery and with it the freedom to dress as they pleased (economics notwithstanding). From then until now, among the most vivid and powerful instigators in our communities has been the preacher. The Right Reverend Such-and-Such, in self-preserving imitation of the White majority, was always dressed in suit and shirt, no matter how humble or threadbare. Black American preachers have a duty to reflect the styles and aspirations of their congregants.

No reverend dare tend his flock looking ratty. Church members expect their pastor to wear the best suit, the finest leather shoes, and the whitest, crispest shirt. Thus encouraged, the church, which has produced so many of our intellects and activists, has also turned out our most stylish dressers.

Marcus Garvey carried his message of Pan-Africanism in quasi-military suits or black suits and white shirts that served as the trunk of his fabulous style tree. He decked his head in outrageous plumage reminiscent of Angolan kings and European royalty. Years later, the Nation of Islam, most famously through Brother Malcolm, became a stylish presence in sober, neat suits on street corners and mosques in Black communities around the country. A revolutionary in

In 1967, Black Panthers protested for the release of renegade Huey P. Newton: Their stark uniform consisted of head-to-toe black *(opposite)*. Reverend Jesse Jackson's hip sartorial edge helped him rally a new generation of Black Americans in the seventies *(left)*. Known on his college campus as "Tweedy" for his good taste, Martin Luther King, Jr. was attentive to the details from an early age: His hand-rolled, monogrammed pocket square proved the point *(above)*.

glasses, Malcolm's serious, brooding face made pre-scriptive spectacles a cool alternative for intellectuals, White and Black, to this day.

It was imperative to the goals of luminaries like Malcolm and the Reverend Dr. Martin Luther King, Jr. that their appearance work for the good of the cause. Their style reflected their divergences—Malcolm's hard-line philosophies matched his stark suits, Martin's pedestrian traditionalist look girded his integrationist message—and their similarities. Both chose the dress of the oppressor, signaling their willingness to move toward détente. The suit chain, however, was broken when Black leaders—present and post Malcolm and Martin—became more confrontational, pessimistic about equality between Whites and Blacks and unwilling to compromise. Whites became more violent toward them in response. So our leaders turned to a style that showed just how disenfranchised they felt from White America. Wearing a suit stood for solidarity with "the man," and what many of our leaders wanted then was to bring "the man" to his knees.

The Black Panther leaders ushered in a new style of dress for success, success in the revolution. Bobby Seale, Eldridge Cleaver, H. Rap Brown, and Huey Newton looked powerful and sexy, all Afros, black leather jackets, and skinny pants. In a country where male sexual allure is equated with power, they became sexier still when armed with a cache of weapons.

Intellectuals and politicians too threw off the yoke of the suit and declared their style independence with progressive thinking and avant-garde clothes they had seen on such African leaders as Stokely Carmichael (Kwame Toure), Julius K. Nyerere of Tanzania, and Prime Minister Michael Manley of Jamaica. The tailored suit, once so splendid, momentarily became the monkey suit, the dress of unstylish stooges, chumps, apes of the White man. Instead, our leaders wore shirt jackets or bushjacs—untailored shirts with square hems which, as the name suggests, were part jacket, part shirt.

The pendulum swung back to classic style as Black mavericks urged us to assimilate, not aggravate.

Fabulous dashiki-wearing Jesse became slick suit-wearing Reverend Jackson. Prominent men such as Andrew Young and Julian Bond favored the suit, and, in the age of integration, their audience preferred this more traditional style as well.

Leaders mirror and shape our own style and the mise-en-scène of our communities. There is both a religious fervor and a showy materialism in the expensively tailored, double-breasted splendor of Minister Louis Farrakhan's wardrobe, which seemed more than appropriate for the simultaneous right-wing puritanism and conspicuous opulence that the eighties unleashed. But, typical of the subtle complexities of Black men's clothing, a voice so disturbing to the power elite comes robed in the most conciliatory garb.

It has been the history of Black men's style to confound. Who but a Black man would have the nerve and wonderfully perverted sense of style to wear a perm and a suit? Reverend Sharpton in his tracksuit, cow chain, and coiffure is a stereotype waiting to happen. In his suit, he gets people to pause. He has not tempered his rabble-rousing message, but for those who snicker, the joke may be on them, since he has used his style to make himself a distinct presence in the community and a mediagenic politician in an age of visual communication.

Few are the prominent men who have incorporated distinctive African touches into their career style. It is a look Mr. Mfume wears both day and evening. But for the most part, celebratory kente cummerbunds and dashing adinkra-print tuxedos come out at night, when the mood turns festive. Perhaps it is too brazen a political statement to wear a Bogolan print shirt or a kente tie in America's boardrooms or academic halls. Our visible Black men already seem to infuse their look with some kind of ephemeral Africanness, which may have to do with the way they wear a suit or even the way they wear their hair.

For several of them—Reverend Sharpton, Reverend Jackson, Mr. West, Mr. Gates, Mr. Mfume, and their philosophical forbears—facial hair has pride of place. Mr. West's playful goatee and Reverend Jackson's carefully clipped mustache are a distinctive part of their style. It is through their facial hair that these men are quietly proclaiming resistance to the system they are fighting against, a system that measures immersion and willingness to toe the line by a clean-cut jaw. Facial hair may be for many of our men—who do not wish to go the more youthful or creative route of balding the head—the ultimate rebellious style statement. Or then again, it may just be that they've had too many painful razor bumps.

Mayor Willie Brown, profilin' with his posse, the San Francisco Police Department: Brown is known as a West Coast dandy and favors pinstriped, double-breasted Italian suits (left). Brown's East Coast counterpart, former New York mayor David Dinkins, is also a dandy, one whose taste leans toward elegant English conservatism (above).

Jesse JACKSON

"LUMINARIES"

The men of substance who I have encountered over the years are not remembered for the clothes they wore, but for a sermon they gave or a statement they made. Men like Dr. Martin Luther King, Benjamin Mays, Howard Thurman, and Dr. Sam Procter believed that ideas were the measure of a person. I believe that a man's clothes should complement his personality, not supplement it. I don't want my clothes to be a distraction. I wear basic colors, striped ties with plain shirts, plain ties with striped shirts. Ultimately, I'm more concerned about where I'm seen than what I'm seen wearing. I want to be seen at a factory fighting for workers. I want to be seen in schools inspiring children. I want to be seen registering someone to vote, or negotiating a business opportunity for Black people. I want to be seen advancing democracy in Africa, or helping an abandoned family in a slum area. And I don't want my clothes to steal the thunder from my actions.

One of my favorite things to wear is my "swear-in" suit. It's a basic short-sleeved safari suit. It's called a "swear-in" because when President William V. S. Tubman of Liberia died, his successor, President William R. Tolbert, who farmed in a similar type of suit, drove all the way from the country and was inaugurated in it. I like the ease it offers me. I don't want to be in a position where I'm afraid to pick up a baby because he might drool on me or to embrace a ditchdigger for fear of getting my clothes soiled. I don't want clothes to stand between me and people.

Nowadays a lot of our kids wear the baggy-butt britches. Britches hanging off their butts, and tennis shoes with no strings in them. As far as I'm concerned, that style comes from jail culture, where inmates can't wear belts and shoelaces because they may hurt themselves or somebody. So jail culture is being recycled in the name of hipness, when in fact that appearance limits your options when you are looking for a job.

Frankly, for many of our people, style has become a substitute for substance, resulting in some of the poorest people wearing some of the most expensive clothes. Unfortunately, our tastes often assure self-esteem deficits. Just look at the statistics: We drink the highest-priced Scotch, drive the most expensive cars. Wealthy people don't wear their dollars like that. Look at President Clinton—he's an American president and he wears plain suits. We overcompensate, covering up a deep feeling of inferiority.

It's not that I don't appreciate some style, but, I declare, to see some of our kids . . . Our kids, the poorest kids, are having style competitions every day, and it's not right. That's the reason I'm for school uniforms. With clothes no longer an issue, the real issues get addressed—for example, can you type? Can you read and write? But then, if school uniforms do become mandatory, I suppose Calvin Klein will start making some. So we need to make sure that we, too, are manufacturing some.

MOSHOOD

DESIGNER

The name Moshood has become synonymous with a style that personifies African pride. Originally from Lagos, Nigeria, Moshood arrived in New York in the early eighties. After years of tireless effort, he opened his first boutique in Brooklyn, New York. It bears his name.

Moshood's timeless collection of clothing combines the traditional beauty of African tailoring with a Western edge. His fluid, decorative designs have been embraced from Harlem to Soweto and by such celebrity clients as Wesley Snipes, Isaac Hayes, and Maxi Priest. While there are no hard and fast rules to dressing with ethnicity, Moshood, based on his bicontinental lifestyle and his appreciation of traditional African fabrics, offers a few guidelines for incorporating multiculturalism into clothes.

Ethnic STYLE

So you want to wear your culture on your sleeve? For some, ethnic style means donning a regal, embroidered Agbada, the traditional dress of many West African men, slipping on a pair of babous, those butter-soft leather slippers worn by many brothers from the motherland, and topping it off with a fila or kufi cap. For others, ethnic style equals the use of just a few exotic elements to jazz up a traditional wardrobe. Regardless of how it's interpreted by the individual, ethnic style is a wonderful means of personal expression.

FABRICS

Part of the beauty of dressing with ethnicity is the opportunity to select from an international array of interesting fabrics—materials that wouldn't typically be part of a Western-style ensemble. Some of the techniques used to make certain fabrics, such as ikat from Morocco, kente from Nigeria, or kuba from Mali, are as interesting as the end result. Kente, for example, is produced by a popular African textile-making technique known as float weave, in which brightly colored threads are floated above the weaving of the main fabric base.

"In traditional African dress," Moshood explains, "it's the fabric you choose that determines whether an outfit is formal or casual." Bogolan, also known as mudcloth, a rugged cotton fabric worn in rural areas of Mali, is considered casual, while aso okes, regarded as the fabrics "of royalty," are reserved for special occasions. Furthermore, fabrics can be used to make an authentic statement, as exemplified by a dashiki made from printed Kanga cotton, or an inspired statement, as seen in Western-style accessories such as belts decorated with Ndebele beadwork. Ethnic fabrics allow the wearer to delve into rich textures and

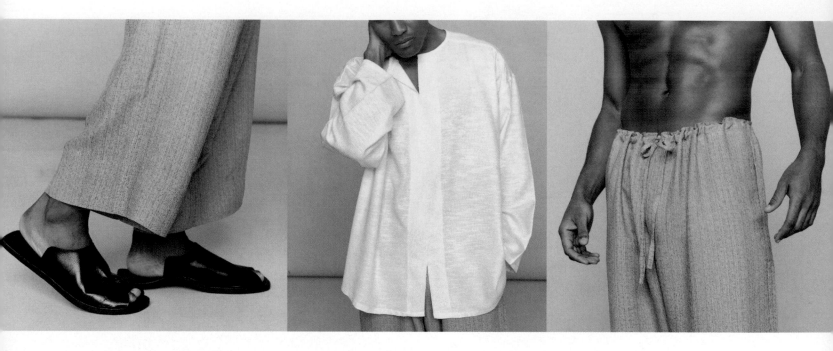

vivid colors. "People of African descent should express themselves in color," says Moshood, "and there are no boundaries when it comes to how color can be used."

PANTS

Ethnic-style pants are loose in construction, with a roomy, non-constricting fit. They may fasten at the waist with a simple drawstring, button-fly, or elastic band. Legs are either tapered or stovepipe-full.

SHIRTS

The most popular choice of ethnic top is the dashiki —the loose-fitting pullover made from either printed or embroidered African cloth. The buba, cut from cotton or linen, differs from the dashiki in its length, which hits anywhere from waist to knee. A Western-style shirt made from an exotic fabric also fits the bill.

FOOTWEAR

Because many of our ethnic looks come from cultures based in warmer climates, sandals are an ideal choice of shoe. Moshood's favorite? "Salubatas from my native Nigeria. They are open-toe leather slides consisting of a sole with a wide strap that goes across the

top of the foot." When sandals are not an option, stick with uncomplicated, organic-shaped shoes that mold to the foot, such as a plain loafer or chukka boot.

ACCESSORIES

Ethnic style offers the option of switching from everyday gold and silver jewelry to more artful pieces made from natural materials such as wood, bone, shell, and semi-precious stones like amber, jade, or turquoise. "I recommend brothers wear bracelets, anklets, and the like," Moshood states. "These types of accessories are not as feminine as most men think. In traditional African dress, men have always adorned themselves with handcrafted jewelry and accessories made from animal materials—medallions made from calf's leather, for example, or amulets fashioned out of fish vertebrae." The mark of handcrafted material is often its imperfection. Such "flaws" make a piece unique, distinguishing it from mass-produced designs. Accessories from Moshood's homeland of Nigeria are heavily embellished with stamped metal plates, stained wooden beads, and cowrie shells—of particular significance, since they were once used as the country's currency.

If it ain't got that SWING

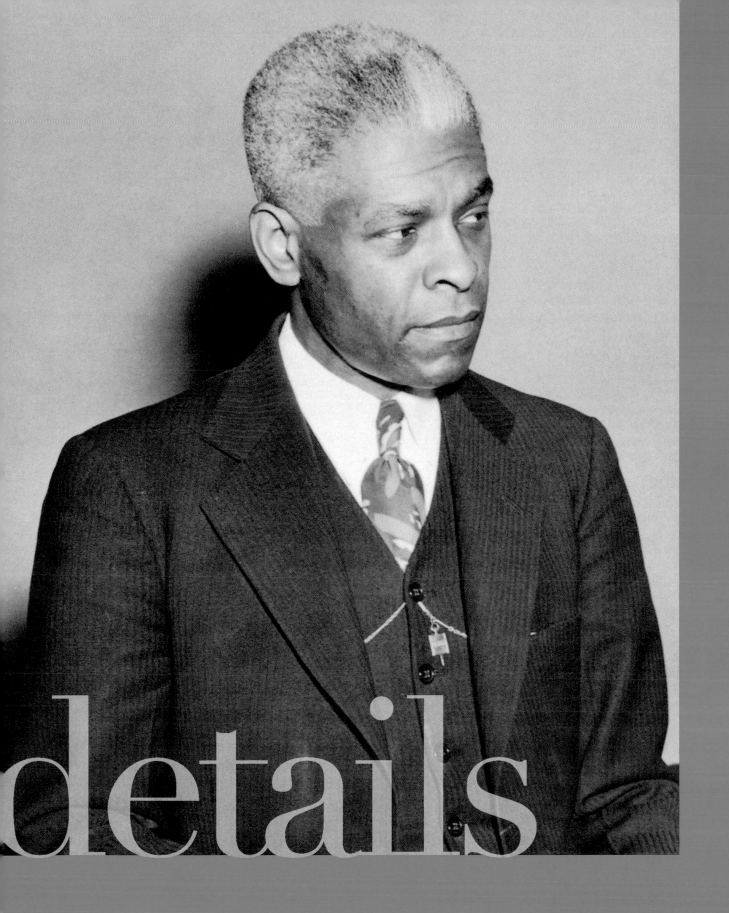

details

"If I'm scheduled to meet you at eight, and I'm ten minutes late, it's because I'm in the third outfit."

WILLIE BROWN

details

PICTURE THE EXCESSIVELY EMBELLISHED

player of the seventies, swathed in jewel-tone silk bandannas and topped with a wide-brimmed, feather-trailing felt "sky." Or the forties zootie, who timed his cool swagger with his long-chained gold pocket-watch. Or Public Enemy's rapper-jester, solid-gold capped teeth spelling out his name, F-L-A-V-O-R F-L-A-V, wall-sized clock pendant telling the people what time it was. Think Duke's thousand-plus necktie collection, Sammy's two-fisted chunky diamond rings, Michael's sequined socks and crystal-beaded glove, Mr. T's feathered earrings and stacks of gold chains. Unique

The details: tonal necktie, pocket fob, silk square *(previous spread, left)*. President emeritus Dr. Benjamin Elijah Mays created the image of the dapper "Morehouse man" *(previous spread, right)*. A full-knotted, striped silk cravat signaled ambition *(top)*. Despite the discomfort it caused, a stiff high collar was de rigueur in the early 1900s *(above)*. In the thirties, a gentleman of means faced the cold in belted bankers coat and bowler *(right)*. Shave, haircut, manicure, shoe shine: Satchel Paige got the works *(opposite, top)*. A leisurely young man sported a costume fit for a little lord: Note the white linen plus fours, silk stockings, and cap-toe lace-ups *(opposite, bottom)*.

accessories can mean everything to a Black man's identity. Onlookers may call it ostentatious, but this meticulous attention to detail is what sets Black men apart when it comes to style.

Accessories such as jewelry, glasses, belts, and neckwear act as messengers, conveying the impressions we want to impart. They're the element of a man's wardrobe that reveals a little more about his personality and tastes. Black men in America have taken full advantage of this opportunity to make such an individual statement.

Having been severed from their African heritage and bound by slavery to America, Black men had little chance of passing down family heirlooms such as treasured clothing or jewelry. Over the course of our assimilation, we embraced the primarily English customs of speech, worship, and dress, as did other immigrants. (Mainstream menswear in America has always taken its cues from British royalty, with its strict dictates on everything from waistcoats to cuff links.) It was only in the early twentieth century that, as Black men began to make their mark in business, sports, and entertainment, led by such pioneers as Alonzo F. Herndon, Jesse Owens, and Paul Robeson, they were able to once again allot some of their attention to their image and, eventually, to their African identity.

Musician and composer Ferdinand Joseph La Menthe Morton, better known back in the twenties as "Jelly Roll," is remembered for wearing a pearl-gray derby, checkered vest, ascot accented with diamond stickpin, spats, patent leather shoes, and signature jeweled arm-band. Such a high level of accessorizing was a sign of respect for his audience. From Nat "King" Cole to Bobby Short, Black entertainers have maintained this tradition for nearly a century. But no one better illustrated this confident elegance and double-take-inducing extravagance than world-champion boxer Jack Johnson. Known for owning hundreds of hand-made shoes, natty hats, and gem-encrusted walking sticks, Johnson was legendary for his fashionable flamboyance. Finis Farr, in his book *Black Champion:*

The Life and Times of Jack Johnson (Scribner, 1964), described the boxer abroad, on a trip to Britain:

"He walked one afternoon down Piccadilly, wearing a biscuit-colored silk suit and a pale, soft golden hat, of the style known as the tribly, after Du Maurier's famous novel. A silk bandanna trailed from the pocket of his jacket, and he tapped the pavement with a black, silver-headed walking stick, almost prancing in shoes made of doeskin and crocodile."

The flair with which notable Black men such as Johnson wore their clothing inspired many and repulsed some. But their treatment of the finishings could not be ignored. Be it in prosperous or impoverished times, Black men stayed sharp. The zoot suit of the forties inspired equally outlandish accessories, such as heavyweight gold-plated watch chains, severely pointed calfskin suede shoes, super-duper wide-brimmed hats, and cartoonishly exaggerated, eight-inch-square bow ties (see: Cab Calloway).

On the political front, the legacy of haberdashery may have been slightly more subdued, but its impact was just as powerful on our collective image. The quiet elegance of some of our loudest voices for

Sammy Davis, Jr., the king of sting, piled on the chunky rocks: It was Mr. D., not Mr. T, who first promoted the layered-jewelry look *(above)***. Fats Domino tickled the ivories with matching wristwatch and pinkie ring, monogrammed shirt cuff, and gemstone cuff link** *(right)***. In 1963, Malcolm X embodied the sparse modernism of the Nation of Islam** *(opposite, top)***. Renauld White made history as the first Black model to appear on the cover of** *Gentlemen's Quarterly* **(opposite, bottom).**

social change was critical to establishing a platform from which, one day, more elaborately outfitted brothers would speak. As an advertisement for the classic American clothier Paul Stuart stated: "A proper function of the business suit is to offer a man a decent privacy so that irrelevant reactions are not called into play prejudice what would be purely business transactions." If only it was that easy.

A graduate of the all-male, historically Black, Morehouse College in Atlanta, Georgia, the Reverend Dr. Martin Luther King, Jr. was a walking, talking example of detail in dress. As did most men in the fifties and sixties, King practically lived in a suit. Whether he was preaching, speaking, marching, or "sitting-in," King was always a well-put-together brother whose details softly shouted pride in appearance: Perpetually shined oxfords, monogrammed cotton handkerchiefs, the ever-present slim gold tie-clip, or the benchmark felt Borsalino hat, dented with only enough flair to keep him a "man of the cloth," Dr. King's focus on the minute details was readily apparent. Fellow "Morehouse man" Dr. Lawrence Edward Carter remembers Martin's nickname at "the house"—"Tweedy," for his clean tweeds. The future reverend was also voted a "best-dressed" student. Having been bestowed with such titles so early in his journey, and by his fellow men, no less, Dr. King had the look of a leader long before he became one.

Accessories never meant more than they did in the excessive seventies, but, for the record, not all Black men were "pimpin', " "hustlin', " or "jive talkin'." Although completely cognizant of the images attached to the aforementioned terms, many Black men, regardless of personal style, were busy continuing the work of the slain Dr. King. One such leader is former speaker of the California State Assembly and mayor of San Francisco Willie Brown, who in the seventies referred to his look as "bold conservative." Infamous for his fastidious self-adornment, Brown felt strongly that "all males should look like peacocks—but not in costume." Notorious for his signature thousand-dollar Brioni suits, his

numerous "best-dressed" mentions, and his politically unheard-of closet photo features in *Gentlemen's Quarterly*, Brown has a talent for combining quality with flash, creating looks that turn heads but could never be classified as trendy. His yellow silk tuxedo or smooth seven-and-five-eighths-sized Borsalino crown have marked him as a man known for style. Legendary for his lateness, Brown attributes the mild character flaw to his love of fashion—indicative of an attention to detail that's 100 percent politically correct.

This commonality of cool threads and fine details connects Black men. Although our existence in America is politically, socially, and economically diverse, most of us consciously maintain a tie to that widely regarded birthplace of style innovation, the streets. Street style is an ongoing movement. It can be emulated but never predicted, imitated but never packaged, because the moment it's spotlighted, it automatically evolves. Black men have been leaders of this detailed beat throughout the twentieth century, and in the sport- and music-saturated eighties and nineties their influence has been all but overwhelming. The distribution of details is apparent in the appearance of acclaimed auteur Spike Lee, who has turned the baseball cap into the American equivalent of the director's beret. It's obvious in the gold-hooped left ear of basketball miracle-worker Michael Jordan. It was out-loud-and-proud in literary expatriate James Baldwin's cosmopolitan silk ascots. Thanks to men of color and style, such previously anti-establishment accoutrements are suddenly considered acceptable. But the originators themselves don't wear their details as expressions of deviancy. Instead, they're statements of individuality, worn with pride. "Accessorizing" in the traditional sense of the word may not do justice to the sartorial accomplishments of Black men in America, for accessorizing implies the incidental addition of minor style details, whereas, for men of color, these supposedly secondary particulars have inspired international trends.

Brothers in the seventies brought on the funk, mixing textures, patterns, and proportions: Wide-brimmed hats, chrome-plated shades, window-pane plaids, bathrobe-wrapped sweater coats, studded leather trenches, high-shined spectator shoes—what was left? *(opposite).* **Actor Wesley Snipes incorporates Afrocentric elements into traditional Hollywood glamour: His silver mask ring acts as a subtle yet striking accent** *(above).*

My style is all about the details, an eclectic mix of influences. If something looks good on somebody and I think I can work it, I'll try it. I steal whenever I can. My favorite accessory is my beret. I only own one; it's navy-blue. But the most basic element a Black man can have in his wardrobe is a light blue dress shirt. There is nothing more flattering on brown skin than classic oxford-blue. You can throw it on under a suit or layer it on top of a white T-shirt and a pair of well-worn khakis. It's a wardrobe refresher.

Renauld WHITE

"DETAILS"

I grew up in Newark, New Jersey, and at the time it was home to a large community of musicians, artists, writers, and bohemians. They had the coolest counterculture style: the sandals that they wore, the black turtlenecks, the corduroy pants, the mufflers, even the occasional pipe. It was definitely nontraditional. My father was also always impeccably dressed in his off-hours. He was a truck driver, but the moment he jumped out of his rig and into a suit you would have thought he was a lawyer. It had to do with the way he carried himself. Being from the South, he had a dignified carriage and a dynamic presence.

My favorite era in Black male style would have to be the early sixties. The influence then of Black Muslims on Black men of any religion! They wore three-button suits, crisp white shirts, very plain ties. Hair was cut close to the scalp. Horn-rimmed glasses completed the look. The overall effect was that of "simple elegance," long before it was in vogue. It was completely modern, and what was so powerful was the fact that, in its most immaculate form, it was direct, authoritative, and intimidating. The Muslims' sharp style details set a new standard. How they dressed!

As one of the first prominent Black models, and the first to be on the cover of a national magazine (*GQ*, November 1979), I felt a responsibility to present the best possible positive image of Black men in print. In my field, being stylish was the equivalent of being professional—this is where the details came into play—and I also just wanted to kick a little ass! When I see the ease with which Black models book jobs today, I see the fruits of my labor. I hope that our collective efforts continue to broaden the scope of our public image and to open doors for brothers behind us. With all of the pain and obstacles, I still love being a Black man.

Tyson BECKFORD

"DETAILS"

My double-breasted navy-blue pinstriped suit reminds me of the Black style of the forties. It says gangster and sexy at the same time. I can't live without it. It's the basis of my wardrobe, the first suit I ever bought. Then I went on to my gray pinstriped, my solid black, my navy.

The details are what make a fabulous suit shine. I wish more men were aware of the importance of owning a custom-made suit. The fit is guaranteed to flatter your physique, and you never need to worry about anyone trying to borrow it from your closet. I also have a thing for dress shirts with French cuffs. Shirts with standard buttoned cuffs are too basic for my taste. I enjoy choosing sophisticated cuff links to complement my shirts. With my ties, it's important that they be knotted to perfection. Whether it's a necktie or a bow tie, I take the time to get it right. It's definitely a challenge to learn how to tie a bow tie, but the end result is well worth the stress. It looks so much better than the clip-on versions many men opt for. I recommend all brothers learn to tie all types of ties and leave those clip-ons alone. When it comes to jewelry, I keep it simple and sport my diamond studs, which always go well with a pinstriped suit.

Black male style is more than what you see on sports stars and celebrities. We are a people of style, a style that is historically rooted in our many cultures. For me, it's a combination of my West Indian roots and my American upbringing. But no matter what we wear, we wear it with a pride that sets us apart. It's something that Americans of all races admire and attempt to emulate.

Leonard BRIDGES

ACCESSORY DESIGNER

Accessory designer Leonard Bridges trained at La Chambre Syndicale de la Haute Couture Parisienne in France. Now based in New York, he has nearly two decades of experience in the industry, creating pieces for such high-profile clients as Calvin Klein, Isaac Mizrahi, Nicole Miller, Liz Claiborne, Pierre Cardin, and Evan Picone.

Accessories are a matter of personal taste. Relying on his razor eye for the minute nuances of men's haberdashery, Bridges shares some loose guidelines on how the man of color should approach accessorizing as a means of expressing individual style.

While clothing is a necessity, accoutrement is an option. Oftentimes, men either overdo the details, or avoid them altogether—for fear of the former. If used incorrectly, accessories can ruin an otherwise solid ensemble. But accessories play a pivotal role in one's total presentation, providing the finishing touches: Picture Cab Calloway's pocket-watch chain glittering against the fabric of his baggy zoot suit pants, or Jimi Hendrix's brass-buttoned military jackets accented with jewel-toned sashes.

BUILDING A COLLECTION

There are few hard-and-fast rules to follow when choosing accessories. The best way to begin is by considering the situation at hand, what sort of look it calls for, and how those demands can be met without compromising your personal style. Accessories should be purchased separately, based on their individual design. It is a common mistake for men to try to buy such items as ties, cuff links, and belts when they're buying a suit. By trying to complete a look in a single shopping trip, the choice of accessories is often based on time constraints or a sense of obligation—in other words, "Well, while I'm here, I may as well pick up a pair of blue socks to go with my blue shirt and my blue jacket." Instead, men should regard accessory-buying as an ongoing process. Bridges concurs, "If you see something that's great, trust your taste and grab it. Ultimately, if you like it, you'll use it."

BELTS

True style leaders know that quality stands above quantity. Some men try to have a corresponding belt for every pant, but it's better to invest in a few pieces made from good leather. Wearing a belt that was included with the trousers is out of the question.

An easy way to determine the craftsmanship in a belt is to try what Bridges calls "the scratch test." He explains, "Lightly scratch the surface of the skin with your fingernail. If this leaves a mark, you'll know the belt is made of a finer leather because it is similar to your skin, it should react in the same way. If it doesn't, the leather is of lesser quality or has been treated with a synthetic coating, such as PVC, to hide flaws." The stitches should be durable. The thread should have some weight, and be closed with a clean finish, to prevent unraveling. And the hardware should simply be a solid metal cast. Plating on buckles and closures has a tendency to wear off with use. Unless that's your intention, to affect a sort of "shabby-chic" look, choose a solid metal such as brass, which actually ages along with the leather, both getting better over time.

BRACES

Sadly, some of us still insist on wearing braces and a belt together. Brothers, once and for all, this is a fashion faux pas, an instant indicator of bad style. Since both braces and belts serve the same purpose—to help keep one's pants up—it is never necessary to use both simultaneously. When choosing suspenders, look for interesting patterns on the ribbon which suit your day-to-day. For quality's sake, only purchase suspenders that are finished with leather buttonhole keepers.

CUFF LINKS AND TIE TACKS

Cuff links and tie tacks are best kept simple: not too conspicuous, and always made of precious metals. If set with a stone, make sure it is enameled. Jewels should be precious or semi-precious.

In place of cuff links, many men opt for the softer silk "monkey knot," which allows for a wide variety of color choices, both rich solids and twisted multicolors. Contrary to popular belief, silk knots are not inherently more casual than cuff links. According to Bridges, "They can be used for all occasions. Solids should be worn with shirts having a small stripe." By the same token, multicolored knots complement solid shirts.

POCKET SQUARES AND HANDKERCHIEFS

Not since the days of Adam Clayton Powell, Jr. have pocket squares been so popular among well-dressed men of color. From silk to cotton, from wild prints to classic, hand-rolled, solid whites, the options are end-

less. "Of course," Bridges comments, "the fabric should be color-coordinated with the corresponding shirt, tie, and suit." The detail is in the folding. The style of the fold is often a matter of personal taste, but Bridges prefers a fold that uses the center of the square as the tip—unless the square is a starched cotton handkerchief, in which case the actual edge of the fabric works better as the point.

TIES

Sartorially speaking, the tie is the equivalent of a calling card. It conveys a message about who you are before you even open your mouth to speak. Simple, straightforward patterns executed in subtle colors come across as serious yet independent. Prints, ethnic patterns, paisleys, and, depending on the time of year, even soft florals state that the wearer is more of a free spirit, willing to take risks and bend rules.

COLLAR STAYS

Collar stays are a stylish gentleman's invisible friends. These small support tabs help to keep a dress shirt collar at attention, thereby providing a crisp "frame" for a necktie. Today, many shirts are manufactured with plastic stays, but these are temporary fixes and are not meant to be reused, although they can be. "Whatever you do," Bridges cautions, "don't iron your collars while stays are in place—their impression will live on long after they're gone." In addition to plastic, collar stays are also available in stainless steel, brass, and, for the decadent, sterling silver. Metal stays make the collar all the more firm, and provide a sharper edge.

SOCKS

"Socks serve the line," says the frequently sockless Bridges. "They act as a liaison between shoe and pant." When wearing socks, it's best not to contrast your shoe or pant. A solid flow of color makes for a cleaner statement. For example, if it's black shoes, it's very dark or black socks.

ROCKS

Jewelry is the utlimate indicator of personal style, but it, too, has its place. Business is business and, other than perhaps a status wristwatch, flashy jewelry just doesn't belong in the boardroom. But depending upon the profession, there is room for expression. Those in arts-oriented fields, such as music or film, may have more leeway with heavy link chains, i.d. bracelets, even various piercings.

CelebrityBIOGRAPHIES

WYNTON MARSALIS (pp. 26–27) is largely responsible for bringing jazz back to center stage in American culture. An accomplished musician and composer, he has recorded over thirty jazz and classical albums and has performed in more than thirty countries. He is the artistic director for the internationally acclaimed Jazz at Lincoln Center program, which he cofounded in 1987. *Blood on the Fields*, Marsalis's epic oratorio on slavery, was awarded the 1997 Pulitzer Prize for music, making him the first jazz artist to be so honored.

GEORGE BENSON (pp. 34–35), popular for his fluid vocal stylings, is also a prodigious jazz guitarist and has performed alongside such notables as McCoy Tyner, Chick Corea, Lionel Hampton, Tito Puente, and Wynton Marsalis. His 1976 album *Breezin'* was the first jazz recording to sell a million copies, and his crossover hits include "On Broadway" and "Give Me the Night." His most recent release, *That's Right*, showcases his instrumental talents as well as his uncanny ability to scat and play at the same time.

BILL T. JONES (pp. 48–49), a 1994 recipient of a MacArthur Fellowship, began his dance training at the State University of New York at Binghamton. After several years of choreographing and performing as a soloist, he cofounded the Bill T. Jones/Arnie Zane Dance Company in 1982. He has originated more than fifty works for such venues as Lincoln Center and the Brooklyn Academy of Music, and has received commissions to create dances for, among others, the Alvin Ailey American Dance Theater, Boston Ballet Company, and Berlin Opera Ballet. Many of his works have been broadcast on national television, including the critically acclaimed *Still/Here*. His memoir, *Last Night on Earth* (Pantheon), was published in 1995.

ISAAC HAYES (pp. 58–59), a pioneer of R&B, paved the way for soul singers such as Barry White, Curtis Mayfield, and Marvin Gaye. Initially a keyboard session player for Otis Redding, Hayes went on to form a songwriting and production partnership with David Porter: The duo was behind all of Sam & Dave's hits and those of many other artists on the legendary Stax record label. Hayes was instrumental in the introduction of Black artists into the field of soundtrack recording and is best known for his theme song from the Blaxploitation pop-culture classic *Shaft*.

ED BRADLEY (pp. 70–71), as an anchor of the award-winning news program *60 Minutes*, has provided viewers with an in-depth look at world events every Sunday evening for nearly twenty years. Prior to joining the program in 1981, he worked as a principal correspondent for *CBS Reports*, a White House correspondent for CBS News, and an anchor of the *CBS Sunday Night News*. He began his career at the network in 1971 as a stringer in its Paris bureau, was transferred to Saigon after a year, and was wounded while on assignment in Cambodia in 1973. He has been honored with Robert F. Kennedy Journalism, George Polk, Alfred I. duPont, George Foster Peabody, and Overseas Press Club awards, as well as eleven Emmys.

BRYANT GUMBEL (pp. 78–79), a veteran television news personality, has reported from all corners of the globe—Europe, China, Australia, Russia, Cuba, Africa, and the Middle East. Before joining CBS in 1997, he spent nearly twenty-five years at NBC, hosting the *Today* show for an unprecedented fifteen. As an NBC correspondent, he covered the outbreak of the Persian Gulf War from Saudi Arabia and the tenth anniversary of the fall of Saigon from Ho Chi Minh City. He is the recipient of, among several other honors, an Edward R. Murrow Award for his interviews with top Kremlin officials, a George Foster Peabody Award for his work in Vietnam, four Emmy awards, and three NAACP Image awards.

SAMUEL L. JACKSON (pp. 92–93) made an indelible mark on American cinema with his portrayal of "Jules," the philosophizing hitman in Quentin Tarantino's *Pulp Fiction*. The performance earned him Academy Award and Golden Globe nominations, along with unanimous critical acclaim. His film credits include *Eve's Bayou*, which he also produced, *Jackie Brown, The Negotiator*, and *A Time to Kill*. His depiction of a crack addict in Spike Lee's *Jungle Fever* prompted the jury at the 1991 Cannes Film Festival to create a special Best Supporting Performance Award exclusively for him. Best known for his work in film, Jackson has also performed for television and on stage: He originated roles in two of August Wilson's plays at Yale Repertory, "Boy Willie" in *The Piano Lesson* and "Wolf" in *Two Trains Running*.

ANDRÉ DE SHIELDS (pp. 102–103) created the flamboyant title character in the 1975 Broadway musical *The Wiz*. An actor, director, and educator, his role in *Play On!* earned him Tony, Drama Desk, and Friends of the New York Theatre award nominations in 1997. His credits include *Hair, The Me Nobody Knows, Warp, Ain't Misbehavin'*, for which he won an Emmy, and numerous other film and television projects. He has served as a visiting professor at the University of Michigan at Ann Arbor and at Southern Methodist University in Texas. During the 1992–1993 season, De Shields directed Carnegie Hall's Jazzed program, aimed at restoring the arts to public schools. He is also an active member of Actors' Equity Association and holds a seat on its national council.

BILLY DEE WILLIAMS (pp. 104–105), with his portrayal of "Louis McKay" in 1972's *Lady Sings the Blues*, became one of the first Black male sex symbols to break barriers and achieve crossover appeal. A pop-culture icon for his roles in such modern-day favorites as *Brian's Song, Mahogany, The Empire Strikes Back, Return of the Jedi,* and *Batman,* with more than twenty-five films to his credit, Williams is also an accomplished painter.

AHMAD RASHAD (pp. 118–119) holds the Minnesota Viking career receptions lead (400) and is second in reception yardage. A first-round draft choice of the St. Louis Football Cardinals in 1972, he went on to play for the Buffalo Bills and Seattle Seahawks before settling in Minnesota for seven seasons. In 1983, he joined NBC Sports as an NFL commentator. His broadcasting résumé includes from-the-field reporting and in-studio hosting as well as analysis and commentary. Since the beginning of the 1990–1991 NBA season, he has also served as a courtside basketball reporter. He earned an Emmy for his coverage of the 1988 Seoul Olympics.

REGGIE MILLER (pp. 126–127), all-star guard for the Indiana Pacers, has been a scoring leader in the NBA for more than ten years: He finished the 1996–1997 season with 1,432 career three-pointers—the second-highest scoring in NBA history—and he became the first player ever to hit over one hundred three-pointers in eight consecutive seasons (1989–1997). He was also a member of the gold-medal-winning 1996 U.S. Olympic Basketball Team. During the off-season, he runs a basketball camp for kids and serves as a commentator for Lifetime's coverage of the WNBA.

GREGORY HINES (pp. 140–141), dancer, singer, and actor, exemplifies the word *multitalented.* He won the 1992 Best Actor in a Musical Tony Award for his riveting portrayal of jazzman "Jelly Roll" Morton in George C. Wolfe's Broadway production of *Jelly's Last Jam.* Other theater credits include *Sophisticated Ladies, Eubie,* and *Comin' Uptown.* Hines has been featured in such films as *A Rage in Harlem, The Cotton Club, White Nights,* and *Waiting to Exhale,* and he is currently appearing on CBS's *The Gregory Hines Show.* He began tap-dancing at the age of two and turned professional when he was five, performing with his older brother, Maurice, as the Hines Kids.

SAVION GLOVER (pp. 148–149) is the hip-hoppin' heir apparent to the legacy of legendary American hoofers. For his 1996 Broadway smash hit *Bring in Da' Noise, Bring in Da' Funk,* he won the Tony, Drama Desk, and Outer Critics Circle awards for choreography, and two Obies for his performance. Glover made his Broadway debut at the age of twelve, playing the lead in *The Tap Dance Kid.* Additional Broadway credits include *Black and Blue* and *Jelly's Last Jam.* At thirteen, he made his feature film debut alongside Gregory Hines and Sammy Davis, Jr. in *Tap.* On television, he was a series regular on *Sesame Street* for five seasons.

LL COOL J (pp. 160–161) burst onto the hip-hop scene when the form was still in its infancy, a rebel MC in sneakers and Kangol hats. Since his auspicious emergence in 1985, he has evolved from rap sensation to seasoned entertainer. With more than twenty million albums sold, he is one of the most successful hip-hop artists in history: He was the first rap artist to release a single and subsequent album on the now-legendary Def Jam Records label, the first to amass six consecutive platinum-plus-selling albums, and the first to go acoustic, performing on MTV's *Unplugged* in 1991. His hits include "I Need Love," "Going Back to Cali," "Around the Way Girl," "Mama Said Knock You Out," which won the 1990 Grammy Award for Best Rap Solo, and "Hey Lover," which received the same honor in 1996. *I Make My Own Rules,* his autobiography, was published by St. Martin's Press in 1997. His acting credits include *Krush Groove, The Hard Way, Toys,* and *Halloween–H$_2$O,* and he currently stars in the UPN's sitcom *In the House.*

RUSSELL SIMMONS (pp. 160–161) launched his career in the music business in 1979, while a student at City College of New York. Recognizing the cultural and financial potential of hip-hop, then a new urban art form, he began managing and promoting a roster of rappers, including Kurtis Blow, RUN-DMC, The Beastie Boys, and Public Enemy. As the founder, chairman, and CEO of Rush Communications, Inc., he oversees an ever-expanding multimedia empire that includes Def Jam Recordings and Phat Fashions. His Def Pictures division coproduced *The Nutty Professor,* starring Eddie Murphy, and *Gridlock'd,* starring Tim Roth and Tupac Shakur; his Russell Simmons Television (RSTV) division produces the popular HBO weekly series *Def Comedy Jam,* a program that has furthered the careers of Martin Lawrence, Bill Bellamy, and Steve Harvey, among others.

SEAN "PUFFY" COMBS (pp. 172–173), the president of Bad Boy Entertainment, has single-handedly revolutionized the popular music industry by resurrecting classics from the sixties, seventies, and eighties and pairing them with new raps: "I'll Be Missing You," a tribute to the Notorious B.I.G. composed of Puffy's rhymes,

Faith Evans's vocals, and samples from The Police's "Every Breath You Take," went triple-platinum in the United Sates and sold more than 4.5 million copies internationally. Combs has produced such blockbuster acts as Aretha Franklin, Boyz II Men, Mariah Carey, Lil' Kim, Heavy D & The Boyz, Mary J. Blige, and The Notorious B.I.G.

MAXWELL (pp. 188–189), a nouveau soul singer, began writing songs as a teenager: He penned more than three-hundred from his bedroom in East New York, Brooklyn. He introduced his sound through his debut album, *Urban Hang Suite,* released in 1996 and certified platinum in 1997. In *Embrya,* his second studio album, his smooth, sensual vocals ride above warm keyboards and honeyed strings, funky bass lines and strong grooves. He interprets ballads, Latin-tinged grooves, soul, and funk. *Maxwell Unplugged,* an EP of his MTV performance, featured acoustic versions of such hits as "Ascension" and "Whenever Wherever Whatever," along with covers of Kate Bush's "This Woman's Work" and Trent Reznor's "Closer."

LENNY KRAVITZ (pp. 196–197), a rock-and-roll chameleon, rejects anything resembling borders, boxes, or limitations, preferring instead to embrace a wide range of influences in his music. His outlook reflects his upbringing: A child of two cultures, he grew up half-Bahamian, half-Jewish, in New York City. A multi-instrumentalist, playing eveything from guitar to mini-moog to beer bottles for percussion, Kravitz produces a textured noise that combines the best of rock, rap, gospel, and funk. His albums include *Let Love Rule, Mama Said, Are You Gonna Go My Way, Circus,* and 5.

CORNEL WEST (pp. 210–211) graduated magna cum laude from Harvard University in 1973 and completed his Ph.D. studies at Princeton in 1980. He returned to Princeton in 1987 as professor of religion and director of the Afro-American studies department, then moved to Harvard, where he is currently professor of Afro-American studies and philosophy of religion. He is one of the first Black scholars to be appointed university professor, an honor held by only 14 of Harvard's 2,200 faculty members. An advocate of community-based political action, West has worked with former U.S. senator Bill Bradley, Czech President Vaclav Havel, the

Reverend Jesse Jackson, Bishop Desmond Tutu, and President Bill Clinton. He is the author of numerous articles and books, including *Jews and Blacks: A Dialogue on Race, Religion, and Culture in America* (Plume), *Restoring Hope: Conversations on the Future of Black America* (Beacon Press), and *Race Matters* (Vintage).

THE REVEREND JESSE JACKSON (pp. 218–219) is one of America's foremost political figures, known for crossing race, class, gender, and religious lines in the name of peace and unity. A student leader of sit-ins during the civil rights movement, he assisted Dr. Martin Luther King, Jr. and his Southern Christian Leadership Conference throughout the sixties. He was ordained a Baptist minister in 1968. Jackson's two presidential campaigns broke ground in American politics, resulting in the registration of millions of new voters and the election of several Democratic candidates. He is the founder of People United to Save Humanity (PUSH) and The Rainbow Coalition, organizations committed to educational, economic, and political empowerment.

RENAULD WHITE (pp. 232–233) has represented the Black man in everything from luxury car commercials to fashion magazine spreads. His mystique as a model has earned him many firsts: He was the first Black model to appear on the cover of *Gentlemen's Quarterly* (November 1979), the first to promote a nonethnic grooming product, the first to have store mannequins produced in his likeness, and the first and only Black model to have his image placed in a time capsule on the moon. In addition to modeling, he has acted on daytime television in such series as *One Life to Live.*

TYSON BECKFORD (pp. 234–235) is the dynamic, unforgettable image of the high fashion industry today. After only a few years of modeling, his exotic appeal has brought him international recognition. In 1995, Beckford landed an exclusive contract with Polo Ralph Lauren, confirming his status as one of the few male supermodels. He has appeared on the covers of *Paper, Arena,* and *Essence* magazines and has been featured in such leading publications as *Gentlemen's Quarterly, The New York Times Magazine, L'Uomo Vogue,* and *Details. People Weekly* named Beckford one of its 50 Most Beautiful People in 1995 and the Sexiest Male Model in 1997.

Essayist BIOGRAPHIES

THOMAS TERRELL ("Jazz," p. 28) eats, drinks, sleeps—and writes about—jazz. His work has appeared in *Jazz Times*, *Vibe*, and *XXL*, as well as in the liner notes of several contemporary jazz albums, including Shirley Horn's *Light Out of Darkness* and Steel Pulse's *Sound System*. Terrell lives in Brooklyn.

DAVID THIGPEN ("R&B," p. 50), a New-York-based reporter at *Time* magazine, covers the music and fashion industries. His writing has also appeared in *The New York Times*, *Rolling Stone*, and *The Chicago Tribune*.

NICK CHARLES ("Black Men and the Box," p. 72) is a staff writer at *People Weekly*, and a contributing writer for "BET Weekend." Prior to attaining his position at *People*, Charles worked as a features writer for *The New York Daily News* and *The Cleveland Plain Dealer*. His articles have appeared in *The Nation*, *George*, *The Village Voice*, *Essence*, *Emerge*, and *Black Enterprise*.

DEBORAH GREGORY ("Keeping It Reel," p. 94) is a contributor to *Essence* magazine, and has written on topics ranging from entertainment to relationships. Her work has also appeared in *Vibe* and *Mode*.

CRAIG ROSE ("The MVP," p. 120) is an independent fashion copywriter who has written for Tommy Hilfiger U.S.A., Inc., and Liz Claiborne. A graduate of Rutgers University, he is currently writing a series of short stories that explore the various constructs of adolescent Black gay male identity.

GEORGE FAISON ("Reborn in Freedom," p. 142) has been a driving force in theater, film, television, and dance for more than twenty years. He first came to prominence as a principal dancer with the Alvin Ailey American Dance Theater, and went on to choreograph such Broadway hits as *The Wiz*, for which he won a Tony award. Faison has recently added the roles of writer and producer to his repertoire: He was awarded an Emmy for *The Josephine Baker Story*.

JULIA CHANCE ("And It Don't Stop," p. 162) is a freelance writer living in Brooklyn. Her credits include fashion and beauty writer for *Essence*, fashion editor for *The Source*, and associate editor for *Sportstyle* and *Salon News*. She is the coauthor with Sam Fine of *Fine Beauty: Beauty Basics and Beyond for African-American Women* (Broadway, 1997), and currently teaches a fashion magazine course at the Laboratory Institute of Merchandising in New York.

MICHAEL A. GONZALES ("Screams of Fashion," p. 190) is a Blaxploitation baby and coauthor with Havelock Nelson of *Bring the Noise: A Guide to Hip-Hop Culture* (Harmony, 1991). He contributes articles on music and pop culture to such magazines as *Vibe*, *Essence*, and *Mode*. He resides in New York City.

CONSTANCE C. R. WHITE ("Luminaries," p. 212), a veteran of the fashion industry, with senior editorial positions at *Elle* and *Women's Wear Daily* to her credit, is presently a fashion reporter for *The New York Times*. She is also a founding member of Fashion Outreach, a group of industry professionals dedicated to helping young African Americans and Hispanics establish careers in fashion. She is the author of *StyleNoir: The First How-To Guide to Fashion Written with Black Women in Mind* (Perigree, 1998).

ACKNOWLEDGMENTS

First and foremost, I thank God for giving me life, the gift of creativity, and for watching over me at all times, especially during the rigors of writing this book. Also, thank you, Lord, for constantly letting me know that my existence is a part of your master plan by placing such wonderful people in my world who always validate me and my endeavors.

For taking on such a long-overdue celebration of American culture with respect and dignity, a tremendous thanks to the entire dynamic staff at Artisan: Peter Workman, Ann Bramson, Leslie Stoker, Debbie Weiss Geline, Nancy Murray, Tricia Boczkowski, Daria Masullo, Liz Hermann, and Kim Yorio. We are all more informed and stylish for it! Much gratitude to art director Susi Oberhelman for seamlessly combining the contemporary with the classic in her design. And a very special thanks to my power editor Siobhán McGowan, who is now an "Honorary Man of Color," for convincing me to give the legacy of Black male style center stage. You alone burned the midnight oil and, line by line, perfected my voice with enormous care, respect, and attention to detail. You are incredible!

Many thanks to my amazing literary agent Faith Hampton Childs and her staff of consummate professionals, including Emily Bernard, Arlene Stoltz, and Lori Pope. Faith, you "got it" from the onset and nurtured it to perfection—no surprise, since you, too, have impeccable style and taste.

Words barely describe the respect, love, and admiration I have for my mother, Lynell Boston Kollar. Mom, you embody a spirit of perseverance that has its own legacy among strong Black women all over this world. You've found a way to be my sister, my mother, my father, and a best friend all at once. Thank you for being my constant source of inspiration and my biggest fan. (See, those painful back-to-school shopping sprees are starting to pay off!)

Thank you so much to Mr. Quincy Jones for believing in this celebration from its infancy. Your talent and vision is a modern-day phenomenon! As a witness to many of our style eras, your blessing my take on all that we've created is not just an honor but a dubbing by Black style royalty! Your words are the homemade icing on this project, and I am forever grateful. An additional heartfelt thank you to the incredible staff at Quincy Jones Productions—Deborah Foreman, Michelle Whittney-Morrison, the stylish Kidada Jones, Helena Greene, and Arnold Robinson—for making *Men of Color* an ongoing priority.

Many thanks to Mr. André Leon Talley for being an educated voice and a dignified Black presence on the international fashion scene. You tastefully represent the living legacy that is Black male style in circles which may not otherwise have the opportunity to witness our soul and spirit in the flesh. I so appreciate you taking time out of your extremely busy schedule to add your blessing and artful words to this volume.

A very special thank you to the impeccable brotherhood of celebrities who took the time to respond to my invitation and join in this historic celebration. Your generosity and incredible presence let me know that we as Black men will always be able to look to you for inspiration and positive validation. Thank you, Nick Ashford, Tyson Beckford, George Benson, Ed Bradley, Sean "Puffy" Combs, André De Shields, Giancarlo Esposito, Savion Glover, Bryant Gumbel, Isaac Hayes, Gregory Hines, Geoffrey Holder, the Reverend Jesse Jackson, Samuel L. Jackson, Bill T. Jones, Lenny Kravitz, Ed Lewis, LL Cool J, Branford Marsalis, Wynton Marsalis, Maxwell, Reggie Miller, Ahmad Rashad, Tim Reid, Bobby Short, Russell Simmons, Clarence Smith, Larenz Tate, Blair Underwood, Michael Vann, Isaiah Washington, Cornel West, Renauld White, and Billy Dee Williams for

being my founding men of color and for trusting your image to my vision.

To my distinguished cabinet of stylish right-hand men and women who sacrificed days, nights, weekends to work on this book, I thank you from the heart for believing in my concept from the start and for rolling up your sleeves to pull together a million loose ends. Your efforts have helped create a timeless book to be cherished by generations to come.

To my project director and alter ego Craig Rose, who didn't rest until everyone who I felt should be a part of the book obliged, I love you like a brother. Thank you for paying meticulous attention to the details, logistics, and prepublication image of *Men of Color*. It could not have happened without your writing talent, management skills, temperance, and style sensibility regarding every aspect of the project. I am forever grateful to you for your hard work and diligence every step of the way.

To my photographer of choice Matthew Jordan Smith, who understood my vision photographically and captured it in each and every frame. I so appreciate you making yourself available to me in the midst of your many other ad campaigns. Thank you, also, for giving me a constant feeling of creative confidence—you saw yourself through the lens and approached every shot as a potential testament to our collective style history. The results of our photo sessions, often pulled together during hurried lunch breaks, will go down in history!

To my editorial coordinator Julia Chance, thank you, "sista," for losing sleep and assisting me in organizing every element of my manuscript, from chapter titles to guest essayists to celebrity interviews. I so appreciate your wisdom, wit, and seemingly endless memory bank of Black cultural references and facts. Your vision has enhanced the literary essence of my book in ways that are woven deep within the fabric of this style celebration. I could not have done it without you, Jules!

To my style director and mentor Mr. Leonard Bridges, a true arbiter of style and the personification of the *Men of Color* sartorial sensibility: I certainly couldn't have created this book without your razor-sharp eye and your commitment to keeping every original image consistent with our collective legacy. Thank you eternally for understanding my vision and for translating it onto the backs of each and every stellar man of color on these pages. You are style!

To my photo editor extraordinaire Debbie Egan-Chin: Your eye was truly my eye deep in the photo annals of Black male history. What we uncovered is magic and will serve as a new resource for young style-seekers to come. Thank you first for believing in my concept and then for your dedication to excellence in every archival photo you helped to unearth. Debbie, you've made our image shine again! Thanks, too, to photo retoucher John Delecki, for working *his* magic on some well-worn images.

I am honored to be in the company of such a distinguished list of contributing essayists who believed my book to be worthy of their words and stories. Thank you, Julia Chance, Nick Charles, George Faison, Michael Gonzales, Deborah Gregory, Craig Rose, Thomas Terrell, David Thigpen, and Constance C. R. White for adding your voices to the style time capsule we've created.

A thank you to my clever and concise researchers, led by the talented and stylish Mr. Larry Ortiz, whose hard work is present on each page of my book. Thanks to Kelly Beamon, Shannon Crowley Cohen, Erica Johnson, Sharon Frances Moore, Bernard Orr, Tanaji Seabrook, and Cassaundra M. Wilcox for all of your time and resourcefulness.

A special thanks to my team of transcribing experts, led by the always fearless Lynell Boston Kollar. Jill Wells, Cassaundra Wilcox, and Brenda Walker translated my sometimes cryptic celebrity and service-expert interviews, whether taped from my cellular phone, recorded from overseas connections, or scribbled on the occasional cocktail napkin. A big thanks to all of you for turning the words around on a dime, givin' five cents back, keepin' time!

A very special thanks to my corporate sponsors, whose generous contributions and belief in my vision have helped to make *Men of Color* a reality: Tommy Hilfiger U.S.A., Inc.; Rush Communications, Inc.; Eastman Kodak; Schieffelin & Somerset, makers of Johnnie Walker Black Label Scotch, and their top-notch marketing team, Ben Stone, S.V.P., Dan Butling, V.P., Steve Meyers and Manne Marie Megiiola, and their ad agency Vigilante, particularly team members Marc Strachan, Danny Robinson, and Kevin Rhodes.

To my second family at Tommy Hilfiger: I am living proof of your corporate mission. For the past eight years, you've embraced me like a son. First, I am forever grateful to you, Tommy, for keeping me at your side and for allowing me a voice and a hand in your style legacy. The best is yet to come! Huge thanks to Joel Horowitz, Peter Connolly, and Catherine Fisher for embracing the book and recognizing its importance to me and its readership. Thanks also to the always stylish staff at "Tommy" who helped me pull this together out of the kindness of their hearts: Carrie Bartlett, Trudy Byrd, Stephen Cirona, Dina Colombo, Alice Flynn, Jen Haas, Andy Hilfiger, Erica Johnson, Koshawn, Peter Paul Scott, P. J. Rosado, William "Rosie" Roseborough, and the entire staff of the marketing/advertising department. A very special thank you to my creative right hand and confidant Carolyn Iglesias, and to her staff, Sam Truedsson and Jackie Wilson, for taking total care of me in my most stressful moments. You style divas are the best!

I am extremely grateful to the *Men of Color* style experts who taught *me* a few things on how to dress: Jeffrey Banks, Leonard Bridges, Martin Cooper, Tommy Hilfiger, Shaka King, Ademola Mandella, Anthony McIntosh, Moshood, Orin Saunders, Rod Springer, and Star. You men are the professional lifeline of Black male style. Thanks again for sharing your expertise with all of us.

A major thanks to my muse and cover model, the dashing Clayton Hunter, for adorning my book cover with his timeless good looks. Clayton, your inside is just as handsome as your outside. Thanks so much for staying with me from the start. And to my legion of strong, attractive models of color—Boris, Charles and Charlton Cannon, James Davis, Gary, Leo Linton, Craig Rose, Daryl Patterson, Rashid Silvera, and Remy Toh—who gave their time to enhance the pages of my book, I say thanks again and again.

To my talented and timely groomers, Craighton, Aliesh Pierce, Robin Hannibal, Sonya Stephens, Cynde Watson for Bobbi Brown Essentials, and Barry White, thanks for lending your talent and creativity to making everyone photographed for the book look effortlessly stunning.

A special collective thank you to all of the talented photographers from far and wide whose archival images document Black male style in America throughout the book. Thanks for seeing Black men at our best and for capturing the moment forever.

To the many publicists, managers, agents, and assistants to my featured celebrities, including Bjorn Amelan, Joe Varr Andrews, Amy Brownstein, Billie Bullock, Cynthia Cooper, Sheila Cox, Gail D'Agostino, Carole Davis, Nevin Dolcesino, Kristine Dugovic, Allen Eichorn, Rhonda Evans, Charles Fisher, Alicia Fuchs, Beverly Garvin, Stephanie Gurevitz, BethAnn Hardison, Dana Hill, Tyson Kelly, David Kim, Dominic King, Sherry McAdams, Cherita McDowell, Benny Medina, Sheila Morrow, Trish Peters, Christina Papodopolous, Gwendolynn Quinn, Tori Reed, Simone Reyes, Margie Rountree, Mark Satlos, Anne Simmons, Michelle Smith, Rhonda Stein, Genevieve Stewart, Helen Sugland, Malika Thompson, Dennis Turner, Kerri Weisberg, Lorraine Westbrook, Christina Wyeth, a sincere thank you for prioritizing my many requests.

A book of this magnitude could not have been completed without the support, assistance, and words of encouragement from friends and associates who believed in my mission and lent a hand wherever necessary. Thank you to all of the supporters of my project. *Men of Color* is all the better because of the kind deeds volunteered by the following people: Michael Henry Adams, Audra Alexxi, the staff at Artista Photo Services, Lewis Van Arnam, Jelani Bandele, Tyra Banks, Michael Barr, Steve Barr, Jash'd Belcher, Bengali, Emily Bernard, Dr. Angela Bolin, Kelvin Bostick, Mr. Gus and Mrs. Mattie Boston, Martin Bradshaw, Renee Scheffey-Brown, Paul Bruner, Stephen Burrows, Michael Carny, Gordon Chambers, Stephen Chin, the staff at Chroma Copy, Michael Clark, Minnie Clayton, Michael S. Cohen, Mr. Rudy and Mrs. Gina L. Bridges Colleton, Marilyn Couvillon, Mark Coventry, Malcolm Crews, Michael Crowley Cohen, Robert Cusido, Terry J. Deglau, Michael Doyle, Pat Durkin, Patti LaBelle and Armstead Edwards, Muhammida El Muhajir, Epperson, Robert Evans, Donna Faircloth, James Fields, Sam Fine, Regina Flemming, Serita Ford, Garret Fortner, Tony Garriett, Thelma Golden, Henry Goodgame, Benny Gordon, Cristina Grajales, Nicholas Granderson, Mark Hardy, E. Lynn Harris, Michael J. Harris, Allen Harvey, West Hill, bell hooks, Kilee Hughes, Renee Hunter, Toyin Hunter, Brian Keith Jackson, Nicole D. Jenkins, Peter Johnson, Tony Johnson, Tyrone Johnson, Wendy Johnson, Lisa Jones, Veronica Jones, Robert Joseph, Stephane Kenn, Jules Kollar, Clarice Lee, Eugene Lee, Joanne Lee, Dr. Marshall Lee, Margo T. Lewis, Quentin Lynch, Steve Manning, Anne Marcus, Craig Marshall, Rebecca Matticko, Sharon Chatmon Miller, Loleta Mitchell, the staff at My Own Color Lab, Ian Allen and Terra Nash, Jutta Newman, David Orr, Robin Ortiz, Derrick Pinkney, Marni Prather, Richard Presser, Len Prince, Christina Sage, Quigley and Carly, Karla Radford, Jenyne Raines, Dolly Rose, Jackie Smith Roye, Yvette Russell, Jonathan Sanders, Lea Sanders, Dr. Howard Schultz, Ron Scott, Stephanie Scott, Barbara Shaum, Keith Shore, Deborah A. Simmons, M.D., Alexander Smalls, Audrey Smaltz, Adrienne C. Smith, Barbara Smith, Michael Smith, Babatu Sparrow, Michele Stein, Michelle Stoddard, Peter Strongwater, Lydia R. Stuckey, Harmonica Sunbeam, Lori Tesoro, Byl Thompson, Deryck Thompson, Hilda Thompson, Fofana Tidiani, Rubi Times, Howard Tomlinson, Darian Trotter, Cathy Tucker, Jeffrey Tweedy, Linda Villarosa, W. Richard Veitch, Cheryl Wadlington, Brenda Walker, Savoy Walker, David Watkins, Eleanor Watson, Jill Wells, Edward Wilkerson, Marc Wilson, George C. Wolfe, Bill Wylie, Gretchen Young, and Zap Messenger Service.

A special mention of thanks to one of my fashion mentors, the late Ellis Smith, for helping me to believe in myself and my goals. Your spirit lives on and is a constant source of motivation.

Finally and most important, to all of my incredible family, the Mason-Johnsons, as well as to my "chosen" family, Craig Rose, Cynde Watson, Darian Trotter, Gordon Chambers, and Julia Chance: You are my foundation and an ever-present source of strength and encouragement. You have continually believed in my artistic endeavors, no matter how "far out" they may have seemed. Thank you for always accepting me as I am and for supporting my projects wholeheartedly. What Sydney started, I will continue, so *Men of Color* is ours to be proud of! The incredible journey of style has only just begun.

Bibliography, Endnotes & Fashion Credits

Baker, Patricia. *Fashions of a Decade: The 1950's*. New York: Facts on File, 1991.

———. *Fashions of a Decade: The 1940's*. New York: Facts on File, 1992.

Barlow, William, and Cheryl Finley. *From Swing to Soul: An Illustrated History of African-American Popular Music from 1930 to 1960*. Washington D.C.: Elliot & Clark Publishing, 1994.

Bergreen, Laurence. *Louis Armstrong: An Extravagant Life*. New York: Broadway Books, 1997.

Bogle, Donald. *Blacks in American Films and Television*. New York: Garland Publishing, 1988.

Brandt, Nat. *Harlem at War: The Black Experience in World War II*. New York: Syracuse University Press, 1996.

Campione, Adele. *Men's Hats*. San Francisco: Chronicle Books, 1988.

Carnegy, Vicky. *Fashions of a Decade: The 1980's*. New York: Facts on File, 1990.

Chaille, François. *The Book of Ties*. Paris: Flammarion, 1994.

Chenoune, Farid. *A History of Men's Fashion*. Paris: Flammarion, 1993.

Cimino, Al. *Great Record Labels*. London: Chartwell Books, 1992.

Colaiaco, James A. *Martin Luther King, Jr.: Apostle of Militant Non-Violence*. New York: St. Martin's Press, 1988.

Conner, Marlene Kim. *What is Cool?: Understanding Black Manhood in America*. New York: Crown Publishers, 1994.

Connikie, Yvonne. *Fashions of a Decade: The 1960's*. New York: Facts on File, 1990.

Cooke, Mervyn. *The Chronicle of Jazz*. New York: Abbeville Press, 1998.

Costantino, Maria. *Fashions of a Decade: The 1930's*. New York: Facts on File, 1992.

Courtney-Clark, Margaret. *African Canvas*. New York: Rizzoli, 1990.

Davis, Miles, and Quincy Troupe. *Miles: The Autobiography*. New York: Simon & Schuster, 1990.

Davis, Tracey, with Dolores A. Barclay. *Sammy Davis Jr., My Father*. Los Angeles: General Publishing Group, 1996.

De Marly, Diana. *Fashion for Men: An Illustrated History*. London: Holmes & Meier, 1989.

Ewen, Stuart. *All Consuming Images: The Politics of Style in Contemporary Culture*. New York: Basic Books, 1988.

Fashion Theory: The Journal of Dress, Body & Culture. Dr. Valerie Steele, ed. New York: Vol. 1, Issue 2. 1997.

———.Vol. 1, Issue 3.

———.Vol. 1, Issue 4.

Feldman, Elane. *Fashions of a Decade: The 1990's*. New York: Facts on File, 1992.

Fisher, Angela. *Africa Adorned*. New York: Abrams, 1984.

Fitterling, Thomas. *Thelonious Monk: His Life and Music*. Berkeley: Berkeley Hills Books, 1997.

Flusser, Alan. *Clothes and the Man: The Principles of Fine Men's Dress*. New York: Villard Books, 1985.

———. *Style and the Man*. New York: HarperCollins, 1996.

Foster, Helen Bradley. *New Raiments of Self: African American Clothing in the Ante-Bellum South*. Oxford University Press, 1997.

George, Nelson. *Blackface: Reflections on African-Americans and the Movies*. New York: HarperCollins, 1994.

Golden, Thelma. *Black Male: Representations of Masculinity in Contemporary American Art*. New York: Whitney Museum, 1994.

Gourse, Leslie. *Unforgettable: The Life and Mystique of Nat King Cole*. New York: St. Martin's Press, 1991.

Gregory, Hugh. *Soul Music A-Z*. New York: Da Capo Press, 1991.

Gross, Kim Johnson, and Jeff Stone. *Men's Wardrobe*. New York: Alfred A. Knopf, 1998.

Haley, Alex and Malcolm X. *The Autobiography of Malcolm X*. New York: Ballantine Books, 1973.

Hamilton, Charles V. *Adam Clayton Powell, Jr.: The Political Biography of an American Dilemma*. New York: Maxwell Macmillan International, 1992.

Hampton, Lionel, with James Haskin. *Hamp: An Autobiography*. New York: Warner Books, 1989.

Harley, Sharon. *The Timetables of African-American History*. New York: Simon & Schuster, 1995.

Harris, Middleton, et al., eds. *The Black Book*. New York: Random House, 1974.

Haskins, James. *The Cotton Club*. New York: Random House, 1977.

Haygood, Will. *King of Cats: The Life and Times of Adam Clayton Powell, Jr.* New York: Houghton Mifflin, 1993.

Hebdige, Dick. *Subculture: The Meaning of Style*. London: Routledge, 1979.

Herald, Jacqueline. *Fashions of a Decade: The 1920's*. New York: Facts on File, 1997.

———. *Fashions of a Decade: The 1970's*. New York: Facts on File, 1992.

Hochswender, Woody. *Men in Style: The Golden Age of Fashion from Esquire*. New York: Rizzoli, 1993.

Holland, Ted. *This Day in African-American Music*. California: Pomegranate Artbooks, 1993.

Holly, Ellen. *One Life: The Autobiography of an African-American Actress*. New York: Kodansha America, 1996.

James, Darius. *That's Blaxploitation!*. New York: Griffin/St. Martin's Press, 1995.

Johnson, Venice, ed. *Heart Full of Grace: A Thousand Years of Black Wisdom*. New York: Simon & Schuster, 1995.

Jones, Dylan. *Haircults: Fifty Years of Styles and Cuts*. New York: Thames & Hudson, 1990.

Jones, James Earl, and Penelope Niven. *James Earl Jones: Voices and Silences*. New York: Charles Scribner's Sons, 1993.

Konop, Carol. *The Shirt Book*. New York: Cappiello & Chabrowe, 1995.

Lewis, Reginald F., and Blair S. Walker. *Why Should White Guys Have All the Fun?: How Reginald Lewis Created a Billion Dollar Business Empire*. New York: John Wiley & Sons, 1996.

Lurie, Alison. *The Language of Clothes*. New York: Random House, 1981.

Major, Geraldyn Hodges. *Black Society*. Chicago: Johnson Publishing Company, 1976.

McDowell, Colin. *The Man of Fashion: Peacock Males and Perfect Gentlemen*. London: Thames & Hudson, 1997.

Merlis, Bob, and Davin Seay. *Heart & Soul: A Celebration of Black Music Style in America, 1930–1975*. New York: Stewart, Tabori & Chang, 1997.

Null, Gary. *Black Hollywood: From 1910 to Today*. New York: Citadel Press, 1993.

Polhemus, Ted. *Street Style*. New York: Thames & Hudson, 1994.

Rampérsad, Arnold. *Jackie Robinson: A Biography*. New York: Alfred A. Knopf, 1997.

Rawick, George, ed. *The American Slave: A Composite Autobiography*. Connecticut: Greenwood Press, 1979.

Richardson, James. *Willie Brown: A Biography*. Berkeley and Los Angeles: University of California Press, 1996.

Salley, Columbus. *The Black 100: A Ranking of the Most Influential African-Americans, Past and Present*. New York: Citadel Press, 1993.

Starke, Barbara M., Lillian O. Holloman, and Barbara K. Nordquist. *African American Dress and Adornment: A Cultural Perspective*. Iowa: University of Iowa Press, 1990.

Thomas, Velma Maia. *Lest We Forget*. New York: Crown Publishers, 1997.

Van Deburg, William L. *New Day in Babylon*. Chicago: The University of Chicago, 1992.

————. *Black Camelot: African-American Culture Heroes in Their Times, 1960–1980*. Chicago: The University of Chicago Press, 1997.

Villarosa, Riccardo, and Giuliano Angeli. *The Elegant Man*. New York: Random House, 1990.

White, Charles. *The Life and Times of Little Richard: The Quasar of Rock*. New York: Da Capo, 1994.

White, Constance C. R. *StyleNoir: The First How-to Guide to Fashion Written with Black Women in Mind*. New York: Perigree/The Berkley Publishing Group, 1998.

White, Shane, and Graham White. *Stylin': African-American Expressive Culture from Its Beginnings to the Zoot Suit*. Ithaca: Cornell University Press, 1998.

ENDNOTES

1. (p. 134) Barbara M. Starke, Lillian O. Holloman, and Barbara K. Nordquist, *African-American Dress and Adornment: A Cultural Perspective* (Iowa: University of Iowa Press, 1990), p. 72.

2. (p. 183) Alex Haley and Malcolm X, *The Autobiography of Malcolm X* (New York: Ballantine Books, 1973), pp. 63–64.

3. (p. 205) George Rawick, ed., *The American Slave: A Composite Autobiography* (Connecticut: Greenwood Press, 1979), pp. 1126–1127.

FASHION CREDITS

Miles Ahead: THE SUIT: pp. 37–38: Canali suit and shirt, Tommy Hilfiger tie, Johnston & Murphy shoes.

Measuring Up: THE PANT: p. 48: Dolce & Gabbana jacket and pants; p. 49: Jean Paul Gaultier shirt and pants; p. 61: Tommy Hilfiger shirt, Canali pants and belt, Church's shoes; p. 62: Tommy Hilfiger shirt and pants, Sulka belt.

Front and Center: THE SHIRT: p. 70: Charvet shirt, Canali tie; p. 81 (clockwise from top left): Tommy Hilfiger shirt and Burberry's tie, Burberry's shirt and Sulka tie, Tommy Hilfiger shirt and Ascot Chang tie, Canali shirt and tie, Sulka shirt and tie; p. 82: cuff links by Burberry's; p. 83: Canali shirts.

Fade to Black: ATTITUDE: p. 92: North Beach Leather jacket, Hanes T-shirt, Malchijah Hats hat; (inset) Canali suit, Barry Keisselstein-Cord belt courtesy of Mr. Jackson, J. J. Hat Center hat; p. 93 (left): Paul Smith suit, Kangol hat; (right): North Beach Leather jacket, Paul Smith pants, Malchijah Hats hats, Barry Keisselstein-Cord belt courtesy of Mr. Jackson; p. 107: Vivienne Westwood suit and shirt, Tommy Hilfiger tie and belt, Jane Diaz pinky ring; p.108 (left): Jean Paul Gaultier halter-back suit, Vivienne Westwood shirt, Sulka ascot, Uncle Sam's walking stick, Juno shoes; (right): all clothing by Oswald Boteng.

Cool Points: RELAXED ELEGANCE: p. 118: suit courtesy of Mr. Rashad, T-shirt by Calvin Klein; pp. 126–127: clothes courtesy of Mr. Miller; p. 129: all clothing by William Reid; p. 130 (left): Donna Karan coat and pants, William Reid sweater, Hanes T-shirt; (right): all clothing by William Reid, Jutta Neumann sandals; p. 131 (left): Donna Karan suit, Vivienne Westwood shirt, A. Testoni shoes, Tommy Hilfiger belt; (right): Donna Karan leather jacket and pants, William Reid sweater, Hanes T-shirt, Turnbull & Asser gloves.

On the Good Foot: THE SHOE: p. 140: Giorgio Armani duster, Yohji Yamamoto pants, Canali shirt, Church's shoes; (inset): Donna Karan robe, Canali shirt, Church's shoes; p. 141: Donna Karan robe and shoes, Canali shirt; p. 151 (clockwise from top): A. Testoni, A. Testoni, Pottery Barn vintage-style shoe last, Sulka, Ferragamo, Sebago; p. 152 (left): Church's lace-ups; (right): Sebago loafer; p. 153 (left): A. Testoni formal slip-on; (right): New Republic Chelsea boot.

Just Above My Head: THE HAT: pp. 160–161: Mr. Simmon's clothing and hat by Phat Farm, Adidas sneakers, LL Cool J's clothing by FUBU, J. J. Hat Center hat, Starter baseball cap; p. 175 (clockwise from top): J. J. Hat Center, J. J. Hat Center, Sulka, New Republic; p. 176 (left): J. J. Hat Center fedora; (right) J. J. Hat Center homburg; p. 177 (left): New Republic bowler; (right): Sulka newsboy.

Say It Loud: HAIR: p. 199 (clockwise from top left): Calvin Klein T-shirt, Tommy Hilfiger shirt, Paul Smith shirt, Ascot Chang shirt, Hanes T-shirt.

Facing the Rising Sun: ETHNICITY: p. 221: Epperson shirt, Malchijah Hats hat; pp. 222–223: Raif Atelier shirt and pants, Jutta Neumann sandals.

If It Ain't Got That Swing: THE DETAILS: p. 232: Donna Karan suit, sweater, and scarf, Equation beret, Common Ground and Craft Caravan rings; (inset): Canali suit, Tommy Hilfiger shirt, Burberry's tie, J. J. Hat Center hat, Hamilton vintage watch, Georg Jensen cuff links; p. 233 (left): Canali suit, Tommy Hilfiger shirt, Burberry's tie, J. J. Hat Center hat, Hamilton vintage watch, Georg Jensen cuff links; (right): Jean Paul Gaultier suit, Hanes T-shirt, Burberry's tie, J. J. Hat Center hat, Hamilton vintage watch, Georg Jensen cuff links; pp. 234–235: all clothing by Ralph Lauren, chairs courtesy of Craft Caravan and Bengali African Expo; p. 237: Sulka scarf, Canali tie (left), Burberry's tie (right), Turnbull & Asser silk pocket square, Burberry's cuff links; p. 238 (left to right): Canali belt, Sulka belts, Burberry's pocket squares, Zona jewelry box; p. 239: Sulka scarves.

SizingCHARTS

SUITS AND SPORT JACKETS

US	34R	36R	38R	40R	42R	44R	46R	48R
European	44	46	48	50	52	54	56	58
Actual Waist	28	30	31½	33½	35½	37	39	40

US			38T	40T	42T	44T	46T	48T
European			94	98	102	106	110	114
Actual Waist			31	33	35½	37	39	40

US			38S	40S	42S	44S
European			24	25	26	27
Actual Waist			33	35	37	39

TROUSERS

US	28	30	31½	33½	35½	37½	39	40
European	44	46	48	50	52	54	56	58

DRESS SHIRTS*

US	14½	15	15½	15¾	16	16½	17	17½
European	37	38	39	40	41	42	43	44

SWEATERS

US	XS	S	M	M/L	L	XL
European	46	48	50	52	54	56

KNITS

US	S	M	L	XL
European	5	6	7	8

BELTS

US	30	32	34	36	38	40	42
European	80	85	90	95	100	105	110

SHOES

US	7½	8	8½	9	9½	10	10½	11	11½	12
European	40½	41	41½	42	42½	43	43½	44	44½	45

° Sleeve length for most European dress shirts is standardized per size; traditionally, European sleeve lengths run slightly long.

Source LISTING

It would be a difficult and dubious endeavor to prescribe a specific style of dress for the man of color: Style is inherently personal, and is best developed by the individual. The following clothiers carry quality Afrocentric and/or traditional European collections. For convenience, they have been grouped according to the chapters in the book. The reader should view the recommended retailers, specialty shops, and department stores as starting points from which to build a tasteful yet distinctive wardrobe. Ask questions, explore options, and choose clothing that best expresses your personality.

Miles Ahead: THE SUIT

Agnès B.
79 Greene Street
New York, NY 10012
212.431.4339

Giorgio Armani
760 Madison Avenue
New York, NY 10021
212.988.9191

Barneys New York
660 Madison Avenue
New York, NY 10021
212.826.8900

Wilkes Bashford
375 Sutter Street
San Francisco, CA 94108
415.986.4380

Bergdorf Goodman Men
754 Fifth Avenue
New York, NY 10019
212.753.7300

Bigsby & Kruthers
1750 North Clark Street
Chicago, IL 60614
312.440.1750

Bullock & Jones
340 Post Street
San Francisco, CA 94108
415.392.4243

Burberry's Ltd.
9 East 57 Street
New York, NY 10022
800.284.8480

Cable Car Clothiers
441 Sutter Street
San Francisco, CA 94108
415.397.4740

Cheo
30 East 60 Street
New York, NY 10022
212.980.9838

Despos
500 Crescent Court,
   Suite 152
Dallas, TX 75201
214.871.3707

William Fioravanti
45 West 57 Street
New York, NY 10019
212.355.1540
(by appointment)

Giacomo
723 North La Cienega
   Boulevard
West Hollywood, CA 90069
310.652.6396

Tommy Hilfiger
468 North Rodeo Drive
Beverly Hills, CA 90210
310.888.0132

Syd Jerome
2 North LaSalle Street
Chicago, IL 60602
312.346.0333

Shaka King Menswear
207 St. James Place #3L
Brooklyn, NY 11238
718.638.2933

Calvin Klein
654 Madison Avenue
New York, NY 10021
212.292.9000

Stanley Korshak
500 Crescent Court,
   Suite 100
Dallas, TX 75201
214.871.3600

Ralph Lauren
867 Madison Avenue
New York, NY 10021
212.606.2100

Leonard Logsdail
9 East 53 Street
New York, NY 10022
212.752.5030
(by appointment)

Louis, Boston
234 Berkeley Street
Boston, MA 02116
617.262.6100

New Republic
93 Spring Street
New York, NY 10012
212.219.3005

Nordstrom
865 Market Street
San Francisco, CA 94103
415.243.8500

Pucci
333 North Michigan Avenue,
   Suite 205
Chicago, IL 60601
312.332.3759

Saks Fifth Avenue
611 Fifth Avenue
New York, NY 10022
212.753.4000

Dion Scott Custom
   Wardrobe Designer
343 South Robertson
   Boulevard
Beverly Hills, CA 90211
310.659.8497
(by appointment)

Paul Smith
108 Fifth Avenue
New York, NY 10011
212.627.9770

Paul Stuart
Madison Avenue at 45 Street
New York, NY 10017
212.682.0320

Ultimo
48 East Oak Street
Chicago, IL 60611
312.787.0906

Ermenegildo Zegna
743 Fifth Avenue
New York, NY 10022
212.751.3468

Measuring Up: THE PANT

Agnès B.
79 Greene Street
New York, NY 10012
212.431.4339

Giorgio Armani
760 Madison Avenue
New York, NY 10021
212.988.9191

Barneys New York
660 Madison Avenue
New York, NY 10021
212.826.8900

Wilkes Bashford
375 Sutter Street
San Francisco, CA 94108
415.986.4380

Bullock & Jones
340 Post Street
San Francisco, CA 94108
415.392.4243

Burberry's Ltd.
9 East 57 Street
New York, NY 10022
800.284.8480

Charivari
18 West 57 Street
New York, NY 10019
212.333.4040

Calvin Klein
654 Madison Avenue
New York, NY 10021
212.292.9000

Nordstrom
865 Market Street
San Francisco, CA 94103
415.243.8500

M. Penner
2950 Kirby Drive
Houston, TX 77098
713.527.8200

Paul Smith
108 Fifth Avenue
New York, NY 10011
212.627.9770

Jack Taylor
341 North Camden Drive
Beverly Hills, CA 90210
310.274.7276

Front and Center: THE SHIRT

Anto
268 North Beverly Drive
Beverly Hills, CA 90210
310.278.4500

Ascot Chang
7 West 57 Street
New York, NY 10019
212.759.3333

Wilkes Bashford
375 Sutter Street
San Francisco, CA 94108
415.986.4380

Bergdorf Goodman Men
754 Fifth Avenue
New York, NY 10019
212.758.7300

Brooks Brothers
346 Madison Avenue
New York, NY 10017
212.682.8800

Bullock & Jones
340 Post Street
San Francisco, CA 94108
415.392.4243

Burberry's Ltd.
9 East 57 Street
New York, NY 10022
800.284.8480

Buttondown
3415 Sacramento Street
San Francisco, CA 94118
415.563.1311

Ralph Lauren
867 Madison Avenue
New York, NY 10021
212.606.2100

Leslie & Co.
1749 Post Oak Boulevard
Houston, TX 77056
713.960.9113

Nordstrom
865 Market Street
San Francisco, CA 94103
415.243.8500

Thomas Pink
520 Madison Avenue
New York, NY 10022
212.838.1928

Saks Fifth Avenue
611 Fifth Avenue
New York, NY 10022
212.753.4000

Paul Smith
108 Fifth Avenue
New York, NY 10011
212.627.9770

Sulka
Waldorf Astoria
301 Park Avenue
New York, NY 10022
212.980.5226

Robert Talbott
680 Madison Avenue
New York, NY 10021
212.751.1200

Turnbull & Asser
42 East 57 Street
New York, NY 10022
212.752.5700

Ermenegildo Zegna
743 Fifth Avenue
New York, NY 10022
212.751.3468

Fade to Black: ATTITUDE

Agnès B.
79 Greene Street
New York, NY 10012
212.431.4339

American Rag
150 South La Brea Avenue
Los Angeles, CA 90036
213.935.3154

Wilkes Bashford
375 Sutter Street
San Francisco, CA 94108
415.986.4380

Camouflage
141 Eighth Avenue
New York, NY 10011
212.741.9118

Charivari
18 West 57 Street
New York, NY 10019
212.333.4040

Dolce & Gabbana
825 Madison Avenue
New York, NY 10021
212.249.4100

Epperson/The E Shop
771 Fulton Street
Brooklyn, NY 11217
718.246.0321

Gucci
685 Fifth Avenue
New York, NY 10022
212.826.2600

H. D.'s Clothing Company
3018 Greenville Avenue
Dallas, TX 75206
214.821.5255

Tommy Hilfiger
468 North Rodeo Drive
Beverly Hills, CA 90210
310.888.0132

Shaka King Menswear
207 St. James Place #3L
Brooklyn, NY 11238
718.638.2933

M.A.C.
5 Quad Lane
San Francisco, CA 94108
415.837.0615

Maxfield
8825 Melrose Avenue
Los Angeles, CA 90069
310.274.8800

Fred Segal
8100 Melrose Avenue
Los Angeles, CA 90046
213.651.4129

Paul Smith
108 Fifth Avenue
New York, NY 10011
212.627.9770

Cool Points:
RELAXED ELEGANCE

Joseph Abboud
37 Newbury Street
Boston, MA 02116
617.266.4200

Giorgio Armani
760 Madison Avenue
New York, NY 10021
212.988.9191

Wilkes Bashford
375 Sutter Street
San Francisco, CA 94108
415.986.4380

Bergdorf Goodman Men
75 Fifth Avenue
New York, NY 10019
212.758.7300

Bullock & Jones
340 Post Street
San Francisco, CA 94108
415.392.4243

Burberry's Ltd.
9 East 57 Street
New York, NY 10022
800.284.8480

Buttondown
3415 Sacramento Street
San Francisco, CA 94118
415.563.1311

Carroll & Company
425 North Canon Drive
Beverly Hills, CA 90210
310.273.9060

Charivari
18 West 57 Street
New York, NY 10019
212.333.4040

Epperson/The E Shop
771 Fulton Street
Brooklyn, NY 11217
718.246.0321

Scott Hill
100 South Robertson Boulevard
Los Angeles, CA 90048
310.777.1190

Industria
755 Washington Street
New York, NY 10014
212.366.4300

Donna Karan Menswear
550 Seventh Avenue, 9th Floor
New York, NY 10018
212.789.1697

Shaka King Menswear
207 St. James Place #3L
Brooklyn, NY 11238
718.638.2933

Calvin Klein
654 Madison Avenue
New York, NY 10021
212.751.0040

Neiman Marcus
400 North Park Center
Dallas, TX 75225
214.363.8311

Nordstrom
865 Market Street
San Francisco, CA 94103
415.243.8500

Phat Farm
129 Prince Street
New York, NY 10012
212.533.PHAT

Loro Piana
46 East 61 Street
New York, NY 10021
212.980.7961

Saks Fifth Avenue
611 Fifth Avenue
New York, NY 10022
212.753.4000

TSE
827 Madison Avenue
New York, NY 10021
212.472.7790

On the Good Foot: THE SHOE

Barneys New York
660 Madison Avenue
New York, NY 10021
212.826.8900

Bullock & Jones
340 Post Street
San Francisco, CA 94108
415.392.4243

Church's
428 Madison Avenue
New York, NY 10017
212.751.0891

Diego Della Valle
41 East 57 Street
New York, NY 10022
212.644.5945

E. Vogel
19 Howard Street
New York, NY 10013
212.925.2460

Gucci
685 Fifth Avenue
New York, NY 10022
212.826.2600

Nordstrom
865 Market Street
San Francisco, CA 94103
415.243.8500

Prada
45 East 57 Street
New York, NY 10022
212.308.2332

Saks Fifth Avenue
611 Fifth Avenue
New York, NY 10022
212.753.4000

To Boot NY
603 Washington Street
New York, NY 10014
212.463.0437

Vincent & Edgar
972 Lexington Avenue
New York, NY 10021
212.753.3461

J. M. Weston New York, Inc.
812 Madison Avenue
New York, NY 10021
212.535.2100

Just Above My Head: The HAT

Arnold Hatters, Inc.
620 Eighth Avenue
New York, NY 10018
212.768.3781

Wilkes Bashford
375 Sutter Street
San Francisco, CA 94108
415.986.4380

Bullock & Jones
340 Post Street
San Francisco, CA 94108
415.392.4243

Cable Car Clothiers
441 Sutter Street
San Francisco, CA 94108
415.397.4740

J. J. Hat Center
310 Fifth Avenue
New York, NY 10001
800.622.1911

Alexander Kabbaz
903 Madison Avenue
New York, NY 10021
212.861.7700

Malchijah Hats
225 Dekalb Avenue
Brooklyn, NY 11205
718.643.3269

Norton Ditto
2019 Post Oak Boulevard
Houston, TX 77056
713.688.9800

Pockets
9669 North Central
    Expressway, Suite 100
Dallas, TX 75231
214.368.1167

Worth & Worth
331 Madison Avenue
New York, NY 10017
212.867.6058

Facing the Rising Sun:
    ETHNICITY

African Color Scheme
4341 Degnan Boulevard
Leimert Park Village,
    CA 90008
213.298.9837

Ahneva Ahneva
3419B West 43 Place
Leimert Park Village,
    CA 90008
213.291.2535

Anyiam's Creations
1401 University Boulevard,
    Suite G114
Langley Park, MD 20783
301.439.1110

Beads of Paradise
16 East 17 Street
New York, NY 10003
212.620.0642

Brenda Bunson Bey
    at 4W Circle of Art
    and Enterprise
704 Fulton Street
Brooklyn, NY 11217
718.875.6500

Elcore Couture
    at 4W Circle of Art
    and Enterprise
704 Fulton Street
Brooklyn, NY 11217
718.875.6500

Epperson/The E Shop
771 Fulton Street
Brooklyn, NY 11217
718.246.0321

Ethnic of Ybor City
428 East Sample Road
Pompano Beach, FL 33064
954.781.1145

Freedom
74–28 South Vincennes Avenue
Chicago, IL 60621
773.488.3733

Everett Hall
5345 Wisconsin Avenue
Washington, DC 20015
202.362.0191

Island Outpost
1332 Ocean Drive
Miami Beach, FL 33139
305.673.6300

Keyi Ko Afrikan Arts
9765 South Wood Street
Chicago, IL 60643
800.295.0248

Malchijah Hats
225 Dekalb Avenue
Brooklyn, NY 11205
718.643.3269

A. Mandella Africa-USA
365 West 34 Street
New York, NY 10001
212.244.2306

Brian McKinney
1178 South La Brea Avenue
Los Angeles, CA 90019
213.933.4148

Moshood
698 Fulton Street
Brooklyn, NY 11428
718.243.9433

Moshood
217 Mitchell Street
Atlanta, GA 30303
404.523.9433

Pan-African Connection
612 East Jefferson Boulevard
Dallas, TX 75203
214.946.4798

Raif Atelier
887 Fulton Street
Brooklyn, NY 11238
718.622.2377

Stranger Clothing Company
610 South Marengo Avenue
Alhambra, CA 91803
626.289.1518

Studio of Ptah
155 Canal Street
New York, NY 10013
212.226.8487

If It Ain't Got that Swing:
    THE DETAILS

Barneys New York
660 Madison Avenue
New York, NY 10021
212.826.8900

Wilkes Bashford
375 Sutter Street
San Francisco, CA 94108
415.986.4380

Bergdorf Goodman Men
754 Fifth Avenue
New York, NY 10019
212.758.7300

Bullock & Jones
340 Post Street
San Francisco, CA 94108
415.392.4243

Burberry's Ltd.
9 East 57 Street
New York, NY 10022
800.284.8480

Cable Car Clothiers
441 Sutter Street
San Francisco, CA 94108
415.397.4740

The Coach Store
595 Madison Avenue
New York, NY 10022
800.262.2411

Hermès
11 East 57 Street
New York, NY 10022
800.441.4488

Alexander Kabbaz
903 Madison Avenue
New York, NY 10021
212.861.7700

L.A. Eyeworks
707 Melrose Avenue
Los Angeles, CA 90046
213.653.8255

Ralph Lauren
867 Madison Avenue
New York, NY 10021
212.606.2100

Morgenthal-Frederics
685 Madison Avenue
New York, NY 10021
212.838.3090

Nordstrom
865 Market Street
San Francisco, CA 94103
415.243.8500

Norton Ditto
2019 Post Oak Boulevard
Houston, TX 77056
713.688.9800

New Republic
93 Spring Street
New York, NY 10012
212.219.3005

Pockets
9669 North Central
    Expressway, Suite 100
Dallas, TX 75231
214.368.1167

Oliver Peoples
8642 Sunset Boulevard
Los Angeles, CA 90068
310.657.5475

James Robinson
480 Park Avenue
New York, NY 10022
212.752.6166

Saks Fifth Avenue
611 Fifth Avenue
New York, NY 10022
212.753.4000

Paul Smith
108 Fifth Avenue
New York, NY 10011
212.627.9770

Paul Stuart
Madison Avenue at 45 Street
New York, NY 10017
212.682.0320

Sulka
Waldorf Astoria
301 Park Avenue
New York, NY 10022
212.980.5226

Robert Talbott
680 Madison Avenue
New York, NY 10021
212.751.1200

INDEX

PhotoCREDITS

Every effort has been made to account for and credit the copyright owners of the archival photographs included in this book. Any inadvertent omissions should be brought to the attention of the author, care of the publisher.

Michael Henry Adams: p. 66, right. Richard Allen: p. 113, top. Allsport: p. 123, Jed Jacobcohn; p. 206, right, Markus Boesch. AP/Wide World Photos: p. 51, bottom, left; p. 67, bottom; p. 212, above; p. 215, above. Archive Photos: p. 122, bottom, left, Reuters/Jeff Christensen. Marc Baptiste: p. 87, top; p. 172. Anthony Barboza: p. 14; p. 23; p. 32; p. 46; p. 68, bottom; p. 91, above; p. 112, right; p. 116, right; p. 156, top; p. 181; p. 186; p. 213; p. 230. Ron Barboza: p. 12, above; p. 42, top; p. 134, above; p. 178. Janette Beckman: p. 122, top, right; p. 164, top, left; p. 164, bottom, left; p. 165, above. Wes Bell: p. 102. Black Star: p. 69, left, Brian Blauser; p. 88, top, Bob Fitch; p. 157, bottom, Charles Most; p. 184, Bob Fitch; p. 205, Bob Fitch; p. 206, above, Connie Hwang; p. 215, left, Bob Fitch. Courtesy of the Brooklyn Museum of Art: p. 203, Consuela Kanaga. Courtesy of CBS: p. 78. William Claxton: p. 30, above; p. 30 right; p. 114; p. 116, above; p. 136; p.190, right. Daniel Dease: p. 25, above, right; p. 169, left; p. 171, top left; p. 207. Courtesy of Doc's Antiques: p. 1; p. 137. Egan & Chin: p. 210. Courtesy of Alvin Fair: p. 57, bottom left; p. 91, left. Courtesy of Mary Fernandez: p. 86, above. Carol Friedman: p. 26. Courtesy of Giant Step Records: p. 34, Dah Len. W. P. Gotlieb/Library of Congress/Gershwin Fund: p. 29, right; p. 29, bottom; p. 66, above. Joe Grant: p. 25, left. Chester Higgins: p. 146, left; p. 158, above. George Holz: p. 57, top, left. Jerry Jack: p. 135. Lou Jones: p. 146, above. The Kobal Collection: p. 72; p. 77, above. Dan and Corina Lecca: p. 166, bottom, left. Dorothy Low: p. 165, top. Courtesy of Robert Mason: p. 67, top. Courtesy of the Collection of Morehouse College: p. 15; p. 21; p. 22, above; p. 40; p. 45, above; p. 45, right; p. 68, top; p. 88, above; p. 89; p. 138; p. 158, left; p. 225. MPTV: p. 44, Gene Howard; p.73, Wallace Seawell; p. 74, top, Marv Newton; p. 74, middle, A. Eccles; p. 76, 20th ABC; p. 77, above, right, NBC; p.77, below, right, Paramount; p. 85, Warner Bros.; p. 96, left, John E. Reed; p. 191, Richard C. Miller; p. 228, above, Gabi Rovia. Michael Ochs Archives: p. 28, top; p. 31, top; p. 31, bottom; p. 41; p. 50, David Corio; p. 51, top left; p. 51, top right; p. 51, bottom right; p. 52; p. 53, above right; p. 54, bottom left; p. 54, top left; pp. 64–65; p. 74, bottom; p. 87, bottom; p. 88, above; p. 88, right; p. 95, bottom left; p. 99; p. 115, above; p. 120, top; p. 120, right; p. 134, right; p. 157, top, David Corio; p. 159, top, David Corio; p. 182; p. 183, left; p. 190, above; p. 192, left; p. 192, above; p. 202. Outline: p. 101, above, Gregory Heisler; p. 104, Nathaniel Welch; p. 122, top, left, Michael O'Neill; p. 122, bottom, right, Gregory Heisler; p. 124, top, left, Steve Sands; p. 124, above, Max Aguilera Hellweg; p. 148, Michael Walls; p. 162, above, Janette Beckman; p. 162, right, Frank W. Ochenfels; p. 168, Michael O'Neill; p. 169, above, Barron Claiborne; p. 187, Andrew Eccles; p. 196; p. 208, above, George Holz; p. 217, left, George Lang; p. 217, above, John Abbott; p. 231, Jeffrey Thurnher. Pham: p. 69, above. Photofest:

p. 19; p. 25, above, left; p.28, above; p. 29, top, left, William Claxton; p. 51, bottom, right; p. 53, above, left; p. 54, above; p. 55; p. 57, above; p. 58; p. 75, top; p. 75, above; p. 94; p. 95, top, left, Kisch; p. 95, top, right; p. 95, bottom, right, Kisch; p. 96, right, Kisch; p. 97, above, Kisch; p. 98, left, right, Kisch; p. 101, bottom, right, Bruce Talamon; p. 113, bottom; p. 133; p. 143, top, left; p. 145, above; p. 164, above; p. 167; p. 179; p. 185; p. 228, right. Len Prince: p. 110; p. 124, bottom, left. Richard Samuel Roberts/The Estate of Richard Samuel Roberts/A True Likeness/Bruccoli, Clark, Layman, Inc.: p. 20, top; p. 112, above; p. 154; p. 157, middle; p. 227, bottom. Saba: p. 101, top, right, Boesl/Action Press; p. 195, above, Tinnefeld; p. 209, Steve Star; p. 218, Majlah Fanny. Photographs and Prints Division/Schomburg Center for Research in Black Culture/New York Public Library-Astor Lenox and Tilden Foundation: p. 6; p. 20, above, Bloom, Chicago; p. 22, right; p. 43; p. 111, The Morgan and Marvin Smith Photograph Collection; p. 120, above; p. 120, right; p. 142; p. 143, top, right; p. 143, bottom, right, Murray Korman; p. 143 bottom, left, James J. Kreigsmann; p. 144; p. 183, above, James J. Kreigsmann ; p. 227, top. Coreen Simpson: p. 155; p.163. Matthew Jordan Smith: p. 2; p. 8, pp. 36–39; pp. 48–49; pp. 60–63; pp. 70–71; pp. 80–83, pp. 92–93, pp. 106–108; p. 118; pp. 126–131; pp. 140–141; pp. 150–153; pp. 160–161; pp. 174–177; pp. 198–201; pp. 220–223; pp. 232–239. Morgan and Marvin Smith Photograph Collection: p. 121; p. 156, right. Courtesy of Sure Fire Productions: p. 188, Eric Johnson. Tar: p. 159, bottom; p. 166, right. Therme/Courtesy of Bjorn Amelan/The Estate of Patrick Kelly: p. 165, left. UPI/Corbis Bettmann: p. 12, right; p. 13; p. 42, above; p. 86, right; p. 97, top, right; p. 97, bottom, right; p. 115, left; p. 145, left; p. 157, top; p. 212, right; p. 214; p. 229, top. Nick Vaccaro Collection, NYC: p. 86, top; p. 117, bottom; p. 180, top; p.180, right; p. 226, top. M. Chandoha Valentino: p. 16; p. 33; p. 47; p. 117, top; p. 139; p. 147; p. 171, above; p.171 bottom, left; p.195, left; p. 208, bottom, right. Donna Mussenden/VanDerZee Collection: p.18, James VanDerZee; p. 66, top, James VanDerZee; p. 132, James VanDerZee; p. 226, right, James VanDerZee. Courtesy of Renauld White: p. 229, bottom. Courtesy of Archives and Special Collections, Robert W. Woodruff Library, Atlanta University Center: p. 84; p. 156, above; p. 180, above; p. 204; p. 224; p. 226, above. Ronnie Wright: p. 166, top, left; p. 208, top, right.

The *Men of Color* staff: Project Director: Craig Rose. Research Coordinator: Larry Ortiz. Researchers: Kelly Beamon, Shannon Crowley Cohen, Erica Johnson, Sharon Frances Moore, Bernard Orr, Tanaji Seabrook, Cassaundra M. Wilcox. Editorial Coordinator: Julia Chance. Interns: Jash'd Belcher, Kelvin Bostick, James Fields, Nicholas Granderson, Quentin Lynch. Photo Editor: Debbie Egan-Chin. Photo Retoucher: John Delecki. Art Direction/Original Photography: Lloyd Boston. Style Director: Leonard Bridges. Groomers: Creighton, Aliesch Pierce, Sonya Stephens, Cynde Watson for Bobbi Brown Essentials, Barry White. Production Assistant: Audra Alexxi for Lewis Van Arnam.

For Harper
Who's the BEST
And EVERYBODY says so
Love Nanna xx

— MH

For Matteo, Samuel and Leo
The Three Musketeers
From Auntie Feli

— FS

First published by Affirm Press, 2020
Published in hardcover by Tundra Books, 2022

Tundra Books, an imprint of Penguin Random House Canada Young Readers, a division of Penguin Random House of Canada Limited

Library and Archives Canada Cataloguing in Publication

Title: Your birthday was the best! / Maggie Hutchings ; illustrated by Felicita Sala.
Names: Hutchings, Maggie (Counselor), author. | Sala, Felicita, illustrator.
Identifiers: Canadiana (print) 20210196351 | Canadiana (ebook) 2021019636X |
   ISBN 9780735271623 (hardcover) | ISBN 9780735271630 (EPUB)
Classification: LCC PZ7.1.H88 You 2022 | DDC j823/.92–dc23

Published simultaneously in the United States of America by Tundra Books of Northern New York, an imprint of Penguin Random House Canada Young Readers, a division of Penguin Random House of Canada Limited

Library of Congress Control Number: 2021937228

Cover and interior design by Felicita Sala
The text was hand-lettered by Felicita Sala.

Printed in China

www.penguinrandomhouse.ca

1 2 3 4 5   26 25 24 23 22

Penguin
Random House
TUNDRA BOOKS

YOUR BIRTHDAY WAS THE BEST!

MAGGIE HUTCHINGS FELICITA SALA

tundra

YOUR BIRTHDAY
WAS THE BEST!
EVERYONE SAID SO.

I JOINED IN ALL THE PARTY GAMES BUT...

i ate
SO MUCH
i FELL ASLEEP
ON YOUR CAKE.

YOU
SCREAMED.

AND
THEN . . .

YOUR BABY SISTER
TRIED TO EAT ME.

THAT'S WHEN ...

EVERYONE SAYS
IT ATE
UNCLE LARRY

AND
AUNTIE SHARON

AND
GRANDMA.

BUT
i WASN'T SCARED.
BECAUSE GUESS WHAT?

IT is MARVELOUS.
IT is FABULOUS.
IT is FULL OF
DELICIOUS THINGS
LIKE...

HAIRY
CHEESE
AND

CAT
POO
AND

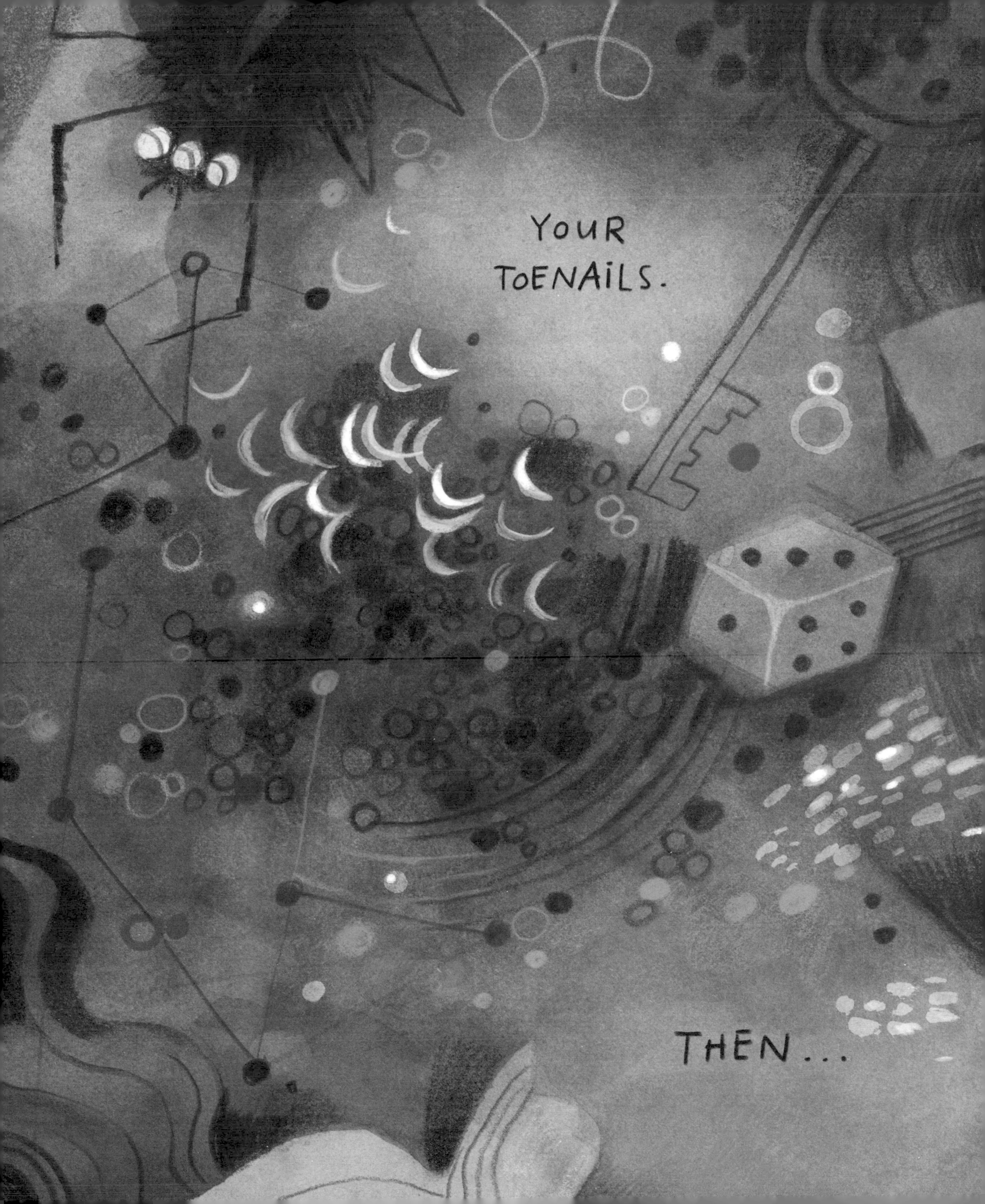
YOUR TOENAILS.
THEN...

I GOT TIPPED OUT
IN THE
BIG OUTSIDE BIN.

WHAT A
WONDERLAND!
AND
GUESS WHO WAS THERE?

UNCLE LARRY
AND
AUNTIE SHARON
AND
GRANDMA.

i HAD THE BEST TIME.

i WANTED TO STAY
BUT...

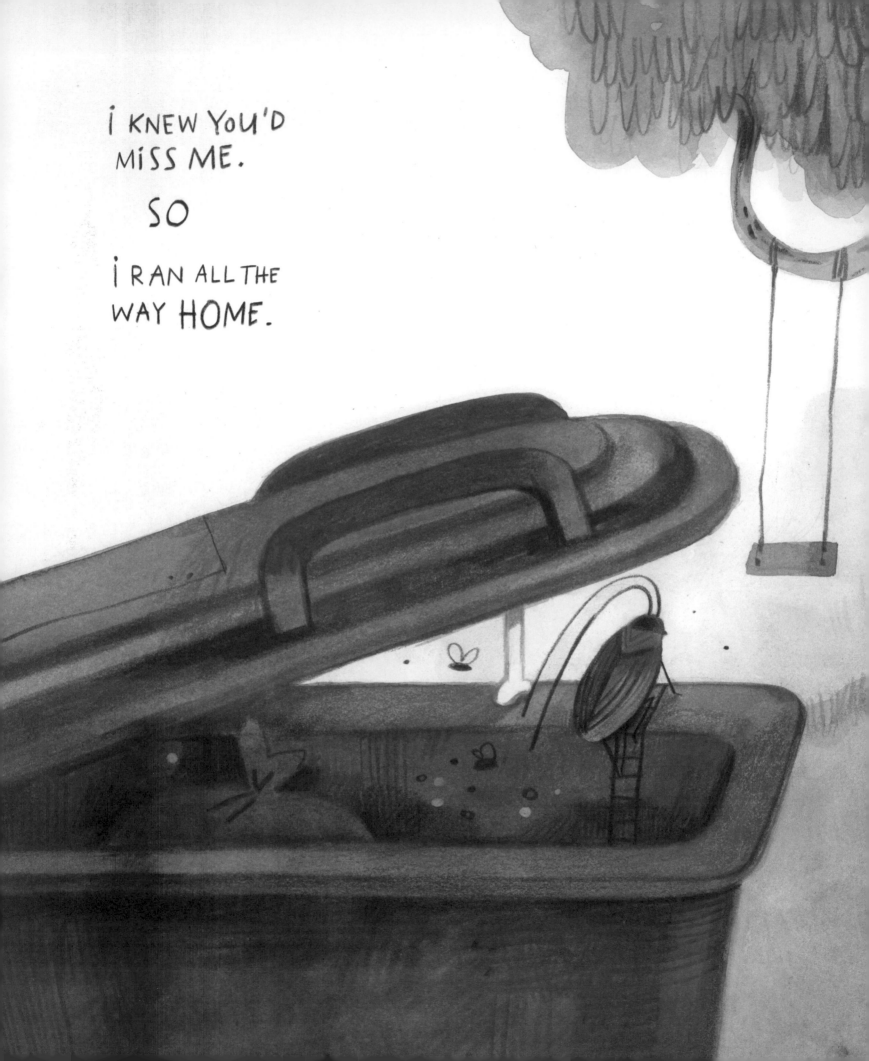

I KNEW YOU'D MISS ME.

SO

I RAN ALL THE WAY HOME.

YOU SCREAMED.

YOUR BiRTHDAY
WAS THE BEST!